© 2019 Gary Wiltshire and Michael O'Rourke.

MO Publishing.

ANGELS, TEARS AND SINNERS

by Gary Wiltshire and Michael O'Rourke.

All rights reserved. No part of this publication may be reproduced, distributed, or transmitted in any form or by any means, including photocopying, recording, or other electronic or mechanical methods, without the prior written permission of the publisher, except in the case of brief quotations embodied in critical reviews and certain other noncommercial uses permitted by copyright law.

* * * *

Also by Gary Wiltshire

Winning It Back: The Autobiography of Britain's Biggest Gambler

The imposing presence of Gary Wiltshire has long been one of the familiar and colourful sights on the racecourses and dog tracks of Britain. Biggest of the big gamblers, Gary has been punter, racecourse bookmaker, and in recent years television pundit, heading BBC coverage of the betting ring. But there are two sides to Gary Wiltshire. One shows the genial, wise-cracking personality revelling in every angle of the betting business, the poor boy made good, with racehorses running in his colours and a personalised number-plate on his Mercedes. The other shows his obsessive punting bringing him to what he unflinchingly calls 'rock bottom'. The story tells how from the age of five he could calculate the return on a bet; how he would serve the Kray twins' family at his father's flower stall in Leather Lane; how he famously lost £800,000 on the day of Frankie Dettori's 'Magnificent Seven' at Ascot and then sold all he had so that he could pay off every penny he owed, and started again. It is a remarkable rollercoaster ride of good and bad fortune, by turns hilarious and heart-rending.

* * * *

About the author

Michael O'Rourke

Michael O'Rourke was born in Staffordshire. He has many eclectic hobbies and interests. His writing style is unusual, as he takes serious subjects and gives them a comedic touch, but without losing the underlying serious essence of the story.

This, his latest offering, is in collaboration with his old friend - larger-than-life bookie, Gary Wiltshire. They have been friends for 30 years, often seeing each other on the race tracks. Michael was an on-course bookmaker himself for five years, and at one time bought two Midlands racecourse pitches off Gary. They are both men who enjoy a punt, so Michael knows and appreciates what Gary has been through.

So, who better to write the big man's follow-up book than a guy who has worked on the "coal face" and experienced the volatile life of trying to make a living by laying bets.

Michael's previous works include the top-selling *Black Eyes and Blue Blood,* which is now considered a classic in the 'gangster genre'. The book details the story of Liverpool hard man Norman Johnson, who was the only man to have worked with both the Krays *and* the Philadelphia Mafia.

Last year saw the release of *Life in the Faz Lane*, and this latest book earned rave reviews. This is the true story of the notorious fraudster Faisal Medani, who had scores of international footballers 'in his pocket'.

Another biography written by Michael O'Rourke due out later in 2019 - *Chef on the Run* - tells the amazing and true story of international TV "super chef" Sidney Sharratt, a man who has seen more death and destruction than Rambo. The book covers his adventures in Africa, Asia and America.

He never falters in his 'laugh-a-minute' quest for culinary excellence amid all the mayhem.

* * * *

Acknowledgements

Many thanks to:
- * Alex Steedman (Racing UK.)
- * Al Lee - 2cheeseburgers.com
- * Adam Sutton - Adamartwork
- * Kevin Casey
- * Johnny Metcalf,

And all the great British racing public.

Contents

		Page
	About the author	4
	Acknowledgements	7
	Angels with Dirty Faces and Golden Hearts	10
	Introduction	16

Chapter

1	HALF THE MAN I USED TO BE	22
2	WALKING IN SHADOWLANDS	37
3	TO POSSILPARK AND BACK	66
4	RETURN OF THE PRODIGAL SON	87
	Gallery	*106*
5	HORSES FOR COURSES	115
6	GONE TO THE DOGS	167
7	BETTING WITH KING BARRY	185
8	RIGHT, SAID FRED	201
9	WINNERS, VALUE, ODDS-ONS AND LONGSHOTS	210
10	CHARACTERS OF THE RACE TRACK (Angels and Sinners)	232
11	TO INFINITY AND BEYOND	261
	Epilogue	273
	Gary's Lucky (Funny) 15	278
	Author's other works	285

ANGELS WITH DIRTY FACES
AND
GOLDEN HEARTS

STEVE ALLEN
Ace point to point mate, like myself, not been in the best of health.

ALAN BALLARD
"The Window Man" my shoulder to cry on from Bournemouth.

IRISH NIALL BERMINGHAM
Great mate, postman punter, one of the boys.

CHELSEA
The girl in Hill's betting shop, Syerston, always makes me feel welcome.

EDDIE DARKE
"The Farmer" another top point to pointer, the pride of Brighton.

FRANKIE DETTORI
Just simply the most charismatic race jockey who ever lived.

JON HOLMES
Not the porn star, but top entrepreneur from Essex, trusted pal.

DAVE JACQUES
Best bathroom fitter in the biz, racehorse owner and sportsman.

BEN KEITH
Head honcho at Star Sports bookies, the next Victor Chandler.

DEREK LAW
Greyhound trainer, still going, we go back years, great character.

DOM MAGNONE
The Italian Stallion, stellar career involving Irish greyhounds.

STEWART-MOORE
Racing solicitors who proved I wasn't at it, in a canter.

PAUL MCNALLY
My poor beleaguered doctor, I owe him so much, a diamond.

GARY NEWBON
My mate - self-proclaimed legend in the Midlands, special man.

ED NICHOLSON
Top man at Unibet, racing could do with a few more like Ed.

ALAN POOK
Another Brighton man, loyal mate, builder cum bookmaker.

BOB POTTER
King of Lakeside, (BDO Darts) always enjoy my yearly visit.

RUCKEROO
Betting buddy, one of life's winners, but not in a dress sense.

PHIL SEARS
The Bulldog, proper old fashioned geezer who stood loyally by me.

GARY SELBY

Very clever man, with lovely family, mum Joyce and son Malcolm.

ANDY SMITH

Bookmaker, a man who knows the game inside out, a gentleman.

TOMMO

Hardest worker in the game, cancer survivor, a man who will never quit.

JORDAN VINE

Young greyhound punter, big future with Gary Noble and Selby.

BOBBY WARREN

Took me under his wing when I first started, miss him terribly.

* * * *

ANGELS, TEARS AND SINNERS

The true story of the man who defied all the odds

by

Gary Wiltshire

with

Michael O'Rourke

Introduction

Well, well, well.

The last six years have flown by since last putting quill to parchment and now I'm back by popular demand following the great success of my last book *Winning It Back*. That was the true story of one bookie taking on the whole of the British racing industry on an unforgettable day of historic achievements at Royal Ascot. That fatal day in 1996 was a clear oxymoron moment in my life, it ruined me but it also made me. I became the unofficial bookie of the people; the little man up against the machinations of the enormous betting cartels.

They said, 'Fight the good fight, Gal.'

Well, I tried and got the mother of all hidings for my trouble. My amicable nemesis, Frankie Dettori, went into the annals of racing folklore, but at the time I was swept down into a dark drain of financial ruin. There were only two choices open to me; say 'I can't pay' and welch on my considerable betting debt, or pay back every penny to all and sundry involved.

You all know what happened. If I hadn't have paid my dues, life as an on-course bookmaker was over, simple as that. Eventually, I returned every last penny owed; sure, I lost all my properties, chattels and assets, but I considered myself young enough to find the million pound deficit and still make a triumphal comeback. Oscar Wilde once said, 'We are all in the gutter but some of us are looking at the stars.' Well, my old learned pal, I wasn't quite that ambitious; I was just looking to get a roof over my head.

I'd leave the twinklers to Captain Kirk.

So, that's where we left off last time. Everyone who had wagered with me on Frankie Dettori Day was paid and weighed in; the Magnificent Seven was put on the back boiler, if not exactly to bed. I had a healthy few bob in the bank and a lovely serene family life with wife Sue and the kids. That's how Disney films always finish at the pictures, but what followed on was more like a Quentin Tarantino blood-lust flick. People say real life is stranger than *Pulp Fiction.*

The next few years had me fighting for my life in hospital. I'd lost an awful lot of self-discipline and the increasing weight had ballooned to a really dangerous level. On death's door, a wonderful man strode into my own, deteriorating world of pain by paying for a very complex operation with no strings attached, it really will surprise you to find out who he is. I had been given six months to lose 13 stones and save my life, so he is an angel, one I can't thank enough. So, miracles do happen; I know I was there, I wore the XXXL t-shirt and I lovingly bore the scars.

At my most vulnerable, the wife decided to up sticks after seeing some friendly phone texts from a female friend; in her mind it was tantamount to having an affair, and all this happened while I was prone on my back, comatose in surgery. Fat chance that an ailing man, vacillating between 35 and 37 stone would be running about gallivanting, I wasn't exactly *hot to trot* in my condition.

That sent me headlong into a ruinous maelstrom of chronic depression that kept me off the racecourse for nearly a year. Ultimately, it became my most difficult opponent, never giving any quarter. But through an unorthodox treatment I put it behind me before being confronted by two further, serious setbacks.

Firstly, I was accused of malpractice in the backing of greyhounds. Disappointingly, too many people were prepared to believe the fake rumours; these folk in my eyes were sinners, happy to see me ruined but not the slightest bit prepared to apologise or be contrite when it was proven I had no case to answer. It made me realise, no matter how popular I was with the general public, certain people would love to see me take a fall.

While that rumpus was going on, *Sky Greyhounds* removed me from the live broadcasts with a promise to have me back when I had cleared my name. Sadly, this never materialised, the phone never rang and the silence was deafening. I could feel bitter and victimised but you all know me better than that; in fact how many could have gone through what I had without cracking up. In this latest, frank follow up there are laughs aplenty, the joy is never far from the surface. I've always been a fighter, when have you ever seen me with out a smile on my face? I owe it to all of you out there who have supported me from the start; everything I do, I do it for you. There could be a number one hit in there somewhere!

In between my forays to the horse and dog tracks, I have developed a fantastic working relationship with two giants of the sporting world in Mr Fred Done and Mr Barry Hearn. These two gentlemen proved themselves true friends when others turned their backs. They deserve all the luck and the plaudits they get, I will never be able to repay their kindness so thank you both.

Although I haven't been the best husband in the universe, my kids are the most important aspects of my life, along with my wonderful partner Sharon and fantastic father, Eddie. I say to Kelly, Nicky, Charlie and Danny; I love you all dearly and I know that I didn't spend enough time with you when you were growing up. That can't be remedied. I was selfishly building my career as an aspiring bookmaker but you all know these days that you always come first. I'm here for you round the clock and I couldn't wish for better sons and a daughter.

So, now is the time to chronicle the amazing circumstances I have encountered since writing the autobiography *Winning It Back*. This is for all the thousands of racing fans who have been asking, what happened next? This is my frank, sometimes sad, amusing and melodramatic account of Gary Wiltshire Esquire: the bookie with big cahoonas, Dad and Grandfather, chronic gambler, charismatic, happy-go-lucky softie, optimist and vulnerable human being but most of all, a big character who repaid all his debts and has all the time in the world for the Great British racing public.

As Kipling once said,

If you can fill the unforgiving minute,
With sixty seconds' of distance run,
Yours is the earth and everything that's in it,
And - which is more - you'll be a man, my son.

I couldn't have put it better myself. Then again, the geezer did bake exceedingly good cakes.

I proudly give you,

Angels, Tears and Sinners...

* * * *

Chapter One

HALF THE MAN I USED TO BE

Winx, the Australian flying filly, takes 14 strides every 5 seconds compared to 12 for her rivals.

Dear readers, what can I say?

After the phenomenal success of the last book, something I owe you all a huge amount of thanks for, life at that choice moment seemed just hunky dory. I was ready to climb the ladder into the upper echelons of the bookies' hall-of-fame, to become a legend in my own lunchtime. In fact, that was just one of the reasons things and events were starting to seriously unravel. I was simply and plainly eating and drinking too much; I could give the Simpsons in the Strand beef trolley a run for its money, all on my own. One could see from photographs early on in my career that I was never going to make a cat walk model but I was enjoying la dolce vita a little too much.

People use the term big-boned which is a nice euphemism for 'you're fat.' I last heard the term when I was working with John Parrott at Royal Ascot for the BBC. A well-to-do dowager approached me by the parade ring, 'Oh my Mr Wiltshire, you are a fine, large, upstanding gentleman. Big boned I fancy, does it run in the family?'

I doffed my topper, 'To be truthful darling, no bugger runs in our family.' She gave a hearty chuckle. I had a friend for life there. The aristocracy do like a bit of rough.

I suppose the term "trencherman" could be more ascribed to my condition; a hearty eater who enjoys his nosebag but then so could the term, 'You greedy, fat bastard.'

Inside my ample frame was an eleven stone, toned, muscled athlete trying desperately to escape. Eating is one of life's great pleasures but moderation is the name of the game. To me, the Great British Breakfast was just a snack, followed by two tubes of Pringles; in fact, most mornings I felt I could eat a scabby donkey between two bread vans, such was my appetite.

I should have spotted the danger signs. An old pal of mine who was nowhere near the weight I was but was still a good few degrees north of twenty stone, tripped over at the top of the stairs one evening. He was totally unharmed (well padded) but his family in the conservatory thought Eastenders was just finishing.

As most of you know, I was living with wife Sue, in Hollywood. Not the crazy, Los Angeles Central neighbourhood, home of the American film industry but the quainter, more sedate Hollywood, south of Birmingham (no not Alabama, I wish the yanks could come up with some names of their own. We should charge them) on the Worcestershire border.

I don't believe in conspiracies but coincidences happen because living just a few miles up the road in Solihull, was Barry Austin; stalwart Birmingham City fan who had been declared, at various times, Britain's heaviest man. It was rumoured at one stage he was 65 stone but got back down to 40 stone, a sterling effort which in itself was a miraculous achievement as I now know from dire, personal experience.

Barry's plight has been well documented in the press and on television. He has my utmost admiration and comes across as a lovely, lovely man. Any flippant, self-deprecating remarks I make about obesity are entirely about myself, mainly as an escape mechanism from the misery it has caused in my life. There are many of you out there with weight problems. We all put on a brave face, the stereotyped jolly, fat man (or lady) who once back home, indoors, cries their eyes out. Some people dread even going out, it's a hard one to conquer but stay with me through all this, there is a light flickering at the end of the tunnel. If I can do it, so can anyone. Bollocks! I've given the end of the chapter away. Still, this ride is just as good as the destination so stay on board partners, the Wiltshire Great Western steam train, including buffet car, is about to come off the rails. Those of a nervous disposition, look away now.

Birmingham City were great with Barry, they even made him a special bench to sit on. This rung true to myself, people were beginning to call me "Gary Two Seats." Cruel perhaps, but accurate; both the cheeks of my derriere had different post codes... but laughing apart, I was lining up for an unwanted appointment with the "Grim Reaper." I knew I was bang in trouble when the talking scales told me one morning, 'Get off fatty, you're 37 stones. Do one.'

That next Sunday evening, feeling like a decomposing dog turd, I was admitted into Solihull Hospital. Lying on the bed, I was in a slough of despair. 'Eat, eat, eat, that's all I do. Why the fuck is this happening?' Those words were constantly repeating through my addled brain. This was a low point; I felt I was lying at the bottom of the Marianas Trench and it was a long way back to the surface.

I was slowly dying in Ward 8, a pathetic figure. I'll never forget it. I couldn't move, I literally pissed myself because of being a premier mark diabetic. I was top weight in the Obesity Handicap by a good few stone. This event was open to people like myself who overindulged, the ultimate trophy being death. I worked out the odds, guess who was the clear favourite?

Time became a blur; whether I was there seconds, minutes, or hours, I can't recall but the ward sister came in at some stage and informed me a private ambulance had been ordered for moi and it would arrive in half an hour. 'You're going on the short run to Parkway Private Hospital, Gary,' said the sister of mercy.

I was an ungrateful sod, 'Why am I going there?' she elucidated further, 'They are going to save your life; you're having an operation to fit a gastric sleeve on Tuesday morning. The intention is for you to lose 13 stone.'

My mind was all over the place. 'I can't afford that, what's going on?' Apparently, the operation had already been paid for; all ten thousand pounds, by a Mr Done. I couldn't think straight; who, what or why but then it came to me... *Fred Done of Betfred*. Why would he help me, a total stranger? But one thing is certain, without that man I would now be brown bread. I can never repay him or thank him enough, my guardian angel.

Thirty minutes flew by and I'd perked up quite considerably but knew this was only the start of a long-haul flight, there would be plenty of turbulence before I landed safely at the airport with no excess baggage. The hospital orderly and three porters sweated buckets trying to convey my ample carcass onto the stretcher. They finally defied the laws of gravity and miraculously got me up, only for the wheeled equipment to start showing signs of metal fatigue, creaking and groaning as it attempted to move off. They just managed to get me back down before the whole contraption collapsed. I whimsically jested that this must be a faulty one but they weren't laughing, so I let that one die a death. The largest wheelchair in the hospital was sent for and two porters eventually got me down to my waiting chariot.

I think they were just glad to see the back of me, one strangely waved me off with a two fingers motion but real crackerjacks to a man. With all their lifting ability, new careers as stall handlers at the racetrack would be a certainty. Moving all that bucking horseflesh would be a doddle compared to what they had just been put through.

We drove through the expectant, Birmingham twilight. The ambulance suspension was well up to the job as I copped a gigantic, illuminated billboard out of the left window; Diet Coke, making people feel better about ordering two Big Macs and large fries since 1982. The cheeky bleeders, I thought. Wiltshire was well on his way to the excellent Spire Private Care Company's flagship hospital, Parkway in Solihull. The forthcoming operation involved reducing the stomach to 20% of its original size which would lessen the appetite and make one feel fuller much quicker. That was the plan, drastic I know, especially as the operation was irreversible but there was no get-out clause. I'd burnt all my bridges, I was definitely going under the knife. I had no one to blame but myself. Still, looking down at the size of my gut, I wondered if a wizard's sleeve would be a better alternative to a gastric one. In two shakes of a lambs tail we were at our destination, promising a new start to life, a new future, and a new and improved Gary. Suffice to say, little did I know what was just around the corner!

The next morning at seven o'clock I walked down to the operating theatre, all modes of transportation were considered inadequate. It was the 6th of February 2013. I had started keeping a diary as things were happening in my life that I hadn't experienced before so I was jotting things down. If it was good enough for Anne Frank, Samuel Pepys and Adrian Mole, what harm could it do? It all felt like being the condemned man in Sing Sing prison going down to the gas chamber after serving 30 years on death row. I only hoped the male anaesthetist wasn't using cyanide. I noticed out the corner of my eye that he had a Spurs tattoo on the back of his hand. As a lifelong Gunners fan, it resembled the Mark of Satan and it might just have ended up being the last thing I would ever see. Horror show. The lad was right on top of his game though and within a millisecond I was floating into the silent land of the big black void. The anaesthetic never fails.

They always tell you, just to keep you calm, that you're going for a little sleep but what they are really doing is putting you in a coma; no dreams, no pain but plenty to gain or in my case, plenty to lose. It was while I was touring "Planet Oblivion" that wife Sue, back in my pre-op room (number 27), went through the texts on my mobile phone, putting two and two together and coming up with five. When I used to own racehorses, a promising lady amateur jockey named Sharon Broadly would occasionally ride for me, over a period of time we became good friends and kept in touch over the years. There were some texts from Sharon including a recent one saying, 'Please God, Gary get through the operation safe and sound.' Plus one from a few months back asking if I knew any people who would sponsor her daughter, Jaimee, for three-day eventing.

All innocent stuff in my mind, but a storm was brewing. After the operation all was quiet on the Western Front and I was taken to the recovery unit where the average recuperation time is half an hour. The operation must have knocked my socks off because I was there for over five hours. Sue shared each and every minute by my bedside but once home she declared that our marriage was over. I thought she was kidding, that it was a bad joke but she was deadly serious. I've never understood the female logic on a lot of things but I was shell-shocked and totally taken aback by the unexpected, unfolding drama. This had come right out of left field. Surely the woman I loved so dearly wouldn't leave me now, when I needed her more than ever? Maybe it was the life I was living? Dave Jacques, who fitted our new bathroom, had asked her once, 'I bet it's a lot of fun living with Gary.'

To which she replied, 'To be truthful, when he comes home through the door after a day at the races, I don't know if we are going on an exotic holiday abroad or having to sell the house.'

I could see that the career I'd chosen didn't always have the best job security but what could I do? Life itself is one gigantic, humanitarian roulette wheel; we all need the ball to fall into the right slot.

At this stage the operation had knocked me back big time, I couldn't even walk. I felt like a cat that had to crawl up the stairs to get a glass of milk, I was down and out and desperate. Sue decided she had to get away for a couple of days to mull things over. I begged her not to go but off she trotted. I was totally fucked. I hadn't got a clue where she went, who she saw or what she did but after the longest two days of my life, she returned. I begged and pleaded with her to believe me, imploring her to give me another chance, even though I knew nothing had happened. On Valentine's Day, I bought her a lovely big bunch of red roses. It always works in the movies, I was frantically trying to keep the marriage alive.

Next day, 15th February, she was gone. Sue was totally adamant I had been up to no good, so it was set in stone; *au revoir, finito benito*. Now, how was I supposed to look after myself? I was a total technophobe, I couldn't even change a plug; I didn't do being alone. I know it sounds pitiful but that was the way I rolled. I eventually rented a flat, quite close to the former family residence. Sue's son Liam and his partner Becky offered me help with a bed and furniture and were both very concerned about my welfare. I'd like to thank them both, from the bottom of my heart. At the time, I was literally on my knees, feeling like the proverbial burnt martyr. I've done a million things wrong in my life but having an affair with Sharon wasn't one of them.

The whole, stressful episode had a strange consequence on my sleeping habits. I just couldn't sleep on my own in an empty bed in the flat so every night I would go out to sleep in the car, something I was comfortable with after many nights coming back from racecourses the length and breadth of Great Britain and not quite making it home.

In the mornings I would return to the flat and have a shower. I know there's nowt so strange as folk but people have crazier habits than mine: like touching a red hot plate when the waiter told you not to because you have trust issues or forgetting a person's name two seconds after you were introduced. Sound like yourself? Yeah, thought so. Igor Stravinsky used to stand on his head every morning for fifteen minutes to clear his brain cells. How many of us do that?

While we are on the subject of sleeping in cars, there are many famous people who have done it including James Cameron and Jim Carrey. At the last count they were worth 700 million and 160 million dollars each respectively so if you see a bearded weirdo with long hair turning up in your neighbour in an old battered Lincoln Continental, it's probably Carrey.

My head was definitely not functioning properly but the weight proceeded to drop off me like the Niagara Fat Falls. I didn't know whether to laugh or cry at this stage and felt like I needed to talk to somebody sympathetic though only to a layman, not necessarily anyone in the medical or psychiatric sector. Then suddenly, I came up with a brainwave and it was right against the run of play. There hadn't been many that had popped up, so I needed to use it wisely and positively. I phoned Sharon up out of the blue, it was the first time for weeks I'd been in contact and I told her what I'd been through, everything that had happened, including all the very latest updates.

Sharon sounded concerned as I reprised my never-ending tale of woe, neither exaggerating or putting on my pity hat. I knew I wasn't in a great place, mentally but I felt better getting things off my chest. She said, 'You can't sleep in a car Gary, it will affect your health. Come up here, we've got a spare room, you can get your head down and relax.'

Truthfully, I hadn't expected that response but what could I lose? At least I could start communicating with people again.

Did you catch the "we've" bit? Yes, she had a teenage daughter, Jaimee. I put in a half-hearted appeal regarding the proposed arrangement saying 'That's not fair on Jaimee, she might not think this is a good step forward.'

But Sharon was adamant. 'You're coming, that's that.'

Now I never stand in the way of an insistent woman who knows exactly what she wants. So, I was back on the road again. Me and Willie Nelson should do a double act; there must be some historic, gypsy blood in the Wiltshire family somewhere, I was constantly on the move. Still, I think a nice, gaudy neckerchief and a pair of gold earrings would suit me handsome; I do like a Norfolk Lurcher.

The new *des res* was a modest two-up, two-down house in Keyworth, Nottinghamshire; far better than the old jalopy and my private room came with bed, electric fire and two-seater sofa. It wasn't the Ritz but at least I could put my napper down and try to wean a trace of normality back. Most importantly, in my own mind, it was a home and a route back from the insanity of the last few weeks.

I wasn't earning at the time so the most I could contribute to the rent was fifty pounds a week. Now if anyone thinks this was a good life, they have it 100% wrong. I look back now and realise that besides the physical scars and malaise, I was actually suffering from acute depression. The black dog had me in its cruel fangs and wouldn't spit me out. My state of mind was such that I didn't want to be a bookie again, total madness; it was the only thing I was half decent at.

I was continuing to lose a stone a month but because of all the shit and detritus that had gone before, I was living in a nether world of despair and darkness. I couldn't see a way out (Fuck me! I'm starting to depress myself again on this chapter. Stick with me kid, the sunshine is out there on the horizon; wagons roll).

Out of the blue, Fred Done contacted me. He wanted a well-known racing name to appear at his new state of art Warrington studios, fronting the horse racing and betting presentations on a Saturday morning. This was my own golden ticket back to the real world. I felt like I was worth something again, that I hadn't been totally written off but in my addled mind of doom and gloom, it was all but the end until this turned up. To have a betting genius, somebody like Fred in my corner and believe in me, was just the jagged spur I needed to set the old adrenaline coursing through my veins again; just like a tornado pushing a five-star Severn Bore.

What can I say about Fred? The man is an absolute diamond, he has saved my life twice now; once physically, then afterwards, mentally. I can state, hand on heart, I'd gone way beyond the point of no return until he dragged me back. I class Fred as my second father; he is a loyal friend who has even given me his personal phone number, a deep-felt honour because it's essentially just for family calls. It's there for me 24/7 in case I fall off the precipice again but I'm not going for the hat trick anytime soon. That man has done more than enough. I can never repay you old chum, they broke the mould when you were born. Great men pop into one's life very rarely; you just know sometimes when you are in their company that the men talking to you are a little bit special.

Fred started his burgeoning bookmaker empire in 1967 when he and brother Peter opened a single shop in Ordsall, Salford. They had backed England to win the 1966 World Cup, so they got into betting through betting. What they attempted to do is extremely difficult, if not impossible, by taking on the long established, old school, moneyed bookmaking chains from humble beginnings and flourishing quickly alongside them.

From that small acorn they have continued to expand, not as much as my waistline, but a sustained and determined crusade has seen Betfred establish nearly 1,700 shops as they march diligently onwards and upwards. Red-letter years include 2004 when they launched their digital platform *Betfred.com* and 2013, when *Betfred TV* was born which re-established yours truly too. They also run *The Tote*, an old, venerated British establishment that's in safe hands while they possess the keys to the door.

They moved their head office from sunny Salford to Warrington and that has proved a cracking decision in my opinion. Every time I visit there it impresses me as a town on the up; an ambitious community, new rugby league ground, beautiful town hall gates, modern and improving infrastructure. Then again, you've always got to wonder why carrot top, Chris Evans left town.

So that is my love affair with Betfred, I won't go on too long or the public will think I'm taking backhanders (I did tell Fred no more post-dated cheques, but what can you do). I love you Fred Done, you are a Mancunian Napoleon, a giant standing on the shoulders of giants, the Isambard Kingdom Brunel of betting, a colossus, lord of lords, king of kings, ground breaker, humanitarian, philanthropist, man of the people but most of all, family man and friend.

One last thing, Betfred puts money back into sport as they sponsor horse racing, football, rugby league and snooker. In a profession full of more sharks than Montego Bay, they are some of the good guys. Don't get me started on the sinners, we could fill the next five chapters.

I was now back on my feet, getting there slowly but surely. I was taking on the game of life with renewed energy and thought it sounds easy, you all know it can be a bitch. God laughs every time we plan the next stage of our lives for the road has many forks, we just have to keep picking the right route. A few months before I went to live at Sharon's abode, her marriage broke up. These things happen and the timing was fortunate for me really. If Sharon had still been married and I turned up at the front door, I doubt that could have helped an ailing relationship. Could you just imagine each time her ex-husband came home from work and found a strange, fat cockney bloke mooching about. Would you give that the thumbs up? No, neither would I.

Now for all the conspiracy theorists out there and I know most of you like a wager, how many think I was with her before my operation? A good few of you would have said it's odds-on but you would have been wrong and done your money. I will go on the Jeremy Kyle show and take the lie-detector test if anyone wants a hefty punt to say otherwise, winnings to go to selected charities. There were no shenanigans going on whatsoever;

we were both good friends and also, what state was I in? I needed two Viagra just to tinkle on my Hush Puppies. The end result of Sharon's marital breakup was a move for the three of us to a small, nearby village. We just about managed to come up with the rental deposit on a little cottage as money was extremely tight but then we were a happy tight knit band.

I found myself reminiscing about how life had changed in the last few years; from living quite an affluent life in Birmingham, going to all the top restaurants with a personal favourite being Cielo, an excellent Italian establishment in a plush part of the city. On the other hand, I would look forward to a small portion of fish and chips from Keyworth Fisheries on a Friday night. It was really lovely, it was different strokes for different folks. I was now a changed character from my past life. Gorging out on a seven-course meal was part of history, the gastric sleeve would never let that happen again. We had to cut our cloth accordingly and I accepted my lot, the alternative was not worth the death certificate it was written on. If I'd carried on my world of excess gorging, I would now be pushing up the daisies and singing with the choir invisible. I was probably the luckiest man in the world but my mental state was still very fragile. Everything in our lives is about making our own evaluation of the present situation. Good or bad, it's what we make of it and move on accordingly.

All the good natured 'nudge-nudge' 'wink-wink' merchants were still barking up the wrong redwood but all that has happened over a rational, extended period of time, most of it stress related on my part, has actually brought Sharon and I closer together. We were and still are good pals but other things have just developed intrinsically and seemed right for us when they did, as it still does today. So, for any non-believers, I say to you in my best French accent, *Honi soit qui mal y pense* (shame be to him who thinks badly of it) or as my old Mum used to say, 'If you don't like it, stick it up your jumper.'

It must have been so hard for daughter Jaimee to suddenly have another man in her life but we got there in the end. She's a good girl and has occasionally worked for me at the races. It's never easy to take on someone else's kids but thanks to a bit of give and take it is very satisfying to be a part of her life. Sharon has been wonderful and has really taken care of me. She still works for the local funeral directors in town; now that's a game that won't run out of clientele.

* * * *

Chapter Two

WALKING IN SHADOWLANDS

In 1929, Mick The Miller became the first greyhound to run 525 yards in less than 30 seconds.

The dark spectres of despair, despondence and depression were still pervading my soul; this depression was going to be my toughest ever opponent making Frankie Dettori resemble a clawless pussycat heading for the catnip. It had beaten or seriously walloped bigger and better personalities than myself. Why or when it comes is something of a mystery but politely asking it to go, do one and make somebody else really miserable never works, you have to smash it to bloody smithereens. In my case I think I got the split decision, two submissions to one; I've got a lovely technique with a classical Boston Crab.

Hollywood actor Owen Wilson had it that bad that he attempted suicide when he was 38 but thankfully he's fine now. Princess Di, Catherine Zeta Jones and Gwyneth Paltrow suffered from it in the past; all rich, privileged people who experienced the suffocating black cloak of misery. Buzz Aldrin, the second man on the moon is another who has had his own personal eclipses. He still regrets saying 'After you, Neil.'

Comedians have a reputation for manic depressiveness indeed Russell Brand is a deep thinker and worrier. Then again he does support West Ham, it's not a barrel of laughs down there at any time. Also, if he told the odd funny joke it might just help him along the road to recovery.

My own personal favourite comedian, Spike Milligan, was in and out of mental asylums with undue regularity. Sometimes his depression would last over a year and he was plagued by repeat attacks all throughout his life. I suppose the only way he could combat it was to have a dark sense of humour himself.

Peter Sellers once called at his flat and Spike lunged at him with a potato knife. Spike never, ever bought spuds again apparently. When his other Goon mate, Harry Secombe died in 2001, Spike declared, 'I'm glad he went before me, I didn't want him to sing at my funeral.' He once said, 'My father had a profound influence on me, he was a lunatic.' He was laughing to the end and his gravestone fittingly has the epitaph, "I told you I was ill." What a man. He suffered more than most and came through on his own madcap terms.

The Queen described 1992 as an "annus horribilis" after witnessing several family divorces and Windsor Castle going up like Krakatoa. Well, 2013 was turning into my own "annus haemorrhoidis turdus," which any Latin scholar could translate as 'a large pain in the Arsenal' and for a change that wasn't referring to Wenger. I was going to have to firmly strap myself in because the rest of the year was going to plummet downwards faster than that large, cylindrical shaped cheese at the annual Coopers Hill cheese-rolling contest in Gloucestershire. Watched by a crowd of four thousand, fifty optimistic village idiots chase the cheese down a steep hill and there's always claret spilt, broken limbs and multiple concussions and that's just in the pubs, après-ski. It's a real, traditional event.

It was a funny old year... though not really, you know roughly what I mean. Before any of the marital debacle I had made the holy pilgrimage to Blackpool Tower Circus Arena for the annual Snooker Shoot-Out.

An extremely difficult tournament to win, the Snooker Shoot-Out is normally a very good and advantageous betting proposition for a bookie. The format consists of 64 of the world's best snooker players, up against the clock, competing in ten-minute frames, an absolute lottery knockout contest. Any of the players could win it, oh happy days. The odds were in our favour, with a fair wind and the anticipated upsets, I was hoping to be coming away with a full satchel but don't forget it was 2013!

Me and Lofty (Steve Cooke) booked into the busy Norbreck Castle Hotel. I handed £200 to the receptionist but he added that he needed another 20 pounds for the dog. I said we didn't have a dog, but he added, 'You've got the dog's room.'

It was going to be one of those weeks.

The snooker fun was scheduled over three days, starting on Friday, January 25th at 6pm. That very same afternoon we did our bollocks in William Hill's. A few stray bets, too many drinks and a suicidal run of bad luck reduced our betting war chest of three thousand spondulicks down to a mere 160. A slow and chastened, tactical retreat that made Dunkirk look like a party on the sand was the best policy. Things were looking exceedingly grim.

Somehow over the three days, we managed to pull back just over a thousand and at that stage I was grateful for any small mercies. It wasn't very professional but at least we hadn't been totally wiped out. Can I laugh about it now? You betcha but then I still fondly remember the Falklands War, the miners' strike and the 1987 hurricane so there's obviously something not right upstairs. But I'm all for pragmatic, rose-tinted nostalgia; it's what makes us Britons great.

So, that was how I was performing early on that year and this was before the *merde* hit the cooling apparatus. It was truly shambolic but compared to post February it looked utterly textbook. I've just felt a chronic shiver go right through me. February could be such a cruel month; snowstorms, blizzards, repeats of Groundhog Day, Kim Jong-Il's birthday (the North Korean nutter who's son is worse), strikes on the trains, no money after Christmas and Arsenal out of the running for the league yet again. Thank fuck it was only 28 days long in 2013; that was more than enough for me.

Sue was gone, that was de facto and I was a quivering wreck but at least February slinked off into history as well. I couldn't take another rank month like that again. They say March comes in like a lion and goes out like a lamb but I never heard a roar, didn't notice it coming in and by the time it wimped out, I was way past caring.

In a normal year come March there are two words that have me salivating at the mouth. No, not Easter Eggs, you cretin! The majestic, the incomparable National Hunt meeting, the one and only *Cheltenham Festival*. The trouble was I must have been feeling more than a touch out of sorts because I couldn't raise a canter for it. In fact, I didn't want to go but every year there is a precursor to the racing on the Monday night that I'd been going to for years; namely the horse racing preview night at the world famous Hollow Bottom pub, in Guiting Power near Cheltenham. If memory serves me correct, one could partake in an exclusive buffet and meet some of the great and good of jumps racing for less than a score.

Top banana.

I forced myself into the car, repeating to the mantra, 'You are going, you will enjoy it when you eventually get there.' And with that happy thought reverberating in my brain I drove south. I was really glad I did because as soon as I walked in, I thought these are my people. I immediately relaxed and really enjoyed the night. There is a well-known proverb that demands the words buffet and Wiltshire go hand in hand but I'd only just come out of the operation a month previously so a chicken drumstick, some quiche and half a scotch egg would suffice just nicely. There would even be a bit more room as the head waiter always used to put out two large buffet tables, one marked "racing guests" and the other for "Gary Wiltshire."

Speakers included retired jockey and smooth speaking Carl Llewellyn, winner of the classic treble for jump jockeys, the English, Scottish and Welsh Grand Nationals, a very tough feat to achieve. His two Aintree Grand National wins came six years apart, the first on April 4th 1992 on the plucky Party Politics. Loads of desperate housewives, once a year virgin betters and those of the conspiratorial, coincidental persuasion backed him into 14/1 as the general election was on the following Thursday, April 9th. That was the year Welsh windbag Neil Kinnock, the Foghorn Leghorn of the Labour Party, was giving it the big one prior to the election only for the quieter man, John Major of the Tories to draw clear in the last furlong. Neither were thoroughbreds, in fact I wouldn't give tuppence to listen to either of those plodders ever again.

Llewellyn won again in 1998 on *Earth Summit*. This animal was an equine stamina machine, particularly if it rained as he was a talented mud lark. He was hammered down to favourite as if defeat was out of the question after it had rained cats and dogs all throughout the morning and then after dinner it was coming down like stair rods. A rumour went round the course that Noah's Ark had been spotted, surging up the Mersey Estuary and he consequently jumped off at 7/1. He resolutely obliged, staying on to win by eleven lengths from the gallant top weight *Suny Bay*. *Earth Summit* matched Llewellyn by winning the Scottish and Welsh Grand Nationals as well. In fact he was so good, I think I could have ridden him to victory that day though Carl reckons if I'd got on board he would have done a "Devon Loch" at the start, cheeky bugger.

Other speakers on the panel besides me were the talented and likeable Twiston-Davies brothers, Sam and Willie. They are two precocious lads, sure to go right to the top. They are definitely chips off the old block and a credit to their father, ace trainer, Nigel.

Always in attendance are the feted, self-proclaimed "Gentlemen Bookmakers" Star Sports represented by the ubiquitous Luke Tarr, their head of public relations. He's a bit of a geezer, a jack the lad but a top man and very knowledgeable about sports betting. He should go on to bigger and better things, maybe a big television sports slot but you never can tell. Even if he doesn't, he's young, rich, intelligent and good-looking. Don't you just hate these lucky bleeders who seem to be able to do anything without trying that hard. Maybe it's all in the genes. Life's not fair.

Star Sports founder Ben Keith is an old pal of mine and like me he's a greyhound man. His solicitor dad took him to the track one night; he had a winner and was hooked. He then started clerking for various bookies. I remember him working for Barry Slaney, a famous bookmaker who had a loud stentorian voice that he used to attract punters to his pitch. Ben later realised his ambition and become a bookie himself.

He started out at Sittingbourne and then Walthamstow before buying some betting shops with varying degrees of success. He found his niche with Star Sports, a company who've developed a reputation for not being scared to lay a big bet. They are now one of the major players and you will always find them at Aintree, Ascot and Cheltenham. Ben is very experienced, articulate and professional and the most sanguine guy I have ever met. He's also a gourmet of fine food though he is quality to my quantity. So, best of luck to Luke and the rest of the crew at Star Sports; they are a cracking outfit and I always look forward to meeting them on my travels, may there be many more great days in the Cotswolds.

After I left the Hollow Bottom I had that sinking feeling again. I was berating myself because I'd just enjoyed the most wonderful night and tomorrow was the start of the greatest horse racing extravaganza on the planet. I should have been over the moon with excitement but I was lower than a snake's belly. I drove home in a controlled daze hoping that a good night's sleep would bring me out of this desperate, unwelcome malaise but my own rationale was going haywire.

That night I tossed and turned. I couldn't sleep, worrying about the next day. It was totally irrational but this is what happens when you are under the power of a greater force. It was once called *manic depression* but the politically correct brigade has re-termed it *bi-polar disorder*. To be honest, that didn't make me feel a whole lot better. Stop bloody changing things you meddling morons. A dustman is not a waste management and disposal technician, a librarian doesn't cut it as an information advisor and a life guard on Baywatch was not called a wet leisure assistant although Pamela Anderson could have called herself anything she wanted before administering me with the kiss of life.

The next morning, I had the classic red-eye. I took one look in the downstairs hall mirror at the creature from the black lagoon and decided it wasn't a pretty sight. The public could have a welcome break with a no show from me; I would stay in bed all day, head deep under the duvet, everybody leave me alone style.

I'd had an uneventful hour under the sheets when a little birdie in my head tweeted, 'If you stay in bed today, you will do so for the rest of your life.' Damn clever those talking canaries. I knew I had to rouse myself and make an effort. Believe me, it was one of the hardest things I've ever had to do. At this stage I wasn't taking any anti-depressants, I was fighting the unseen enemy on my lonesome and he was battering seven bells out of me. I was clearly out my depth.

On the journey to Cheltenham I had no sense of fun, excitement or awareness at all. Two or three times I nearly turned back but eventually I drove into the West Car Park and pulled up the handbrake. It's about a five-minute walk to the entrances, outside hundreds of people were milling past the car in all directions but I had absolutely no intention of joining them. Looking down on the passenger seat there was an unopened, pristine Racing Post dated Tuesday 12th March 2013. I'd bought it at a petrol station earlier when things had seemed lighter and much more whimsical but that was an hour ago, the cumulus nimbus storm clouds had since drenched and addled my poisoned mind. I still can't tell you who ran and won that day and to tell you the truth, I couldn't have cared less.

I waited until every man and his dog were inside Prestbury Park Racecourse then broke down and cried my eyes out. I was sobbing for hours on end but I found it a really cathartic experience; it was like purging my blackened soul, I actually felt a lot better. I suppose if the late Ken Dodd had popped up on the radio singing Tears that would have broken my channel of thoughtful calmness and I'd have probably head-butted the dashboard.

One of my mother's favourite songs from the early 1960s was Julie London's *Cry Me A River*. Well I'd done my fair share that afternoon; I'd probably cried the Zambezi, Orinoco, Nile and Danube as well as the River Sow, a small tributary of the Trent that runs through the centre of Stafford. I threw that one in because my writer likes to give his hometown a mention in all of his books. I can't fathom why, in my opinion the best thing that comes out of that town is the A34, though to be fair, it is a good stop off point for anybody on their way to Uttoxeter Races. Now that's my kind of town.

I sloped off the car park one race before the end. There were a few lost souls wandering around aimlessly, they'd obviously done their money before the finale. Boy I knew that feeling but at that moment I couldn't spare any solace for them. The man I was fond of more than most; me, Big Gary, was in a quandary, there was a mortal battle to fight, I had to win it; that was the very least. I owed to my kids and close friends; Wiltshire would need to be the warrior supreme.

In early March I'd been kindly invited to a knees up by Fred Done, a special birthday party for his wife Mo. The cabaret was fantastic and the food was out of this world. I was there as a single man, bereft of all confidence and imagining I was the only singleton in the ballroom despite there being dozens of people there on their own. But in my mind it was just me, I was torturing myself with worst scenario delusion. Back at the hotel I slid up the stairs, shuffled into my empty room, shut the curtains, switched the lights off and retired to bed.

In the pitch black of the night I had a lachrymal lie down with the Johnny Nash song, *Tears on my Pillow* replaced by "Tears on both Pillows" by Gary Wiltshire. The world, at that moment, was a cold, dark and lonely place.

It was time to see the doctor. I'd tried an apple a day and that was total bullshit; my whole body was sore and aching, I needed a professional, medical bod in my corner. Being a typical man I'd been avoiding a trip to the surgery but the pain was so bad that I couldn't put it off any longer. Ladies reading this probably know their husbands, brothers or fathers will only go to the medical centre as a last resort. Why do we all react like this? Who knows, it must be something in our DNA.

The upshot was the man in lily-white doubled my prescribed dosage of Voltarol dispersible tablets. Between you, the bedpost, and me I'd been on those bad boys on and off over thirty years, mainly for arthritis and inflamed joints. I know that revelation will come as a massive shock to most of you but could I help it if I wasn't the natural athlete you all thought I was? For the severe depression he put me on a regimen of strong SSRIs (Selective Serotonin Reuptake Inhibitors). Of course, why hadn't I thought of them? Mainly because it was bloody unpronounceable, I just concentrated on swallowing the little sods.

A couple of days later I wasn't exactly in the pink but the pills had semi worked their magic. I even smiled when next door's cat took another sloppy dump in my garden; last week he would have been dropped kicked over the gate, two points for St Helens style. For all cat lovers, that was just a joke. I never missed an episode of Top Cat when I was a kid; Officer Dibble was always the bad guy. In fact, no animals were harmed or injured during the writing of this book.

On Friday 22nd March, I had the great honour of being invited to the TV studios for *At The Races* with ex-jockeys Luke Harvey and Jason Weaver.

What a double act, they put Hale and Pace to shame but then again the bubonic plague was funnier than they were.

Jason the "Weaver Shark" is a canny wee tipster and a natural, *bon vivant* while Luke is the perfect foil, regularly taking a fair smattering of light hearted abuse. Luke's marriage only lasted 16 months and he still gets his leg pulled about this and other situations but he calmly takes everything that's bowled at him in good spirit and deftly deflects them to the boundary.

The day Barney Curley came storming over to Luke and John McCririck was television gold. Curley's horse, *Cristoforo* had drifted out like the proverbial barge from odds on favourite to 3/1 throughout the day and then ran a shocker, being beaten a long way from home. Big Mac was giving it large on air but as soon as he saw Curley looming up with intent he quickly changed into a contrite little choirboy. Luke was just being himself; the man hasn't got a bad bone or act of malice in his body.

How many of us would have reacted as well as he did when Curley was in his face, shouting, 'You were an under achiever in life, never was a rider, you know nothing about racing and shouldn't even have a job.' Now Barney, don't sit on the fence; say what you mean. Talk about being direct and to the point.

Anyway, the remarkable thing was Luke never turned a hair, adopting the stance of a calm, consummate professional. McCririck eventually came to Luke's aid, pontificating that he was a brave man who once took risks jumping fences but Curley obviously didn't see it that way and demanded that the interview be terminated. If you haven't seen it then give *YouTube* a gander, it's hilarious.

Jason Weaver made the transition from world-class jockey to television pundit with effortless aplomb; the man is a natural communicator, broadcaster and frontman. Many of us are lucky to have a decent stab at one job but in his first career Jason also rode over a thousand winners, was stable jockey for Mark Johnston's top establishment and is one of only a small number of riders to break the 200 winners mark in a season.

I recall he actually rode a winner for me one previous season at Southwell Races. While everyone was busy patting him on the back in the winners' enclosure I whispered in his ear that I'd got something for him on the car park in half an hour. His little face lit up agog with excitement. I'd had a touch that week and got my hands on a score of foreign Sat Navs with speed camera warnings off a pal down the market, Del Boy style, cheap and cushty. He came sprinting out of the jockey changing rooms, I handed him a box and he opened it then feigned happiness. Well what did he suspect, a wad of fifty-pound notes? I was Gary Wiltshire for fuck's sake, not the Aga Khan.

So they were the men, my boys, my buddies with whom I was participating. That evening the central feature of the show was a popular concept called *Get In!* It was a tipping competition where the public would select horses for the chance of winning a £200 free bet. I can confidently say that I enjoyed myself very much. It was the first time that year I completely forgot about all my travails and troubles, such was the effect of being in magical company with close-knit camaraderie and just experiencing the sheer contentment of being in a safe and secure environment. I really didn't want it too end but the happy hours came and went all too fleetingly. Still, I suppose it's perfectly natural to want the good things in life to go on longer and bad times to never materialise so I wasn't fretting too badly as I left the studio. I mused that I just might have turned the corner.

A few positive actions then hoisted me up to a better level of fulfilment, starting with the move up to Sharon's house in mid April. It wasn't totally ideal but a step up on how I'd been living, nay, existing previously. It was still a fight though because the darned depression was lurking in the background. If there's one thing I can't abide it's a lurker, nothing good ever comes from that covert standpoint.

So if you ever meet me on a racecourse or at an event then absolutely no lurking please. I can tolerate loitering and lingering or even the odd bit of amateur mooching but Gary Wiltshire's pitch these days is a non-lurk zone. In the past a lurker would occasionally get through if they were bearing gifts like an 99 ice cream with double flake or jumbo hot dog with onions; that would definitely neutralise any lurk ban but my standards are a lot higher now that the appetite has waned considerably.

The antidepressants might well have been having a placebo effect on my thought processes. I was probably overestimating their potency because if they were as good as they were cracked up to be then I wouldn't have suffered so badly on my worst days. They never even registered on some occasions. I soon realised they were not the ultimate panacea or universal remedy, as my worst moods were down in the dungeons of despair and darker than Whitby Jet.

Spring turned to summer and my moods were capricious, bouncing up and down more than a fiddlers elbow; the world lightened then darkened and vice versa. Though not at the top of my game I was coping by going racing and winning a few bob, at least I was keeping the wolf from the front door (and not that long haired wally from *Gladiators,* either).

The Investec Derby Festival that year put a few quid in the old satchel. Oaks day on Friday 31st May was mighty dandy as the aptly named *Talent* won the showpiece race. It was nice to see one of the smaller stables at the time winning a classic with Ralph Beckett's flying filly coming home at 20/1.

I was optimistic enough to hope for more of the same the next day for the big one, The Derby. This race was slightly different from the previous day's Oaks when there had been three or four fancied runners. The Derby was all about one horse, the Jim Bolger trained, Dawn Approach. He was the one the bookies feared and they were all running scared. I had an opinion that only the distance could beat him and could he handle the undulating one and a half miles of the unique Epsom Downs? This was conjecture of course and the upshot was that he was priced up ridiculously skinny at odds of 5/4. For all of you out there who misguidedly thought I'd take it on, thank you so much for your faith in me still having balls of steel.

I was older and wiser (and poorer) so let some other young buck make the headlines. I decided to leave well alone, I'd had more burnt fingers than Captain Birdseye had fish fingers. For all the wise after the event merchants, I know he trailed in last, I know he ran too freely and I know he didn't get the distance but I only surmised that just before the race. Many times before the start I'd harbour an opinion and quite a few times I'd be bang on the money but more often than not I'd be on a different tangent. We are all human, fallible and prone to bad luck as well as unforeseen circumstances.

Anyway, the Aidan O' Brien third favourite *Ruler Of The World* won the race at 7/1, not totally unfancied but I made a small profit on the book. I was up a good few quid over the festival but I wasn't feeling that great; my head obviously still wasn't right but I'd just have to carry on regardless.

The notion that anyone making a lot of money cannot get depression is sheer bunkum. Stan Collymore was earning five figures each week playing for Aston Villa when he went under with it. John Gregory the Villa manager was not sympathetic about it, saying to the papers, 'What's he got to be depressed about, he's earning thousands.' He just didn't get it. It's not about the money. The money is irrelevant; getting better is all it's about. Collymore became suicidal; he said the illness was withering his soul.

Piers Morgan, everyone's favourite presenter, waded in and announced Collymore should "man-up." The late, great Eric Bristow (RIP champ, darts legend) would later have his Sky TV darts contract terminated for using the term "wimps" for footballers who had been sexually abused years earlier by coaches (watch this space, Wiltshire is another to soon have a run in with Sky). Double standards spring to mind. Every time you switch on the television Piers is hosting this and that or being a guest speaker elsewhere while poor old Eric, a genuine sporting superstar, was banished, never to be seen again.

Bristow become an honorary Staffordshire man having come up to Stoke from The Smoke before moving on to the rugged moorlands town of Leek. Eric became a wallaby hunter, searching for a large colony of them on the bleak terrain. They were released in the 1940s from a private zoo and flourished for many years. Eric never found them and they are all extinct now after the last one died in 2009. People still report seeing them but that's mostly late on a Saturday night, falling out of The Red Lion after downing ten pints of Old Peculiar.

The best way to explain depression to all the cynics, doubters and flat-earthers out there who think money overrides all, is this:

Replace the word depression with the word cancer, aids or cirrhosis and then just ponder; would having a million pound in the bank make life worth living? It might do for small periods but knowing you had a chronic illness that was ruining your life, your future and your very existence would nullify all the money in the world. I hope and pray none of you ever come face to face with any of those terrible afflictions but on a lesser scale, who wouldn't give a week's wages for agonising toothache to just disappear or for a persistent irritating cough to evaporate into the ether. We don't like pain, we like pleasure, we are pleasure seekers and there is no pleasure at all in depression; it is a pain in your brain, a scourge of the mind. I hope people can accept depression as a serious illness because over the years, right up to the present day, blasé breakfast presenters still get away with 'man-up' jibes. The modern forward- thinking majority have recognised the condition for what it is but media wise, individuals think they know so much, but they seem to learn so little.

The week after The Derby I was trotting along to Bolton to price up the players for the UK Open (PDC) Darts knockout at the Whites Hotel at the Bolton Wanderers stadium, at the time called The Reebok but now known as The Macron. It always attracts a huge field but from my past experiences, the cream always seems to rise to the top. The tournament was played over four days, 6th - 9th June and on the first day alone there were fifty matches with the field eventually whittled down to the best eight in the quarter-finals on the last day.

I tried to work it as best I could as I was having concentration issues but the old noggin pulled me through. In each and every match I was siding with the higher ranked player and in the final Phil Taylor beat Andy Hamilton 11-4 in the battle of the Stokies so no surprise there. It hadn't been a bad week but my life existed on a day-to-day self-appraisal; four seasons in one day was never so apt.

Saturday night at the dogs would always give me the buzz so you would think The Greyhound Derby Final at Wimbledon Stadium on June 29th would have me jumping around like a nest of hornets but you'd be wrong. I was about as lively as Monty Python's *Eric the half-bee* and he'd been in a serious accident. I was doing the punditry for Sky TV but behind my jovial on-air manner, my head was up my jacksy; I was walking around like a George Romero zombie. I only just managed to hold it all together but I was totally apathetic about most of the results that evening, even though there was plenty of serious prize money to be won.

The final is the one and only thing I can recollect with a biggish priced dog *Sidaz Jack* winning fairly comfortably at 6/1. I was delighted for the winning trainer, the legend that is Charlie Lister, triumphant for the seventh time. I wasn't quite so happy with my own predicament. I was starting to beat myself up mentally, becoming unhinged which is a very dangerous stance when you hate yourself and your life. I'd been through the mill and I was being ground down to desperation.

Straight after the last race I didn't drive home to the Midlands as a subconscious urge took me south, towards Eastbourne and first to Pevensey Bay. I hadn't been there since I was a kid in happier times. I walked along the beach front for about 15 minutes then got back in the motor and headed for Beachy Head.

I drove into The Beachy Head Pub car park from where it was a fair walk to the white cliffs and lighthouse. Did I have the bottle though to cross over to the other side? A staggering twenty people each year on average jump to their deaths here. They are the highest chalk cliffs in the country; it's a long way to fall. I looked at my watch and it had gone midnight; did I want to be another statistic? I would probably be the best-known geezer to say Goodnight Irene at this suicide hotspot and it would be all over the red tops and sports channels. I would certainly be the heaviest; it wouldn't take long with my weight to plummet onto the cruel rocks below.

A desperate person also has to be a brave person to take his or her own life but that person at this moment wasn't me. I'd come down here to test my resolve or lack of it and discovered there was still plenty of fight in the old bulldog. Tomorrow was another day and it was a day I wanted to experience. God knows what Sharon thought when I stumbled through the front door at half-five in the morning.

It was now the heart of summer, Saturday July 13th and a sizzler brought a great throng of piscatorial punters, all heading for sunny Stoke on Trent. Their destination was Cudmore Fisheries in the borough of Newcastle Under Lyme, just off the road to Market Drayton. Fishomania was in town; the F.A. Cup of angling and really big prize money was on offer. Those who once opined that fishing was a worm on one end of a stick and an idiot on the other end were at home watching TV and crying into their handkerchiefs, they had obviously missed their fishy vocation.

Barry Hearn has brilliantly masterminded this event, as only he can and it's hard to believe that last year 2018 was its 25th anniversary. Matchroom Sports will sponsor events such as this, sports that fall somewhere between fringe and mainstream like fishing, darts, snooker, pool, ten-pin bowling and table tennis. Love him or not (I worship the ground he walks on), nobody out there can say he isn't the king of promoting. He sees potential in sports no one else would touch and without him some of those sports would be dead or in moribund state.

He, like Fred Done, is another giant of sport who has saved my skin. I won't gloss over it here because he gets embarrassed when people like myself praise him in public (he often likes me to do it with a private audience though). A man from the distant past, Alexander of Macedonia usurped Barry's title long before Bazza was born but if he came back today, I'm sure he would resonate that he was the one not worthy. The one true heir should be Barry the Great, now that has a nice aura to it. I personally would get everyone at Matchroom to address him like that, even make it compulsory. Cheers me old mate.

Back to the fishing and Barry, in his infinite wisdom, had me there at Cudmore as the sole bookie. I couldn't fault him but it was yet again not one of my going days. As glorious as the weather was my heart and mind were as black as a Newgate knocker. At this stage you are all probably saying, not again you miserable twat, can't you cheer up for one event? I must admit, it was incredible how many times I wasn't right for a big day's sport but maybe the anxiety of the whole occasion affected my moods as well. I just don't know. If I did, I'd surely be part-time bookie and full-time psychiatrist where the money is much better.

What I did definitely know was that I felt like shit and with all the money cascading in for Wirral angler Jamie Hughes he was the one to watch, so I kept shortening him up to keep my losses to a minimum. The swine meanwhile just kept pulling fish out of the water non-stop; it was like they were throwing themselves onto his hook (there was a rumour afterwards that he had a waterproof I Pod music player in the lake pumping out Des O'Connor's greatest hits and the fish just couldn't take it). He readily outclassed the top quality opposition and eventually won in a hack canter, to the delight of a huge partisan crowd.

I hadn't lost a lot but it wasn't about the wonga, I just wanted to be somewhere else. If memory serves me right Jamie won 30k prize money that afternoon. The guy was a big lump like myself, a fine example of manhood but I've seen pictures of him recently and he's shed a bit of timber. We're both decreasing in girth. He actually won again in 2015 and 2017 and that proves he is an exceptional angler because at Fishomania an unfavourable draw can kill your chances stone dead. It is the equivalent of an outside draw at Chester or Wolverhampton in races over a sprint distance of five or six furlongs. Some trainers will even try and withdraw their horses on medical grounds if they feel they can't win with a draw out in the car park.

His winning haul was an incredible 68 kilograms, which was more than Jesus served up in the miracle of the five loaves and two fishes when he fed the five thousand. So, if there was no divine intervention from the big man upstairs all I can say is Jamie, you are the master of modern angling. Good luck to you Sir and I wish you a lifetime of tight lines, or as I like to say, bent rods.

Talking of the dead draw or even death, this was the first time I'd let that insidious thought enter my mind since Beachy Head. After the event I was looking slantendicular at the uninviting, murky water of the lake and pondering whether I should jump in and do everyone a favour. A belly flop from me would probably cause a tsunami that large it would take out half the villages on the Shropshire, Staffordshire border and I didn't want that on my scorecard.

Then I recalled watching Billy Connolly reminiscing about a school trip to the seaside. The teacher was encouraging the kids to go swimming in the freezing North Sea while young Billy hadn't so much as dipped his toe in. 'In ye go Connolly, ye big jesse', commanded the teacher.

'We don't belong in there Sir, we don't belong,' came the reply. He was spot on as well. I'm definitely a *terra firma* man, the nearest I like to get to fish are the battered ones on my plate.

I'm actually a poor swimmer, always have been. A width at the local baths would be like swimming the English Channel for me. In fact on the holiday leisure front abroad, I won't go in the water for the first few days, being the size I am and chalky white; in case somebody thinks I'm Moby Dick's younger brother and launches a harpoon at me. Which has just reminded me of a bookie colleague of mine. His mother-in-law was a big woman who got a job on a Norwegian whaler but she didn't bother with the traditional methods of dispatching the whales; she used to dive in and strangle them, he's petrified of her.

2013 was still playing its little perverse game. On the best racing day of the month, Saturday 24th of August, I was quickly booked into Little Aston Hospital, Sutton Coldfield to go under the knife again courtesy of a bloody large and painful gallstone that had to be removed. At this rate there was going to be nothing left of me (oh yeah) but little did I know all that had gone on in the previous months would pale into trifling insignificance. If there was proof of such a thing as preordained kismet, I must have been a terrible scoundrel in a past life because fate's size twelve Dr Martens were determined to give me a damn good booting. The year would be going out with a bang.

September, October and November came and went, all benign months for me mood and temperament wise. I was occasionally down in the dumps but generally things were looking a tad more favourable. I could handle being discombobulated now and then so maybe a dystopian future was not inevitable.

On Wednesday 11th December I was even invited to the Bookmakers Afternoon Greyhound Services (BAGS) Christmas lunch at a restaurant in Victoria, Central London, just around the corner from the BAGS offices. A very agreeable repast was enjoyed by all with quite a few of the board present including company secretary, Graham McLennan from Tring. After lunch Tom Kelly (the Chief Executive of BAGS) approached and he very kindly presented me with a bottle of quality French champagne. It beat hands down the reduced price demi-john of Pomagne I'd been liberally slurping back home.

We were relaxing after lunch, all pals together like pigs in Chardonnay, comrades in arms and jolly good chaps to boot. Three weeks later everything would turn to enmity, current chums would show their true colours and morph into fair-weather friends, especially the aforementioned Tom Kelly. I could describe him as a snake in the grass but that would be doing reptiles a disservice. The bottom line was I'd be queuing up again at the bloody Co-op for my weekly supply of Pomagne. I came, I saw, I conked out.

On Friday 27th, the day after Boxing Day things got a whole lot worse. I was playing the dogs as a punter and one would think that after watching thousands of greyhound races, I'd have some semblance of backing the right ones. That theory paddled down shit creek when I dropped £1,700. If Sharon had found out she'd have cut my goolies off and stuffed them somewhere cheeky.

The next day I went back to the same bookmakers in Carlton Hill, Nottingham for some more action. As mad as a hatter or a strategic genius, at that moment the jury was out. A lot of people after that bad Friday would have steered clear but I was made of sterner stuff. There is an old saying, form is temporary; class is permanent. It was pointless going in pussy-footed, there was a lot of money to pull back. I steamed right in with multiple forecast doubles and trebles; hard to pull off but very lucrative if one could get a small percentage of the bets in. At close of play I'd won back over £8,700, Big Gary was back in business. What a way to end the year and a trip to Tenerife would be just the tonic to revitalise me after a thoroughly bad twelve months. Meanwhile, in the hinterland, without any of my knowledge, events were unfolding in the most apocalyptic way for yours truly.

The earliest I could get a flight out on short notice was New Years Day so on the 29th I decided to stand at the Cottenham point-to-point meeting which is just North of Cambridge. On the way down I cashed in one of my two winning betting slips at the bookies for over 4k. Lovely jubbly, my pockets were overflowing with crisp, new bank notes. It was reassuring to have multiple Adam Smiths and numerous Charles Darwins on my person, all seemed fine in this green and pleasant land of ours, ignorance was such bliss.

Sharon couldn't get all the time off work to go abroad so I took the admirable but freeloading Lofty instead. It would be blooming marvellous to feel the sun on our backs after a miserable start to the winter. I gave Sharon a thick wad of money for some lady retail therapy; it was extremely satisfying to have pulled off a nice touch, they didn't come around that often.

The second day on the island was Jan 2nd and it's a day I will never forget. We were slowly unwinding by the swimming pool having settled in nicely after the journey and were contentedly watching the world amble by. My mobile phone startled the life out of me when it unexpectedly cranked into gear. I'd only brought it in case there was an emergency back home. I expected to hear Sharon on the other end and was half relieved when a man's voice said, 'Gary is that you?' It was only Joe Scanlon, member of the BAGS board and also on the board of Betfred. I'd known Joe for thirty years, why was he ringing?

'Fuck me, Joe, this had better be important, I'm on holiday.' He was apologetic, he had rung my home and Sharon had given him the mobile number. My heart began to sink. Joe was a serious man, a tough-talking

Southerner who had moved North in a professional capacity. I could tell by the tone of his voice that he was about to deliver bad news so I squinted, clenched my buttocks and waited for the coup de grace.

'Gary you have to get back as soon as possible, this is an emergency. We need to see you at the Betfred head office. There have been accusations and allegations, it needs sorting out pronto for the sake of all relevant parties.'

I didn't like the sound of that so I relayed back to Joe that I'd be on the first available flight out of Tenerife back to Blighty. This was the last thing I needed. I'd made good progress during the autumn and winter months, my condition had improved and consolidated. I was now stressed to high heaven again. Certain people were coming for me; maybe they didn't want to see my headstone in the cemetery but homeless and penniless would do them for starters. I wasn't as weak, physically or mentally as I had been early doors the previous year but I would still need every ounce of muscle strength, every last scintilla of rational thought to repulse their destructive onslaught. Even then, my very best efforts might not be enough to hold them at bay, their big guns definitely trumped my catapult but the white flag wasn't for hoisting anytime soon.

I arrived at the Betfred head office to be greeted by managing director John Haddock. I turned up like the condemned man. Tom Kelly of BAGS had been alleging that he had been waiting 17 years for me to get my come-uppance.

Apparently he still had a cob on from when Frankie rode his magnificent seven, inferring that I single-handedly stopped Fujiyama Crest shortening even more, costing him and other bookies piles of money. I recall losing a fair wedge myself but if that was his reckoning he was obviously rank delusional. One thing was not for debate though; he held a bloody long grudge.

I felt like a betting heretic in front of the Spanish Inquisition with Kelly playing the part of the murderous, mad monk, Torquemada.

Down to the nitty gritty. I was alleged to be the ringleader of an underground betting ring in Nottingham: capo of capos, frontman for nefarious types who would stop at nothing to win by hook or crook. All total bullshit of course. I asked John Haddock, was I masterminding a brilliant hustle the day before I won all the money when I'd done my bollocks? He alluded that that would have been a strange way to have gone about it.

More ludicrous allegations followed for which there was absolutely no proof of any wrongdoing at all, not even any circumstantial evidence. If this had been a court, the term kangaroo certainly sprung to mind but although there would be no sentencing, I was left in no doubt that there would be repercussions. I wasn't going to jail or anything like that but BAGS were a very powerful and influential player in the betting industry. I put over my point of view, answered questions as truthfully as I could and swatted away any nonsense regarding skulduggery. It was like a bad dream where everyone had an agenda against me.

All I could do afterwards was go home, try and relax and hope that common sense would prevail. If there were many more sharing Tom Kelly's point of view then I'd be persona non grata, if not brown bread, colloquially speaking.

BAGS have just celebrated its 50th birthday. Whoopee doo! Lets bake them a cake, pass me the bunting. But in all seriousness they are a formidable entity with hundreds of staff, five million pounds of assets and a cool million in their bank account. They can and do persuade other players in the murky maelstrom of greyhound racing politics to see things their way, as I was all too painfully aware. And they'd put down their own version of events regarding my situation.

It had obviously gone against me when Sky Sports management informed me that I wasn't wanted that week. Have a break Gary was a euphemism for grab your P45 Porky, you is history. I loved that job, travelling the length and breadth of England, doing the greyhound punditry with my great mate, the wonderful Dave Smith. What a buzz to go to all my favourite dog tracks and get paid for the privilege though it wasn't mega money they were paying me. I had to pay my own petrol bills and it's a long haul up and back from Sunderland on a foggy winter night but I wouldn't have swapped it for all the tea in Tenby.

Gary Newbon was another who was a delight to work with and very knowledgeable on many eclectic subjects as well as being a great man to boot. I want to thank John Parrott and Clare Balding too at this juncture for the many happy times we had on the BBC at Royal Ascot, I will always treasure those days. These were the good guys and dolls and there were many more but it starts to get boring if we go all the way down to Ethel the tea lady and Harry the toilet attendant who once told me, 'Folk look down their noses at me because I specialise in the removal of faeces. Don't these people realise that turds are my bread and butter.'

I was over the moon to receive phone calls from both John Parrott and Gary Newbon asking if I was all right and telling me I would go on to bigger and better things. It was greatly appreciated at the time but I still had to fight like a cornered tiger to clear my name. Who would have believed that a former staunch national ally of mine would sneak up and stab me straight between the shoulder blades and this was before I'd lifted a finger to air any of my personal, mitigating circumstances in public.

The last organisation I suspected would ever stiff me was *The Racing Post*. I'd had a good relationship with them for donkey's years but there's nowt so strange as the press when they smell blood and even they couldn't resist turning the screw. It was like our partnership on the first book *Winning It Back* never existed. They didn't bother to consult me about any of the rumours and falsehoods that were doing the rounds in the betting world.

Jim Cremin, now retired, wrote the damning article. I will give him his due, he does know his way round a greyhound track but that doesn't give him the right to spread false allegations about me and the life I lead. He seems to have a good relationship with my bête noire, Tom Kelly. He has interviewed him for The Racing Post before and there is even a picture out there of Kelly presenting Cremin with an award. Pass the sick bag Sharon, I feel distinctly queasy. One didn't need to be Einstein to work out where much of the offending drivel came from before it landed on Cremin's desk. What is it about a scoop falling onto a grubby reporter's lap that changes him from Jekyll to Hyde?

The good news was that three weeks later The Racing Post issued a full and frank apology. It was nice to be vindicated and they had belatedly done the right thing but the little spark of affection I had for them before this debacle has probably dimmed forever. I'm still a fan of the paper; one can't help being extremely impressed by their invaluable input into this great sport of ours. I still hold them in the highest regard as one of the mainstays of the betting world but it just goes to show that where money is concerned, you have to play it the establishment way or the consequences can be life changing. It's a tough old world. Damon Runyon once said, "I came to the conclusion long ago that all life is six to five against." Too true me old son, too true. The man wasn't a bad judge.

My relationship with the other nemesis Tom Kelly and BAGS was and is strained to say the least. Maybe we can build bridges in the future. One can never say never but it looks a Foinavon long shot.

I later contacted Kieren Fallon's solicitors, Stewart-Moore in London, who were experienced in sporting allegations of this kind. I wanted help to officially clear my name and all told it cost me a five-figure sum. All the while the BAGS juggernaut was still trying to prevent me making a living. It seemed if I became the owner of a ten-year-old whippet or even sniffed a greyhound's backside they would officially object. Blimey O'Reilly!

I hadn't murdered anybody but the bottom line was they didn't want me within a certain vicinity of any greyhound stadia. It's a long, greasy pole you slide down when the betting Gods are against you so for now, because of them, "Belly On The Telly" had lost his status and become "Belly Off The Telly." It just didn't have the same ring or sparkle.

* * * *

Chapter Three

TO POSSILPARK AND BACK

Sea Biscuit was small and ran in three races where he could have been claimed for $2,500. He wasn't.

As you can imagine, the stressful standoff with BAGS wasn't exactly helping my depression saunter off into the distance. I wasn't the happiest bunny in Watership Down to begin with but all the negativity going on had grossly shrunken my brain down to the size of a frazzled walnut.

It got to the point where I didn't go horse racing at all. Each day after Sharon had gone out, I'd sit in the greenhouse for long tedious hours on end, I just couldn't face going to the track. This went on for about six months. I could name you every pot plant from an African Violet to a Zebra plant; Percy Thrower wasn't in my league. In mad moments of paranoia and delusion I saw myself on Mastermind, scoring a maximum on the splicing and propagating of exotic plants (Gary Wiltshire, you have no passes, score 24), lovely stuff.

I had plenty of time on my hands to dream and reminisce. I regressed back to Bishop Stopford Secondary School where somebody with a warped sense of humour put me in charge of the school greenhouse at dinner times. So, history was repeating itself, the only difference was back then as a teenager I was always looking to bunk off to the bookies as soon as possible.

In my present situation I wanted nothing to do with Racing. I was sick in mind and spirit but the greenhouse was my sanctuary, my place of retreat where I could be alone with all my pals, the geraniums, petunias, flags and pansies. At this juncture, you're all saying Old Gal's lost the plot. Well you could blow me sideways and call me Auntie Mabel because you'd be spot on. It was going to take a minor miracle to nurse me back to normality. For the time being, all I had was my memories, good, bad and indifferent.

The many hours I cogitated and reflected on past events, my family and relationships were always to the fore. I hadn't been the greatest dad to my kids. Could I or should I have taken another kinder, more benign approach to the people I loved the most in this world? There was no changing anything in my real existence but maybe if I looked back pragmatically, I wouldn't repeat any of the damning mistakes that I'd made in the past, that was presuming I had a future at all. It meant in betting parlance at that present time, all daily, race meetings had been abandoned until further notice. Due to unforeseen circumstances, all bets were off,

My first serious relationship as a teenager was with a Glasgow lassie, Phyllis Shearer, no relation to the Geordie legend, Alan. At the time, I only had one love and that was gambling, so nobody was more surprised than me when I found myself experiencing a holiday romance. I'd gone for a break with my mate, Stirling, to Benidorm, staying over at the aptly named Don Juan Hotel.

A coach full of sixty Glasgow factory girls arrived two days after we'd settled in, of course the whole demographic of the hotel then changed. Leapy Lee's little arrows hit me on the blind side and I spent a lot of time in her company. I promised Phyllis, when the holiday was coming to an end that after I'd sorted a few things out in London, I would pack a few togs and come up on a mini excursion to Glasgow. It's been fabricated so many times before, after a week of passion, allied with sun, sea, sangria and sexy time, that two people from opposite ends of the country will carry on again, once back home. It's never the same though. The shitty weather, the yawning distance between them and the daily grind always gets in the way of a budding holiday relationship so it rarely happens for most. For one thing it's too much bleeding mither.

That flippant holiday promise 'We'll keep in touch' must join 'The cheque's in the post,' and 'I'll respect you in the morning,' as things that seldom materialise. I surprised myself though after I returned to The Smoke. I was genuinely missing Phyllis, so I decided to make the long run up to the land of the haggis and thistle. I was so smitten that I'd walked barefoot over mountain and valley to get there.

It was a real eye-opener, the district of Possilpark in Glasgow. Just north of the mighty River Clyde, it could make Aleppo look like Belgravia. With much trepidation, I parked up the car and briskly walked the 100 yards of Glasgow's mean streets (a Gary Wiltshire personal best) right up to Phyllis's tenement block. It was another world up there, as different from London as any city could be, notwithstanding the teeming populations of both Metropolises.

I made quite a few forays up there. I wouldn't say I ever became an honorary Scot but Gary McWiltshire had certain majesty about it. In my late teens I wasn't in bad shape, my previous football playing and training had always kept me trim (I would give an arm and a leg to be as fit now), my fighting weight was just south of thirteen stone. You don't realise what you've got until it's gone. Of course, I was occasionally sampling the famed Scottish cuisine up there, which certainly didn't help my waist measurements. I was losing the odd trouser button but in those days my metabolism was burning off any excess weight.

I've never been rude or remiss, that just wasn't in my nature. I once willingly experienced the obligatory local snack, deep-fried battered Mars Bar. On the second trip up there, myself, Phyllis and family friends shared a ten-inch battered Margherita Pizza. I was quite a daredevil then but contrary to popular opinion, everyone in Scotland isn't a chip shop junkie. I was getting the taste for Irn-Bru. As they say when in Rome but it was nothing I couldn't capably handle. The matriarch of the family, Margaret, was a wonderful Glaswegian, she was like a mother hen round me and her Sunday dinners were legendary. I noticed little local nuances in the food; a lot of the bangers were square, if I recall they were called Lorne Sausages, very tasty indeed. Scotch pies were popular, delicious minced mutton in pastry but the crème de la crème was dessert. Margaret would serve up single nugget wafer ice cream and I've always had room after a hearty repast for a sweet (no shit, Sherlock) but these were to die for.

Margaret would always politely enquire if I could manage a wee dish of afters, I'd modestly contemplate for two or three seconds, then nod. She knew the score, was the Pope a Catholic? It was an odds-on certainty but one has to go through the motions of etiquette. The said dessert was a Scottish delight, consisting of vanilla ice cream on a chocolate wafer filled with mallow and smothered in raspberry sauce. I'm salivating as I'm writing this. Every time I returned home a few pounds heavier than I went, mum would say, 'They really look after you up there Gal.' Little did she know it was my patriotic duty, I was the unofficial English cultural attaché.

The most striking thing you can say about the Scots (never say Scotch, they don't like that, that's their whisky, not nationality) is that they are a one off, a country full of contradictions and anomalies.

They produced many great thinkers and inventors like, Alexander Graham Bell, Adam Smith, James Watt and John Stuart Mill while their poorer contemporaries were living in the slums of Glasgow and Edinburgh, suffering with poverty, illness and violent behaviour off criminals. The Saracen Foundry in Possilpark was a major employer for over a hundred years; it used to export top quality metal products all over the world to each and every continent. One of its best-known sellers, developed solely in this country was the classic K6 street telephone box designed by Sir Giles

Gilbert Scott. All that came to a shuddering halt in the mid-sixties. Britain was struggling and the manufacturing sector was closing sites and cutting jobs. Shipbuilding suffered greatly and the Clyde ship workers were laid off in their thousands as those in both Newcastle and Belfast could attest.

In the economic void left behind came a return to hardship but the Scots have always been resilient people. What they lacked in creature comforts they made up with friendly camaraderie and humour, it was one of the happiest periods of my life. I would often go on long walks with Phyllis, the parks and the architecture were stunning, every man and his dog seemed to know her. Like every city, you went out after dark just keeping your wits about you; we are all located somewhere between saints and sinners. The Scots have a sub-class of their own, the equivalent of the English chavs, up there they call them NEDs (Non-Educated Delinquents).

One breakfast time we were short of milk so Margaret asked me to nip to the corner shop for two pints. I merrily went on my way. It was a chilly, beautiful, sunlit morning. It was half-past eight, the streets and walkways were sparse of people, it was obvious not many of the local denizens in the area were clocking on. I sauntered confidently into the shop and came back out only to be accosted by a Ned. He was a gangly youth sporting cheap tattoos. 'Ha'e ye got some change for a coffee, big man?' I pressed a pound note into his palm, 'Brand new, big man. See you,' and off he bounced like Skippy the Kangaroo. He wouldn't have long to wait for the Off-licence to open. That was the best pound I spent up there, he was happy and so was I.

I had to laugh because Margaret always had copious amounts of fruit in the house, an apple or orange were never far away. The Cornflakes and Weetabix in hot milk were always accompanied by slices of banana. On the veg front they knew their onions from their shallots, maybe it's a myth about healthy eating up there because I never encountered a dearth of farm field produce.

The rumour about lack of fruit and veg in the Scottish diet being the equivalent of Kryptonite to Superman never ever materialised. Maybe the poorest families struggled to put it on the table but I presume it would be likewise in England. The average life expectancy for men in Glasgow is surprisingly over 71 years old, that's amazing really. If people are eating poorly it just shows the fantastic durability of the human body. If you put that much crap in your motor, it would break down within the month.

Against all my earlier expectations, I became extremely fond of the area. Peter Capaldi, Jim Watt and Kenny Dalglish had all gone to school here, Lena Martell, had apparently been born two streets down from us. These were real dyed-in-the-wool Scots, not like Rod Stewart, born in London or Sandy Lyle from Shrewsbury but tough men and hardy women who knew the meaning of a tough upbringing and the value of a pound note. The Jocks have always had a reputation for being careful with their wonga, Phyllis told me an account of a local man who had suffered bereavement.

Dougie was a typically dour Scot. His beloved wife Morag had gone to meet her maker and he wanted to place the most economical death notice in the local paper. He arrived to fill in the lodgement form and he was a man of few words, so it simply read, "Morag died." The receptionist informed him that they had a minimum charge which would give him three more words, so he cogitated and then added them. The amended obituary thus appeared in Friday night's edition and read, "Morag died. Toyota for sale." Absolutely brilliant.

As much as I was enjoying my time up there, the logistics of driving from London to Glasgow and back was wearing me out and putting thousands of miles on the speedo, so I decided to start flying up. At that time my finances were quite healthy so it made sense for someone else to do the steering. I could even get a nice bit of shuteye on the flight, lovely stuff. I used to fly from Gatwick with British Caledonian. I think they went bump about thirty years ago which was a bloody shame because it was always a pleasure to admire the stewardesses in their beautifully tailored tartan uniforms with

Tam O' Shanter caps, my all-time favourite trolley-dollies.

From Glasgow Airport I'd hop into a cab and drop off at Fruin Street, Saracens Cross, Possilpark, job's a good-un. One particular New Year's Eve stands out. On a previous taxi drive I'd enquired of the good cabbie if he knew of any greyhound tracks in the vicinity. I was reliably informed that Ashfield dogs, a flapping track, was favourite because of its close location to Possilpark. I'd timed my run up to Glasgow to take in some pre-Phyllis recreation. On entering the stadium, I asked a couple of experienced regulars for a few odd pointers. Once happy to have got the lay of the land, I was ready to start betting.

I was carrying 900 sobs, a heck of a lot of money in those days, but after backing the first four winners I'd turned it into a cool £1,400. I bought a few drinks for my new Caledonian pals; at that moment I was the new and unofficial King of Glasgow. Eight losing races later, my crown had slipped, I was now a down and out friendless Englishman who had just enough for the taxi fare back to Possilpark. The new, official Prince of Fools forlornly got into the back of the cab, I was utterly dreading telling Phyllis I'd done my bollocks again.

On arriving at Fruin Street I saw that Phyllis had spent ages getting ready and was all glammed up. That didn't make me feel any better, let me tell you. I put all my cards on the table. I was close to tears. She just opened her purse and handed me sixty quid. She said, 'Don't worry, we've still got enough for a good night.' What can you say about a great woman like that? Most people at this moment would be saying, don't ever lose this woman, she is the right one for you but just like a man in his new orthopaedic shoes, you all stand corrected.

The sheer scale of the distance and the time I was away from London finally forced my hand. The relationship slowly petered out. I was gloomy at the time but it wasn't the end of the saga, we would gloriously unite again in the near future. On my last flight back down, I imagine just South of Hadrian's Wall, I thought to myself those sneaky old Roman Emperors knew a trick or two. They had blitzed and conquered all of Western Europe but decided to call it a day on the outskirts of Northern England. The Roman legions would never venture into bonny Scotland which was probably for the best, they would have probably got their bloody heads kicked in had they attempted to move in on those hard, doughty Scots.

I brought back my love of Irn-Bru but gradually weaned myself off it. The drink was much harder to get back then in England, there weren't a lot of shops stocking it, thank God. To this day, Coca Cola is the number one selling soft drink in every country in the world bar one. I'll let you hazard a guess where it is only number two and what drink trumps it.

Shortly after I got back, I put a few nice winners together at Fontwell Park and returned home carrying more than a monkey. I'd been seeing a well-to-do Jewish girl at the time and it had got to the stage where I had to make a stark choice. Her family liked me and wanted me to go the whole hog and become a fully-fledged member of the Jewish faith. The indoctrination was many hours of studying the Torah but then undergoing the cruellest cut of them all.

The money in my pocket held my destiny and instead of circumcision, circumnavigation was the answer, all the way down to Weymouth Docks for a ferry to Jersey. I had no idea why or what I was doing but my needy independence was calling all the shots and after a few days on the island I applied for a job. The local paper contained a vacancy for an MC at the Hawaiian Club in Portelet Bay, South Jersey. How hard could it be? With a bit of bullshit, a touch of bravado and thirteen stone of bollocks the job was mine. It was a blessed relief at the time to relax and have time away from serious relationships. My head was pointing me in the right and proper direction, I was obviously not ready at that moment to be putting a band of gold on someone's finger and settling down.

There was a Billy Butlins holiday camp down the hill so I used to go there after the night's entertainment for a beer and some female company. I looked the dogs in my resplendent evening suit. The holidaymakers were always very impressed especially after I threw in a few porkies about being the cabaret singer and comedian. Little did they know I was only introducing the acts. At the time I was scoring more than Charlie George but it's true, just like a kid in a sweetshop, you soon get fed up of a good thing.

A year of hula girls, ukuleles and Hawaiian shirts, drinking beer and gratuitous sex should be enough for any man but I was the charitable sort so someone else could do it. God works in mysterious ways. I felt the calling to spread my new-found knowledge and experience on the mainland again. London was beckoning and soon it would be answered by a fully-fledged Gary Wiltshire return to a brave new world.

I knocked sheepishly on Mum and Dad's door. I shouldn't have worried; my mother was ecstatic, they hadn't a clue where I'd been, they thought I was dead. I realised at that moment how selfish I'd been. At that age we think we are immortal and the solar system revolves round us, we don't always think about others. My father had actually phoned up Scotland to speak to Phyllis. Quite correctly, she informed him euphemistically that she hadn't seen or heard jack shit from me but that call had got her worrying about me. We always hurt the ones we love.

That short sojourn in Jersey was actually the catalyst for getting Phyllis and myself back together. I phoned her up and invited her down to London. We got on again like a house on fire, everything looked in place for a Scottish Anglo alliance and we duly got married in 1977. I was only twenty-two but you know me, I'd give it my best shot (no Vicar, it's not a shotgun wedding, cheeky old sod), it was the happiest day of my life. Our first haven of married bliss was Ranelagh Road, Tottenham and the rent was all of six quid a week. Phyllis got a job with a local manufacturing firm,
I was working down Leather Lane Market with Mum and Dad selling fruit and veg, flowers or anything else I could lay my hands on and flip a profit.

That rough and ready market is still going strong today, one of the few that is. You can buy anything down there from a turnip to a jumbo jet and there's no shortage of cafés and diners either, long may it continue.

We wanted to start a family but our humble bijou abode in Tottenham didn't fit the bill. Then Phyllis fell pregnant so we applied for a move down at the local council offices. This is no word of a lie; on the form there were many various postcodes across the length and breadth of Greater London where you could apply for a move to. Chelsea and Kensington (as if), Hendon, Hounslow, Harlow and Hillingdon were some more but it didn't matter, the only place they would ever send you was South Ockendon in Essex, just the other side of then M25 car park. Kelly, our first baby girl arrived, we had money for all the baby essentials but we didn't have a suitable gaff to bring up an ankle biter.

That was the dilemma. I double-checked that the medieval plague wasn't still there but on seeing no lepers, we picked up sticks and made the holy crusade East to a land time had forgotten. Our new council, two-storey flat was underwhelming but with a lick of paint, some delicate lighting and a visit from the South Ockendon Feng Shui Society we were ready to rock. With both of us working, we had saved a nice little nest egg. We now had our larger property and even though the locale wasn't the most salubrious area at the time, we had plans to move to pastures greener when the opportunity arose. The Ock, as I fondly called it, modestly resembled a modern day Jaywick, another Essex deprived hotspot that has been widely documented but at least they had a beach!

We got our heads down for a few months, worked hard and like a young Donald Trump, I was spotting new residences to have a shy at. They were only council houses at the time but I felt like a property magnate as we moved to Springfield Boulevard, Milton Keynes, concrete cows et al.

I was working my first proper job, betting ring clerk at Milton Keynes Greyhound Stadium. I loved all the hustle and bustle, the sounds and smells of the betting environment. I had decided two years earlier that this was my quest in life. I now had the experience to go for my first bookies licence and the rest is history. At this juncture, my ambition to get where I wanted to would eventually kill any semblance of a normal family life. My early career is well documented, I was picking up pitches on horse and greyhound tracks like confetti at a wedding but the more popular, successful and richer I got, the less quality time I spent with the family. My relationship with Phyllis plummeted downhill to the bottom of the glen. I was hardly at home and there were two more mouths to feed after my darling sons Nicky and Ross were born but the three kids had the best of everything. The only thing they didn't have was me. I was away empire building and in my selfish mind it was impossible to structure a balance that suited us all.

They say that money is the root of all evil; if you don't control the money, the money controls you. Wherever it's sighted, you are on a train, boat or plane chasing it. Phyllis had done brilliantly bringing up the three children, you couldn't wish for better kids but I hadn't seen them grow up, had I? The most important thing you can give your offspring is time, I bitterly regret not being a bigger part of their early lives but they all know I love them dearly.

One morning the light bulb of fate turned on in Phyllis's head. We hadn't been getting on so we both decided I should move out. The spark had gone; I was living a marriage of convenience. I bought her a nice house in an area called Woughton-on-the-Green, South Central Milton Keynes. It was a lovely part of the world. I have to laugh now that at the age of sixty-three, all my ex-wives have had their own lovely places and I'm currently renting. The old adage, there will come a rainy day was never more profound. Mind you, I must enjoy self-flagellation because the saying "There is no fool like an old fool" keeps coming back into my mind. Still what is done can't be changed, one can only look to the future with hope.

After parting from Phyllis, I was a lonesome cowboy for a while. Not in the Brokeback Mountain sense as I had nobody lifting my Stetson and tickling my hair though I love a tickled follicle. Then a lady named Jackie Foord (the surname originates from ancient times from the county of Devon) came unexpectedly into my life. I was returning from Hinckley Greyhounds one profitable evening as I'd amassed a large portfolio of midland track pitches and was creating positive momentum up the bookmakers' league table. I'd been having terrible trouble with my feet; they just wouldn't walk past a chip shop. I've had a lifelong weakness for scotch eggs, (long Legs) and hips (fish and chips). Sure enough, I hit on a win double; Jackie was in the shop with her sister, they say rust never sleeps and I wasn't backward at coming forward. I asked her out after ordering my fish supper, she accepted and another episode in my journey was playing itself out. I believe everyone's life is mapped out, fate is final. What is decreed will happen; you just have to go with the flow, kismet is just too powerful to bend.

My time with Jackie was the most lucrative period of my betting career. Those were seven, golden years that coincided with the birth of my fourth child, Danny in 1985. There were absolutely no money worries, the Wiltshire betting empire had gone from strength to strength but my roving eye wouldn't give over. What was wrong with me, it must be a genetic flaw. I was certainly no George Clooney but women seemed to want to show their maternal instincts, then again it could have been my rapier wit and charisma. My own vanity precludes holding folding being the reason, certainly that has never come across in any of my relationships, then again, I could just be naive, a lot of us men are when it comes to the crunch.

The aforementioned Sue Hogan, in fact had her own stash of wonga and the Tote lady was firmly in my sights. They say blondes have more fun and I wanted a piece of the action. After I left Jackie, I made sure she was financially secure for life. She was probably experiencing a sad, emotional train wreck in her own personal feelings towards me after the break up, it took me years to realise how mean I'd been. Sue and I set up together and I thought, yet again, she was definitely the one. But as the previously documented text gate involving Sharon blew everything out of the water, we were all where we were. I was with Sharon and sitting day after day in the solitude of the greenhouse. I couldn't live the rest of my life through this unhealthy, ethereal reminiscence but the way I broke out of it came via a totally unexpected chain of events that still staggers me to this day.

I'd been on gardening duty for about six months and Sharon needed a little runabout so I drove into Nottingham. I'd heard good reports about a local firm, *NottinghamCar.Com* who were neither dear nor pushy when making a second-hand car sale. I had the good fortune to bump into the boss himself, Charles Sumner but no relation to Sting from the band *The Police,* whose real name is Gordon Sumner.

Universally known in the car game as *Champagne Charlie*, I emphasised to him that the car was for '*Er indoors* and I didn't want to be returning a wrecker in a week's time. What Charlie said next astonished me, 'I don't want to sell you a car.'

I took umbrage at that and demanded to know why. He said, 'You've been ill haven't you? In fact, right now you're still not well.' I came clean and told him about my depression. He knew exactly what it was because he had suffered the same fate himself but, unlike muggins here, he had gone proactive and sorted it.

Just on the turn of the new millennium Charlie was a total bankrupt, he'd lost all his assets and houses, the whole shooting match. One day he was a very rich man, the next he was potless. His biggest property was the last thing to be repossessed or so he thought. Sitting on the bonnet wing of his car, quietly contemplating his uncertain future whilst having a final gander at the old house slipping through his fingers, he was unexpectedly approached by the chief bailiff. 'Charlie, you're a lovely bloke, I don't know how to tell you this but the car has to go as well.'

He slid off the wing and handed over the car keys, he was now on the streets where he quickly hit the bottle and was in the land of the paralytic, living dead.

A chance meeting saved his life, a psychoanalyst called Terry Leahy mentored him over a couple of sessions and put him on the right path again. Charlie handed me a card with an address on, 'Go and see Terry, then I will sell you a car.' I was sceptical, I'd never been a big believer in mind games but Charlie said the talks had given him a new outlook on life, to the extent that he had just won businessman of the year. I thought that would ding-dang-do for me. What harm could it do? Just talking to Charlie had put a spring in my step.

On returning home, Sharon was not nearly as convinced. I was met with a stern, 'Did you get a car for me?'

After an awkward, short hiatus and silence, I quietly explained what had happened. She just pointed to the push-bike in the passageway, I had to act and act quickly. In the morning I was up with the dawn cockerel and drove to a little cul-de-sac in Radcliffe, it was an old folks sheltered accommodation. At that moment I vowed to strangle bloody Charlie Sumner.

When I got to the first-floor door I was met by Terry Leahy. He was early to mid-seventies but his blue eyes sparkled like a young man's, 'Come on in Gary, and tell me your whole story. Would you like a cup of Rosie Lee? We have Earl Grey. Let's see if I can help. Would you care for some chocolate digestives?'

I gave it frank and I revealed more than I really wanted to but having fired both barrels, it felt great to get it all off my chest. I finished and sat back, curiously waiting to hear the magical edicts of the wisest sage in Nottingham.

It was all over in less than an hour, I can't remember exactly everything he said but I came out of that flat feeling like Superman's stronger brother. He demanded to know why I hadn't been racing, urged me to get out and about; there was nothing to be frightened of, it was what I was good at. He kept repeating, 'Gary Wiltshire had and has the very best name in racing.' If I followed a few simple steps, I could live beyond my wildest dreams. I was now the master on the helm of the ship again, I would steer it through any impending storm, until I reached my destination. I was a convert to positive thinking, returning home feeling high up on cloud nine.

The very next day I returned to Worcester races, an audible gasp went around the ring. Dave, a bookie mate, sidled up to me, 'Bloody hell, Gal, we were convinced you were brown bread, we all had a whip round for a wreath. I'm just gonna get my tenner back.'

This happened everywhere I went. The great thing was people were genuinely happy to see me, shaking hands, clapping me on the back. My million-dollar smile was back as well, for the first time in many months. I didn't have to force it. I knew I could carry on where I left off on the horses, but the dogs were a different matter altogether. BAGS were up to their old tricks again.

In 2014, Lord Hesketh and his Chief Executive Kevin Ackerman consulted me about the new greyhound track they were constructing. It was to be incorporated into the middle of the Towcester Horseracing Stadium. We met at the London Dorchester. Lordie (as he is known to friends) likes the finer things in life and who could bloody blame him. Famous for having his own Formula 1 racing team fronted by the late, charismatic James Hunt, Lord Hesketh has also served in the House of Lords for the Conservative governments of Margaret Thatcher and John Major, before swapping his alliance to UKIP.

He has also produced his own brand of motorbike, before acquiring Towcester Racecourse. They showed me their plans for Britain's newest dog track; they were out of this world. I told them they couldn't fail with that set up; it was a blinder. Out of the blue, they asked me if I wanted a pitch there? Do me a favour, I didn't need asking twice, things were on the up but BAGS were to have the last word in this one.

Towcester Dogs had its first meeting that year on the 6th of December. I had applied for a pitch but BAGS vetoed it right away. Ackerman phoned them on my behalf and they said I could be involved with a pitch but in no way could I stand on the course. So, I arranged for Sharon and son Nicky to man the pitch while I would communicate through a walkie-talkie back in the car. You couldn't make it up. It just wasn't the same as being up front myself. In just six weeks we had done some serious money so we wisely raised the white flag and retreated to the long grass.

Towcester got the Greyhound Derby in 2017 with the closure of Wimbledon. All in all, it was a cracking decision by Lord Hesketh and Kevin Ackerman; all meetings were well attended, with the acquisition of The Derby bringing the classic golden egg. The future had looked bright and assured but the recent closure has shocked so many in the sport. If Towcester could fail then nowhere is safe from going under. I wish I had the solution but we all must keep persevering.

The main thing was that thanks to Terry Leahy my black depression at that moment had all but disappeared. Whether it will come back any time soon in the future, nobody knows. Terry had given me certain little practices to follow, so I was confident next time the dark, sodden storm clouds gathered, I could metaphorically blow them away. All through my trauma I had felt like that dude from Greek mythology, Sisyphus. Condemned by the gods to push an immense boulder up a mountain but every time he got near the top, the boulder would roll down to the bottom and he had to do this for all eternity.

I only suffered for a few years but I know what he went through. I still had the hump over the tin tack from Sky but everyone gets their cards at some point, John McCririck was a classic case. He took his dismissal from Channel 4 badly but fair play to him, what a fighter. Love him or loathe him, he can't be ignored. I for one think racing is the poorer for him not being on our screens.

Shortly after my dismissal from Sky, my old pal Gary Newbon left. What a character. I first met him at the dog track at Hall Green, Birmingham where he introduced himself, 'Hi Gary, I'm Gary.'

I thought clever clogs eh? I knew who he was but just to keep him on the defensive I replied, 'Who are you mate?'

He came back with, 'I'm a legend in the Midlands on ITV.' I burst out laughing and we hit it off instantly, socialising frequently over the years.

Some people probably wouldn't know that Jeff Stelling was a presenter for Sky Greyhounds early on and if there is a better frontman for any sport out there, I've yet to see him. Jeff is a "monkey hanger," a life-long Hartlepool United fan. The team, who have dropped out of the Football League into the National League, are struggling but Jeff is Premier League class, irreplaceable.

I got my break on Sky through producer Dave Lawrence who gave me my first chance. I'll always be eternally grateful but nobody knows until now why I left the BBC Ascot Racing coverage having paired up with snooker legend and Evertonian, John Parrott. It was all down to my old nemesis, calories in, less out. My weight allied to the oncoming depression put the dampers on my career with Auntie Beeb. If only I'd have known at the time that 'desserts' spelt backwards is stressed.

It was the hottest day of the year at Royal Ascot, absolute anathema for a big lump like myself in topper, shirt, waistcoat and jacket. It was bloody murderous out there; I was sweating like a glass blower's arse. A lot of you would have noticed in my last testimonial season that I was carrying a fair excess of timber, I think I was weighing in at about 35 stones, dying would have been a relief.

I literally sweated a gallon of water that day, I'm not bloody kidding.

Halfway through the live programme that afternoon I was totally cream crackered, sitting in the shade of the BBC production van. The call went out for me to meet John Parrott on the rails but there was no way I could physically walk from the van to the bookies section. I'd like to say I was thinking on my feet but it was more like thinking on my backside when I bunged the National Car Park attendant a score to give me a private taxi ride on his golf buggy up to the rails.

The chickens had come home to roost. There was no way I could go through that ordeal again, I had to resign. The BBC was very good about it but my increasing weight was becoming a big problem. I wasn't in the best shape health wise; it was a warning shot across the bows.

I felt close to death out there. Don't forget the racing was shot live; imagine how good would that have looked on afternoon TV, me being taken out on a stretcher. If I'm going to pop my clogs on a racecourse, I'd rather it be Yarmouth or Warwick. It looks a bit pretentious going out at Royal Ascot but at least I would have looked the part in my suit.

There is an old adage, "bread is like the sun; it rises in the yeast and sets in the waist." I had never been a salad and fruit cocktail man but the years of comfort munching were harming my career. The two things I loved most apart from my family, namely food and betting on greyhounds, had cost me two jobs on the television. I was off both The Beeb and Sky but I had so nearly become a household name in 2009 on ITV in a programme called, *The Colour of Money*. I'm convinced I would have gone on to be an international sex symbol... but let me tell you what happened. The format of the show was winning increments of a thousand pounds and knowing when to stop before going over your limit.

I went down there for a week's trial where my participation was as The Fat Banker. I had to give the contestants advice as they progressed to larger amounts of money and the pilot shows were going very well.

The show's host was another mate of mine, Chris Tarrant. He reckoned I was a certainty to get the gig and that worried me as he wasn't widely known for picking winners. The fly in the ointment was the gorgeous, intelligent, willowy blonde, Millie Clode; she was the one standing in the way of my beckoning prime time television career. Now who would you rather have beaming in to your living room live on a Saturday night; two geezers talking bollocks or a bit of rough and smooth in the shape of Tarrant and Clode?

You are way ahead of me; Millie got to co-host the show. She had the physical attributes and was far more intelligent than me, congratulations to her. Sadly, the show lasted only eight episodes. The viewing figures were dire, could The Fat Banker have turned it around? We will never know but I would have given it my best shot. Millie has also read the news on the Sky Sports Channel, I'd like to think she was following my lead but I was probably never out her shadow.

So, with 2014 coming to an end and better in so many ways than the previous year, I could fondly look back and hope with my newfound confidence that the Wiltshire bandwagon could storm up the highway again. I'd had a few kicks in the groin but the future lay with sporting gods Barry Hearn and Fred Done. Terrestrial and satellite television were hopefully only on temporary hold but only God, Nostradamus and Mystic Meg could see the future.

With all the doom and gloom of the past it was time to enjoy life again, to smile and laugh and frolic. And that reminds me of the Irish jockey getting his last-minute instructions off the trainer. 'Well Pat, we need to win this one, the owner's had a monkey on,' Paddy cussed under his breath as the trainer continued, 'The wife has also put a pony on.'

A desperate Paddy retorted, 'Jaysus guvnor there's not gonna be much room up there for me.'

It was a good time to move forward, do not adjust your sets.

A new and improved Gary Wiltshire was, as the Americans say, about to kick ass.

* * * *

Chapter Four

RETURN OF THE PRODIGAL SON

Scurlogue Champ won 51 times from 63 greyhound races in the mid 1980s.

That first meeting back was at sunny Worcester. I say sunny but on a few previous occasions I turned up it resembled Atlantis. There was a hosepipe ban one summer but I don't know where most of the water went because Worcester Racecourse was often under a lake the size of Windermere. There were mallards, Canadian Geese and swans; someone was even canoeing past the grandstand, all it needed was Mark Spitz and Duncan Goodhew giving front crawl and breaststroke lessons for a full regatta.

As mentioned, the reception I received after my enforced sabbatical was extremely heart-warming and a real fillip on my comeback quest. The love, real happiness and enthusiastic greeting of the bookies and public brought a tear to the eye, even to a tough old stager like myself. It was all I could do not to choke up and dab my mince pies with a wad of Pavarottis. It was a bittersweet moment. Dave and his merry band of bookie mates feared the worst in my absence but just like Lazarus, I had returned, not from a tomb but from the garden greenhouse. They don't write them like that anymore. The one bugbear was that I had let people who weren't in my corner dictate their own terms through accusation and hearsay causing me to endure a painful hiatus away from the wonderful race-going public.

I know BAGS and The Racing Post were not totally responsible for my missing year but consequently I now keep my friends close and my enemies closer. It felt like a spell in Wormwood Scrubs and Bags still won't give me any slack or parole. All that enmity and rancour disappeared into the ether that day at Worcester when I first walked out as proud as punch. They sure as hell weren't going to rain on my parade.

It was like I'd never been away. The first race and my very first punter asked for £400 to win £700 on the jolly. You're all getting excited now, the big man is back; 'Go on Gazza, get that money in the satchel.' Well in a perfect world, that was exactly the sort of bet that had stood me in good stead for years. The only problem was, as you know, that current year had been about as prosperous as buying shares in a pork pie shop in Tel Aviv in the middle of a swine flu epidemic and a Middle East embargo on pigs.

The path to the racecourse had been tortuous, long and winding. I'd had to beg, borrow and steal, pawn a few bits of jewellery and go down the back of the sofa, I kid you not. I eventually pieced together 800 big ones, so after I paid my badge money, 80 quid, I had £720 in my pocket. That was my dilemma, if I took the wager and the favourite won, I was left with a score to play with. You know I couldn't cut the geezer back; I was fucking Gary Wiltshire for Christ's sake. It wasn't just the money though, if I showed vulnerability, I was finished.

At the final hurdle the favourite was neck and neck with a 10/1 shot and they went hammer and tongs all the way to the winning post. It was unbearable but the outsider got up to win half a length; my adrenaline rush was out of this world. That's why we bet more than we can afford to lose; it's not called the sport of kings for nothing. I could have bloody French kissed that horse after the race, what a beautiful animal. But I realised there and then what I'd been missing, as infuriating as the game was, it was still in a league of its own.

The rest of the day was nip and tuck. I was mentally shattered after the last race but at least I hadn't done my bollocks. I carefully counted up all the scrunched-up fivers, tenners and twenties; just shy of 900 quid profit after all expenses taken off. I would've settled for a measly nicker but the day had been a great, all-round success and the extra money was the morello cherry on top of the big, Belgian bun. I had a quick look at my mobile, twenty-four missed calls and eight unanswered texts from Sharon. I'd been that wound up and engrossed in the racing that I hadn't heard the phone once all day. I belled her back immediately and she was crying down the phone, it was very emotional. She kept repeating, 'You're back, you're back.'

That was a bit too close to a Gary Glitter revival for my liking but I knew exactly what she meant, it had been a red-letter day for both of us.

As Confucius once said, "one swallow doesn't make a summer" so I had to keep bringing home the bacon. In the schemes of the solar system I hadn't been away for that long but little things in the upcoming weeks didn't seem to be quite as good as previous. Have you ever had that sixth sense that something isn't right or there could be a problem waiting to happen? Something murky was in the air but at that precise moment I couldn't put my finger on it.

I eventually surmised that the bottom was beginning to fall out of the on-course game, there just didn't seem to be as much money about on the track or in the bars and the eateries. Was the time before my breakdown not as I had recalled it? Was I looking back with nostalgic, rose-coloured glasses? The pre- illness takings after deductions certainly weren't a bonanza or boon time but surely it was better than the current financial climate. In 1929, Churchill lost his front bench position all the way through and up to 1939 after which he was recalled to the war cabinet. He described that long lonely decade as his wilderness years.

I was only absent a tenth of that time but did my year in the wilderness coincide with a tipping point for British racing? Was it all swirling down the sink plug with no return? The jury was out but it was indicating a movement towards tighter belts and that was no problem to me with my weight loss. I had a bit more slack to give but I needed another recession or downturn like Telly Savalas needed an Afro comb.

It was definitely harder making a living back on the racetrack but what factors had caused this? Were they irreversible and was there anything that I could do personally to alleviate some of the negativity flying about our unique, wonderful industry? We were all living in a world of austerity, like it or lump it.

The first official bookmaker Harry Ogden had operated on Newmarket course in 1795, he would be turning in his grave at the demise of the modern bookie. At least his great-great-great-great grandson, Stan liked a bet on Coronation Street. For donkeys years we bookmakers worked the horse and greyhound tracks although everyone knew where to find the illegal back street bookies who had runners in all the town factories and department stores. Then in 1961 the game changer came; Harold MacMillan's Conservative party legalised high street bookmakers, he wasn't known as Super Mac for nothing.

At one stage there were over 15,000 betting shops operating in Great Britain at the height of the industry's power, now after a long, slow decline there are less than 10,000. Most of these are the well-known giants of the game, the smaller independent bookies are becoming like dinosaurs, a toothless T-Rex or a badly beaten Brontosaurus, extinct or for the very few left, on their last legs.

Most of shops on the high street are the usual suspects, the household names in Ladbrokes, Coral, William Hill and my old favourite, Betfred. It's a big boy's game now; a cheeky few million is not enough, they are investing in billions now. Bet365 saw the writing was on the wall. They sold their 59 shops in the potteries to Coral. They have since concentrated on online betting which has grown yearly to billions of pounds of turnover. That might be the shape of things to come. The Coates family have worked hard to push their business into the 21st century.

A lot is spoken about addictive gamblers in betting shops. As a man who has lost a few bob myself I have every sympathy for them, but how far can the government go to prevent someone gambling away their future: It's a very hard question to answer.

Don't forget, people can still walk into a real casino and bet a grand or more on black or red. God has given us the ability to make choices, right or wrong, good or bad, it is up to the individual. The last thing we want is a nanny state, I still like to have the power over how I spend my personal money (that's put me up Carey Street more times than I'd like to admit but no one else was to blame bar my good self).

High street bookmakers have certainly changed since 1961. Sure they were once mysterious, clandestine buildings which you couldn't see into and anyone over eighteen who entered was hit by a blanket of fug, tobacco smoke, staleness and the obligatory BO but it did what it said on the side of the tin; the establishment would legally take your wager. Very few women would ever venture alone into those shops. The odd wife or girlfriend, accompanied by her man might spend a few minutes inside but for many years the atmosphere was not female friendly. To be fair, the pub trade was exactly the same; it was a man's refuge.

'But Gary, it's all good now surely? In this brave new world shops are now light, airy and hospitable, you can even get a snack and beverage. We've come a long way, we're out of the dark ages and are betting in comfort, even the ladies are coming in for a punt and not being intimidated, jobs a good un.'

Well, yes and no. If you like your action coming right at you, fantastic but some older stagers like myself need time to ponder. We need to study form, to decide which horse will be our selection. Then again, how many times have we gone to back a horse after careful consideration and at the last moment had one last shufti at The Racing Post, read a positive comment from a no-mark, so- called racing expert about an opposing horse and changed our minds. We've all done it, invariably our original horse wins doing handstands while our hard-earned money is on the donkey out with the washing suggested by The Racing Post Man. It must have happened a million times.

It might be a positive with so many races going off every five minutes but it doesn't give you time to reconsider what you thought was the likeliest winner. It's probably me but I still hanker for when there were only one or two greyhound meetings through the day, two or three horse race meetings; a slower, more peaceful time when every shop had a man chalking up the changing odds and no television screens, just a tannoy giving out commentary. It brings back happy memories but definitely not practical for today's electronic age.

Of course, the bookie wanted your money in the old days too. I know a lot of modern bookmakers would rather keep it simple but with the crazy overheads on the high streets these days it would be impossible to implement. We are where we are. One incredible improvement about modern betting is the fantastic sources of information that are now available. Any sport you want to follow and wager on there are now up to date reports on everything from an injury to a star striker to the change of going at a race meeting in the last half hour. We have all the data we need and more to find winners.

The new miracle of betting has been online gambling with the first online casino opened in the Caribbean in 1994. Has it really been nearly a quarter of a century? Where does time go when you are losing your money? The online poker rooms started dealing about 1998 and that was slightly different because you were playing like-minded people although you could never get a poker "tell," as you couldn't see or hear your adversaries. There was no advantage for players who could read into opponent's behaviour in live games. In my own humble opinion, a good poker player will always beat a lucky player over a sufficient period of time, whatever the format.

The turn of the millennium brought the Aussies in, those bushrangers would bet on two wombats swimming in a shark-infested creek. They are huge punters down under. The Melbourne Cup, the richest two-mile contest in the world is known as the race that stops the nation but all I want to know is why all Australian men with ginger hair are known as Bluey? They can't all support Chelsea, surely? Up The Gunners!

The number of people playing, even in those early days, was eight million, not shabby at all. This phenomenon was not going away. The USA banned online gambling but the consensus is that it will explode again there. The holy crusade that was prohibition didn't work but it's a strange country where it's easier to get a gun than a drink and a bet.

Today in Britain more than half of us play the odds-on line and 3% of all gamblers are pathological. To these blighted people I say try to follow what an old bookmaker once told me but I personally never took a blind bit of notice.

I doubt if you will take heed but it is sound advice, 'The safest bet is always to keep the money in your pocket.' The world would not be as exciting, a trifle boring in fact but for problem punters it would be a lifesaver. I feel for all of you, I've been there, done it and worn the t-shirt. I've lived and died by the sword, I'm too thick headed and long in the tooth to stop now. If it's in your DNA what can you do? Go by the grace of God and hope there are more blessings than chastisements.

Now, depending upon your point of view, we move onto either Anti-

Christ or the Archangel; the betting-exchange. Another millennium creation, Betfair came into all of our lives in the year 2000 along with its smaller baby brother, Betdaq. That time of upheaval was probably the biggest change the world of betting has ever undergone, morphing into trading situation mode.

Once, all track bookies would price up the day's runners based upon on their merits and past performances. Of course the more experienced pros would lead and the newer fish would copy but not to the extent that every board was a clone of every other. Some bookmakers would go long or short on a horse they either rated or didn't regard as the winner. This was based on opinion, you lived and died by that but at least there was a good variety of prices. Watch bookies price up today and they all go in just under the prices of the betting exchanges, very few put their head above the parapet. This must be one of the reasons fewer people are going racing. Don't forget you can now sit in the comfort of your front room and be your own bookmaker with no travelling far and wide, no fuel money, no entry money, no fiver for a pint of warm beer, or indeed battered minnow and ten chips.

The old adage that you never ever see a poor bookmaker was true years ago but things have changed at breakneck speed in the last few decades. With all those advantages of sitting at home, in Mount Pleasant Villas, Wonga Town, Goldshire, Land of Milk and Honey, why do you think I still possess 70 pitches? They are all in poor positions, some I never go to, none of which I will ever get rid of.

'Gary, you know more about racing than most, why don't you stay at home in the warmth? No overheads, no distractions, no more miles on the speedo, just press the right magic buttons to become a millionaire, it would be easy for someone like you.'

Let me tell you this, you couldn't be further from the truth. What bookmakers do on course when they accept your bets is lay. While most of the win bets on Betfair are slightly favourable, the lay bets, especially at longer prices are ruinous. A lot of double carpet on course (33/1) are over

100/1 on the site.

Remember this, when you win Betfair always take its commission off your winning returns, between 2% and 5%. To be fair most people used to pay that lower rate but Betfair have changed rates recently. Still, they never go short on a bet; if you lose, someone with a polar opposite view, a winner, will pay the commission on your lost wager. It's a very nice business. Do I wish I could have been involved from the start? Not likely. You wouldn't see me pushing Scarlet Johansson away to get to Rita Webb, would you?

The people who started Betfair are tinged with genius, you have to take your hat off to them. Has it been good for the betting industry? Well, for on course betting it's been another nail in the bookmakers' coffin but perversely it has made betting from home and on your smart phone with the online bookies as easy as falling off a camp bed.

I don't play Betfair at all. It is a wonderful innovation but it's not for me. Let me explain all. When I lay a bet, I like to know who I'm laying in bed with. You could be taking on owners, trainers, people in the know and all faceless people. Your security blanket flies out the window. On the track I know who I want to take a chunky bet off and I know who to gracefully knock back sometimes; it's called bookmakers intuition and comes from years of experiencing life on the coalface.

There was a guy years ago who would bet at the London greyhound tracks called One Armed Lou and knew his dogs inside out. He went to all the trials so a Lady Godiva from him on an outsider was like a tip in itself. You would take his bet, lay it off and chalk the dog down a few points, he was rarely wrong. Another guy from the West Midlands who resembled Roger De Courcey minus Nookie Bear (I think he owned an engineering company) would flounce up waving a wad of notes right at the death when the last horse was being put into the stalls. I never knocked him back. Sure he had some winners but even Port Vale win now and again.

I prefer to look a punter in the eye. Very occasionally Betfair will go down, just part of this modern age but everything freezes. It's not ideal but if you are trying to lay off a good lump of money it could send your blood pressure up a tad. There is also an app called Bet Angel that works hand in hand with Betfair, fantastic software that gives you the ability to bet in running. Many people bet this way but again DANGER; television screens are two to five seconds behind the real event and shrewdies on the racetrack have already bet when you are punting with horses running into the final furlong while on track they are actually approaching the winning post. A huge advantage or disadvantage depending which side you are on.

The easiest way to explain it is the sun is 93 million miles away. If you glance up in sunglasses one is seeing the sun of 8 minutes ago, likewise a horse race on television halfway down the final furlong is seconds behind real time, the horses in reality have already passed the winning post. People are betting on a developing race at home that other people have witnessed finishing. I know I wouldn't get involved in a situation like that. We, the bookmakers, are also responsible for our own downfall. To a man we have Betdaq on our pitch; we bet and lay accordingly, some bookmakers even green up. This is a button that once pushed gives every horse in the race the same profit. We have ceased being bookmakers; we are now traders. I don't want arbitrage and I don't need arbitrage. I want a bloody good profit on a jolly or second favourite when it has got beat. Maybe I'm the dinosaur, an iconoclast who is not willing to change. I still yearn for the days of the tic-tac men, the racecourse spivs, the characters, the ambiance, the day out to a big meeting where we all travelled together on the same coach or railway special.

I just missed him but loads of my older bookmaker friends have told me about the racecourse legend that was Prince Monolulu. This was a man who claimed he was the chief of the Falasha tribe of Abyssinia but he was really born in the 1880s in the West Indies. The man was an outrageous liar but could pull it off through charisma, colourfulness and unbreakable confidence.

His real name was Peter McKay but that wouldn't have cut the mustard as he started appearing on British racetracks just after the First World War. He wore gaudy, unusual clothes, always bedecked in a plume of brightly dyed ostrich feathers on his head. He definitely would've stood out in grey, early Edwardian England.

His big break came in 1920. He had been making a living on courses, drumming up a crowd with his clarion war cry, 'I gotta horse,' sometimes he would append on, 'To beat the favourite,' occasionally he would call out, 'Black man for luck.' He was the sole black face in a sea of Caucasian boat races so he was very much a novelty and one-off character.

Spion Kop put him on the mainstream map when he won the Epsom Derby that year by over two lengths. Mainly unfancied by the racing press, Prince Monolulu gave it to all and sundry, at a price of course. He used to have a bag or briefcase full of sealed envelopes containing handwritten tips of horses. Whether on a normal day he gave different horses to win the same race we will never know, he takes that one with him to the grave. He was a crafty old rascal. Anyone who bought a tip from him was given a personal caveat emptor and he would whisper in their ear, 'If you tell anyone the horse will lose.'

That golden Wednesday put him eight grand up, a fortune for those days. Was it just good luck that he came up with it? Maybe he was a closet Liverpool fan but that horse coming in at 100/6 (just shy of 17/1) was the making of him. The contemporary common perception of him was he was no better or worse than any other tipster but no one could deny he was the most flamboyant.

Allegedly, he was married six times; the man was a maniac.

He made me look like a Trappist monk and of course that many women in one's life cost a pretty penny. Between 1920 and 1950 he was rumoured to have won and lost a hundred and fifty thousand bags of sand; he was either a real lady's man or a sucker for punishment. We've all been there and me more than most.

He was a black superstar of the time, a national icon, definitely not a shy man and full of eccentricities. He was the first black man to appear on the BBC when it started its initial service in 1936 and he can be seen on cigarette cards of the day. There is a good one depicting him in all his glory on a Churchman's cigarette card. I spotted him on YouTube appearing on a Groucho Marx quiz show in the late fifties; the man was always up for a bit of self-promotion.

Racing was good for him and vice versa. He had a little rhyme that went,

God made the Bees,
The bees made the honey,
You have a bet,
And the bookies take your money.

Bloody sauce but not without a hint of truth and much better than Pam Ayres in my opinion. What an amazing character. His life was not without incident mind. In 1930 he came up with the Derby winner again, *Blenheim* ridden by "The Head Waiter" Harry Wragg. It was a good day though not nearly as lucrative as 1920. On his way back to his residence he was confronted by three ruffians who duffed him up and stole his money. He staggered home where he greeted his wife at the gate. She asked how he had fared then opening his hand all he had left was a solitary threepenny bit. I know that feeling.

Like all of us he had his ups and downs. He used to have a Sunday stall in Petticoat Lane, something else I can relate too. It just highlights what I've always said, enjoy the good times because life is tough but fond memories last forever. The Prince's health and fortune were on the wane in the 1960s and he was admitted into the Middlesex Hospital where he was visited for an interview by racing journalist Jeffrey Bernard on Valentine's Day 1965. The scribe had brought with him a box of Black Magic chocolates for the great man but unfortunately a rogue strawberry cream stuck in his throat and he choked to death. It gives a whole new meaning to the term 'killed with kindness' but the Prince was a showman, only he could have gone out in those circumstances.

He is sadly missed by the racing fraternity and is someone who could never be replaced on the racecourse but if you are ever passing the National Horse Racing Museum in Newmarket, pop in and have a gander at two amazing, colourful jackets on display. Only Prince Monolulu could have gotten away with wearing those in public. RIP big man, gone but never forgotten.

A more contemporary, colourful chappy who once prowled the racecourse is my old mate, John McCririck. He got the bullet from TV in 2013 when I was retreating into my black hole, a sorry affair at the time and one I couldn't give a lot of thought to because of my own, personal circumstances.

John was educated at Harrow (along with fellow racing journalist Julian Wilson) where he was the unofficial school bookie, taking bets off his fellow pupils. It makes me laugh when I hear someone who can't string a sentence together call people like Big Mac and Boris Johnson (who was head boy at Eton) "buffoons." These men are highly educated but because they don't conform to the boring, grey suits approach to life, certain people vilify them.

John originally worked for a bookmaker before dipping his toes in deep water and swimming a few lengths as a bookie himself. He would magnanimously admit that he was a failure as a turf accountant but anyone with a high and mighty opinion of themselves would never do that. He later turned to being a tic tac man (another colourful facet of a day at the races gone forever but we will delve into these mystery men later).

He also worked as a racing journalist for the Daily Star and the Sporting Life, winning awards before working for the BBC and ITV in various capacities involving racing. His big break came when Channel Four Racing took over from ITV. They saw his potential and expanded his remit to reporting from the betting ring. He was an immediate success, sporting as he did, a deerstalker, sideburns, a Cuban Cigar, colourful jackets and a big ego for a big man. Think about this logically, Prince Monolulu was a towering figure, colourful, opinionated and not lacking in any confidence. All McCririck did was step into his shoes. A different role of course but racing had a flamboyant, controversial frontman again.

Big Mac has always divided opinion. Some say he is grumpy, sexist, rude and chauvinistic, others say he is knowledgeable, pro- racing, direct and entertaining. I would say he was the sum of all those parts, which, love him or loath him, made him a great ambassador for horse racing. His rapport with fellow presenter "legendary jockey" Johnny Francome was sublime, a brilliant partnership of ad-libbing with both of them interacting with the public. Francome came across as a very dry wit and he's since gone on to become a successful racing novelist.

When Channel Four didn't renew his contract in 2013, John took it to an employment tribunal claiming unfair dismissal due to ageism, which unfortunately he lost. There was still life in the old dog but another character was gone and Channel Four's new line up of young, knowledgeable, smart and glamorous newbies don't connect with the public. In fact they were as dull as ditch water. Shame.

A big part of my early racing life and experiences were with the tic-tac men. All bookies had an association with them then but now that the betting exchanges and 21st century technology rule the roost they have all disappeared into the ether. Most of them had nicknames like Codhead and Harold the Hat; they were intriguing individuals. Some people used to watch them all day transfixed by the hand movements and secret signals.

In 1999 the writing was on the wall; only three exponents were left on the Southern tracks in Micky "Hokey" Stuart, Billy Brown and Rocky Roberto. All the bookies knew these guys but we were helpless for them in the face of so-called progress. No one man could stand in its path.

Rocky Roberto was a particularly fascinating character and a very good pal of mine, we go back years together. Born of Italian descent, his Dad's name was Dante Roberto who had two Derby winners in *Dante* (1945) and *Roberto* (1972) emulate his name during his lifetime. Rocky was always destined to have a racing career after that. A softly spoken, erudite man, Rocky could recall travelling to meetings on the train which was also the bookies' favourite mode of transport. It's impossible these days with the weight of their equipment but then they would all play cards using the buffet trolley as an impromptu card table.

Rocky took his tic-tac to the Epsom Derby every year and this was when the downs were teeming with people with row after row of coaches, every man and his dog seemed to be there. And of course there would be a huge phalanx of bookmakers to accommodate them. On Tattenham Corner there was a tic-tac called Winkle who only had one eye. It must have been a good-un because it was a long way to the grandstand.

All the tic-tac firms had different coloured cards so a bookie would know a blue card was a certain firm and so on. But just to make things a bit more complicated the cards were known as twist cards, meaning the tic tac firms would have the numbers in different positions, as in twisting the numbers. Now you might think this is all tantamount to disaster but very few things went wrong. These people were honest men; a contract was opened and closed with the wave of the hand, amazing really. At a really busy meeting like the Derby, accounts were settled the next day with many tic tacs burning the midnight oil making sure everything tallied. The system worked so well mistakes were a rarity. There was never any need for arbitration as any mishap was always settled amicably. Can you imagine it going as smooth as that these days? Not on your Aunt Nellie.

Roberto was a man after my own heart. He loved the dogs and he had a penchant for Harringay dog stadium, which sadly shut in 1987. One night was a real pea-souper and the dogs were struggling to follow the hare; it got so bad, the dogs lost sight of what they were chasing, turned around and came charging back the wrong way. Of course, the meeting was abandoned but afterwards someone had the ingenious plan that if it happened again they would tie a torch facing backwards on to the hare with rubber bands. Not sophisticated but the show must go on in the betting industry.

There were a lot of football players who enjoyed going to the dogs back then. Rocky Roberto mentions QPR players Stan Bowles and Don Shanks who I understand shared a flat together. They seemed to be at every London greyhound meeting, both great lads with outgoing personalities. I spotted them one night at Wimbledon where Don Shanks had a gorgeous blonde on his arm. I thought bleeding hell, he's punching above his weight there and he was as well. It was only Miss World, Mary Stavin who had won the title in London and went on to become a Bond Girl. I don't know how long the Swedish stunner stayed with Don but I read she later had dalliances with Graeme Souness and George Best so she did like a footballer.

Stan Bowles was a one off but a suicidal gambler. Poor old Stan couldn't keep a wad; it was always burning a hole in his pocket. He had a deserved reputation for drinking, womanising and gambling but that didn't stop him playing for England and being voted the best QPR player in history. The word maverick could have been invented for Stan. He would often be seen 15 minutes before a home game kick off, across the road at the bookies putting his horses on. During the match he would drift to the wings where the supporters could tell him if his selections had won. When Tommy Docherty took over as manager he informed Stan that he was a man he could trust. Stan came back with, 'I'd rather trust my chickens with Colonel Sanders.'

His mum had him sussed though, 'If our Stan invested in a cemetery, people would stop dying.'

My personal favourite was his landlord banging on his front door. Lodging money hadn't crossed his palm in a month due to gambling losses apparently. 'I've come looking for the rent.'

Without batting an eyelid Stan retorted 'Well, come on in Bert, we can look for it together.'

Stan's contracted Alzheimer's in his late sixties, sad news but at least he's got good family and friends. He's still a legend down Loftus Road where they also have something going on for him so he gets by. It's a real shame but not uncommon for footballers who played in the sixties, seventies and eighties retiring with no money.

A couple of ex-Norwich Premier League players, Grant Holt and Steve Morison are big into dogs. I'm sure they are running some sort of club in the midlands that involves greyhound ownership which is great, the game needs all the help it can get, more power to their elbow.

If anyone is interested in the halcyon days of dog racing there is a very interesting short documentary on *YouTube* entitled "Tic Tac Man" featuring an affable young man, Dean Valentine who was a standing dish at the very busy Walthamstow Greyhound Stadium. He explains some of the price signs like 3/1 which comes from when someone was sentenced in court to 3 months It was called a lay down hence carpet and 33/1, double carpet. The term "a Monkey" came from the old Indian 500 Rupee bank note that featured a monkey on one side. British troops returning from the sub-continent quickly gave it parlance for 500 quid. The Stow, as it was affectionately known, shut down in 2008. I think Dean is still involved in the betting industry while Rocky Roberto went from poacher to gamekeeper and bought a batch of bookmakers' pitches, working under the trading name, Kelross. I wish them both well and all the luck in the world.

PS: When I lost all my money in 1996 on the Dettori Seven, I actually owed Rocky twenty thousand pound. I rang him up to tell him I would get his money to him shortly but not before pretending to be a policeman.

'Excuse me Sir, this is Detective Richard Evans, do you know a fat gentleman who is currently in our cells? He has a twist card with your name on it.'

'Oh no, that's Gary Wiltshire,' I tried to continue, but burst out laughing. Rocky got his money and I could still smile.

What a mad, crazy life we all led, things were never dull when the big man was around.

* * * *

PHOTO GALLERY

GALLERY 1

With the man who changed my life - Frankie Dettori

Me and little Frankie Wiltshire

GALLERY 2

Fred Done, Michael Ball, Mo and Alfie Boe - party time!

Michael Van Gerwen with Jaimee and Sharon at the Dorchester

GALLERY 3

Oi, Oi, lobster time!

With the legend, John Conteh

GALLERY 4

My daughter Kelly and family

Lofty - *BEWARE!*

GALLERY 5

Me and my Danny

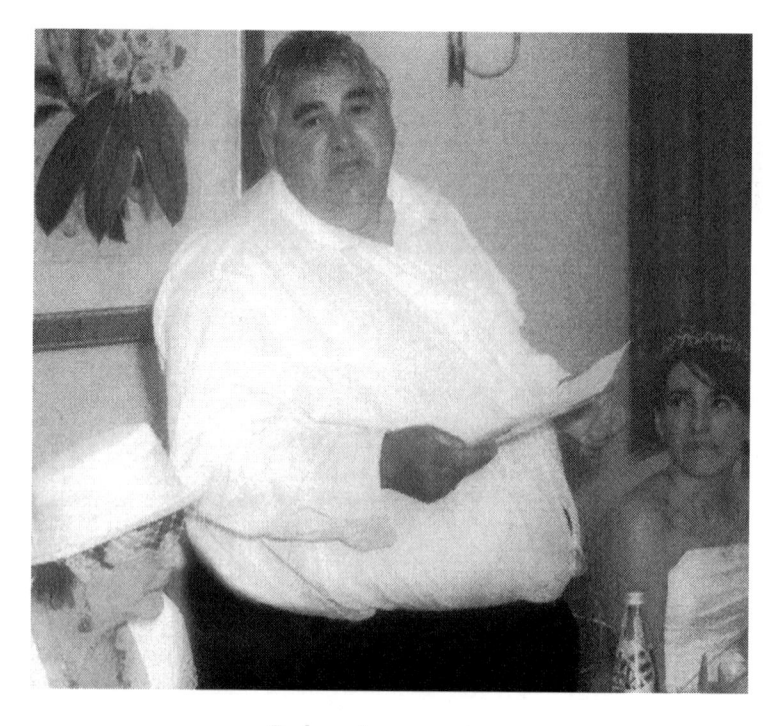

Before the operation.

GALLERY 6

Tenerife, still eating well

Sharon in her jockey days

Looking for the value

GALLERY 7

007 Stuart next to me, still not smiling, bet he used to with the Russian

Me and sister Jackie, with husband Richard

GALLERY 8

Fred with *Mo Twentyone*

Fred's grandchildren with *Mo Twentyone*

Son Charlie with Bethany and baby Frankie

Chapter Five

HORSES FOR COURSES

After Shergar won his first race, racing correspondent Richard Baerlein pronounced, 'At 8/1, Shergar for The Derby, now is the time to bet like men.'

I hear people say there's another recession coming but to be candid, I reckon we are all living in a permanent downturn. Prices go up while wages stagnate. Now you know I'm a betting man, I don't get into politics but can any of us truthfully say that these are the best times to live and bring your kids up right. The technology and huge rapid advances in science have made the day to day chores easier to perform but we all seem to be working round the clock to stand still, we are spending what little we have so much easier than saving for a rainy day. The reason is that the storm clouds seem to be with us on a permanent basis, we have accepted it as the norm but it's no way to live. I just wish I had the answers.

As a child of the 1950s, I became a bookmaker in the 1970s, Thatcherism was on the rise and a lot of working-class people were riding the profitable tsunami wave. For the first time in history, ordinary Joes and their wives were buying their council house or a new build or even, God Forbid, a suburban semi-detached. What chances have most of the kids now? The lucky ones might get a deposit from the bank of Mum and Dad but even still London is out of the question for most, half a million doesn't go far in the capital. The term mortgage is derived from the French *la mort*, meaning death, payment until you die. On that happy note let's get back to the betting, which like every other business, was being squeezed until the pips squeaked.

As much as I enjoyed going racing again, every day was like going down the coal mine; not in physical terms (I take my hat off to all those brave men who ventured deep into the bowels of the earth to retrieve the black gold) but for the sheer pressure of having to pay the daily overheads and come out ahead after the last race result. It was all down to me. I remember Lee Trevino the golfer once saying, "nobody but you and your caddie care what you are doing out there and if your caddie is betting against you, he doesn't care either." So, it was me versus the world. I didn't mind those odds; all I needed was a fair roll of the dice. That wasn't too much to ask surely?

One of my lifetime ambitions was to stand and take wagers at every British racetrack on the mainland or visit the course and have an enjoyable day out punting with the public. This I've managed to do and here is my own personal, Gary Wiltshire A-Z of the horse racing tracks. It put many miles on the speedo and laughs a plenty, sometimes coming home with the caviar but often only good old battered cod.

* *

AINTREE: I had a pitch there on the rails but I sold it. Apart from the three-day Grand National Festival there are only five or six other days racing, so when I was offered good money for the pitch, I took it. Grand National day itself is a long-lived British institution, a fantastic occasion with the people of Liverpool and beyond coming out in force but you take nothing over a fiver in wagers, so because it's on a Saturday I prefer to be at another big meeting. Another reason I baled-out was the horrendous amount of walking. You have to walk miles from the car park to the turnstiles then on to the office to get your badge and finally over to your pitch. None of your destinations are anywhere near the others. I don't walk that far on holiday.

ASCOT: I have over a million reasons for passing this one. If you are an Alien from Venus or have been in asleep for thirty years then get your hands on *Winning It Back*. It's the inspiring saga of one man against the world, a literary classic.

AYR: I always enjoy going up to Ayr, be it for the Flat or jumps. The bracing sea air coming in from the Firth of Clyde, a friendly atmosphere (with many coming down from Glasgow) but I remember it for just one Friday-Saturday Scottish Grand National meeting in particular. I'd driven up with an old bookie pal Andy Smith from Bristol. We were teaming up to take some of those infamous Scottish £100 notes back over the border but the script quickly turned south as on the Caledonian punters were rampant on the first day. In truth we had a poor pitch. I think it only cost £200 to buy it outright, so to drum up some business we went slightly longer on some short-priced, fancied horses. As we packed-up we were nearly on our knees, all six favourites had won. We were down to the tune of 58 grand. Andy was out of it, struggling to breathe let alone speak and I was all for driving straight back to the land of sensibility but Andy eventually found his voice and suggested we go back to the hotel for a few drinks as we had already paid for the night's accommodation.

A few stiffeners at the bar put everything in a better light. Andy had some inside info on three or four fancied runners for tomorrow so if we just took the opposite tack from today's disastrous results and kept his fancies shorter than all the other bookies then we only needed a couple to win to get at least parole from jail.

That Saturday was one of my most successful days on the Racetrack. The first five races we got five winners from Andy. We kept all these horses short; every single one was a skinner, not a bent groat for any of them. I don't even recall what happened in the sixth race, by that time we were past caring. The big man upstairs was certainly looking down on us with benevolence that day, after all expenses we were down £120 which was a result. It was a loss on two day's work but a magnificent fight back.

BANGOR ON DEE: One of my favourites. A lovely little picturesque track, overlooked by the Welsh Hills and the people are charming and friendly. It's an arena for racegoers but strangely doesn't contain a grandstand. I've always done well here, no edge to the place at all. I would highly recommend a family day out alongside real racing folk. On the way up I always stop at Ma Baker's Cafe at Prees Heath, just south of Whitchurch on the convergence of the A41 and A49. In the pre- op days, I would always opt for the big breakfast; two of everything on a platter about 15 inches wide with free refills of coffee, a lovely start to the day. Now, Lyn the manageress will knock me up anything a trifle healthier even if it isn't on the menu, all part of the service before a great day's National Hunt racing. Didn't we have a lovely time the day we went to Bangor? (my apologies to Fiddlers Dram)

BATH: The highest Flat course in the country on Lansdown Hill has a stiff finish that comes up quickly after a sharp bend. That can disorientate some inexperienced sprinters and races can be won and lost negotiating the best route into the straight. You find a lot of winners coming over the top and wide towards the grandstand. It always looks firm going here so maybe they haven't paid their water rates but what do I know? Actually, they haven't got a watering system so that explains it! I retain one pitch here and I always get a pre-racing dinner in Bath at The Fishworks on Green Street for a lovely bit of battered fish. This is a once a year track for me but only if the mighty Wurzels are playing in concert. You can't beat a bit of "Combine Harvester" and "I am a Cider Drinker," top scrumpy and western. Good crowds arrive from Bristol and Bath... old Adge Cutler would be *so* proud.

BEVERLEY: I've been going for years but never seen a hillbilly yet. It's a stiff, uphill finish and a high draw in five-furlong sprint race makes winning next to impossible. There's always a good, enthusiastic Yorkshire crowd but I've never done well here. Just bad memories, especially a traumatic night years ago when I copped off with a local looker (I said, "looker"!) but she turned out to be a nightmare. At this sorry juncture I would just like to erase all memories, not a course for me.

BRIGHTON: Now you're talking. There is nowhere in the whole world quite like Brighton, cosmopolitan would only be scratching the surface. I've been going there since I was a little kid; every Sunday in the summer the family would make the jaunt from London to Southend-On-Sea or Brighton, I loved them both dearly. The best seafood stalls are there on the front promenade selling lovely shellfish while I regard it as the home of the Dinky Donuts. What could be better than munching a bag while walking to Brighton Pier to experience the rides and amusements? I'm not reminiscing now, I'm talking about today.

The Brighton racetrack is quite unique, the horseshoe shape resembles only one other and I often refer to it as the workingman's Epsom. If your horse runs well at Brighton it will probably run well at Epsom and vice versa. A mate's horse Multahab won nine times; seven of them at Brighton, which is where the term horses for courses comes from. Chester is another track that brings the best out of certain horses. The Americans have a term for it as well; they call it "smart placing." It's no real wonder we invented the language and they try their best to contribute the odd snippet. Some days the sea fret comes inland off the English Channel, a wet mist that can hamper visibility. The fret is one of nature's mysteries, it comes in its own time and sometimes you are lucky to catch sight of the horses a furlong out. The television commentator can only describe the start of the race and the last knockings at the finish so what they are doing mid-race is anyone's guess. All said, it's quite unique. Memories are made of this.

CARLISLE: A sole appearance here for me. I had one of my own horses running at the track, Winter Lightning handled by ace trainer David Wintle. I don't think I returned home with any prize money that day though. I caught the early train up from London Euston, sampled a beer or ten on Thomas the Tank Engine and I don't think the day got any better than that. If I can remember rightly, the Carlisle finish was uphill as was most of the surrounding area. Gary Wiltshire and small mountains go together like Greenpeace and the Japanese Whaling Fleet. I was not built for fell running. There's a lot to be said for all the nutters who believe the Earth is flat, I salute their optimism but don't ever go to the Lake District.

CARTMEL: Local monks to the south of the Lake District originally set up the races here. It felt like you were driving up to Scotland, especially given I lived in London. It was always well attended, on bank holidays it was absolutely rammed and sometimes the attendance was 20,000 plus. Obviously some people hadn't just come to bet but to have a jolly old day out, it all added to the marvellous atmosphere. I'd been a bookie up there once but the sheer logistics of travelling and the vast multitude of bookies meant I had to let it go. I always did ok on this racetrack and unlike many others; it threw up winners at all prices. If I lost (or won), I used to console myself afterwards in Cartmel village with a large portion of the world-famous sticky-toffee pudding. I'm salivating just thinking about it. It was very enjoyable; I had many happy days there including one very funny story that I can't divulge! I would probably end up in Pentonville Prison if I did but never say never. Most journeys back home were with all the petrol paid for and a little bit more for the big man so never take a licking, just keep on ticking.

CATTERICK: Another North Yorkshire racecourse that didn't give me any sparkle. It was a long trudge up the never ending A1 before seeing the ominous road sign, "Catterick Garrison". If I want to be surrounded by squaddies, I would enlist (can you imagine me on the assault course), or move to Aldershot. My only salvation was that I never opened a book here. I went once and regretted it. A course to swerve in my opinion.

CHELTENHAM: What can you say about the greatest National Hunt venue in the world? I think half of Ireland comes over on a flotilla of ferries, people save up all year to make the sacred pilgrimage. There's a true story of one Paddy who had put a stipend away every week religiously, the wife had been kept short and the kids had gone without. He boarded the ferry at Dublin, proud as punch with the equivalent of seven thousand sobs in his bulging pockets but he got into a card school, never won a hand and lost his whole stash. As soon as the ferry docked at Holyhead he caught the first one back. Very sad but funny in a perverse sort of way and at the same time, a warning to all us fearless gamblers.

I never miss a day, apart from my depressive period when I couldn't raise a gallop. I actually have five pitches there, one in the silver ring and four in tatts but they're in bad positions. It's an odds-on certainty nobody else will ever want them. The Cheltenham Festival every March is ingrained in the soul of most gamblers, the mighty Cleeve Hill back dropping the roar of sixty thousand voices at the outset of the first race. That still sends a tingle down my neck and long may it last. Cheltenham is one of the Great British sporting institutions, God bless Prestbury Park.

CHELMSFORD: Originally called Great Leighs Racecourse, it was Britain's first new racecourse in over 80 years when it opened in 2008 but it suffered problems and went into admin early 2009. It was the brainchild of entrepreneur John Holmes who looked to be on a winner when he first got a license but for some reason the attendances were disappointing, surprising really when you consider it was the only racetrack in the county of Essex.

It reopened again for racing as the Chelmsford City Racecourse in 2015 when a syndicate led by my old mate Fred Done worked it's magic to get the venue buzzing again. I don't think anyone other than Fred could have done it. The whole place felt jinxed and in the six years of inactivity many had tried to get a license for racing but they had all come up short. Fred had made old pal Joe Scanlon, Betfred's Director of Racing, so he would be overseeing the new operation and what a fantastic success they have both achieved with the racetrack.

When it was Great Leighs, I used to represent Totesport there along with son Nicky and local Tote girl Pam Sharman. It was a shame it closed because it had great potential. Once reopened, I was straight back in representing Betfred on wages. I've got a great relationship with the punters in Essex, I like to think we have the busiest pitch and give the best value. Being Essex, a lot of the bets are twenty quid plus; they might be flash but they do know their racing down there. It certainly makes a change from a cavalcade of the two-pound punters. In truth, there is nothing at all wrong with that but a few hefty punts remind me of the good old days when they used to run at you with big wads of cash. Maybe I'm just an adrenalin junkie.

I'm at Chelmsford throughout the all-weather season. After the last race has been run and I make the journey home, win, lose or draw, I always bell Sharon to see if she wants any Oriental goodies. I've never known her not to because they are the cat's pyjamas. I ring up the best Chinese restaurant in the country, Cinta in Godmanchester, which is just south of Huntingdon, to pre order, the food so it's ready when I arrive. Nine times out of ten we have buttermilk prawns and seaweed, it's the best thirteen quid you can spend. If local man, the Lord Protector Oliver Cromwell had been alive today he definitely would have dined there. A night out might have mellowed him to the extent of not chopping off the head of Charles 1st.

When I finally get home to Nottingham with the food and after a six-hour round trip, I'm absolutely cream-crackered. If I'm really lucky I might get a kiss and a cuddle but usually after she's finished her repast I'm snoring for England, such is life. The Essex venue is one of my favourites; great people, great racing, great company and great facilities. As the Kelloggs' Frosted Flakes legend Tony the Tiger likes to say, 'They're Grrrreat!'

CHEPSTOW: Home of the Welsh Grand National, always the first one run in December before the English, Scottish and Irish. There have actually been four postponements in the last decade due to flooding or frosty conditions. Every time John Parrott and myself worked for the BBC here I was freezing my bloody Jacobs off, it seems to be colder in South Wales than anywhere else in Britain.

That said, it's a dual-purpose racecourse catering for Flat and National Hunt racing and has excellent facilities. I still have a pitch here but don't come that often because I begrudge paying that rip-off toll at the Severn Bridge just north of Bristol. I think it was nearly seven quid. I bet Isambard Kingdom Brunel is turning in his grave, now that honorary Bristolian could build a bridge. I remember years ago when you could cross for half a crown, that's twelve and a half pence to all you young millennials. What makes me laugh is that the toll is only charged one way, the bloody English are penalised for coming into Wales! It's been a border tax if you like but amazingly it's been scrapped so you might just see me up in the valleys a whole lot more.

'We'll keep a welcome in the hillside, we'll keep a welcome in the glen, now you've scrapped that poxy bridge tax, Gary's back on the road again.'

CHESTER: This course, The Roodee, is a Bobby Dazzler. Said to have been a venue for racing since the 1500s, the course is definitely one of the smaller venues at one mile, one furlong. Horses who have won here before tend to go in again, it's a real specialist track with the home stretch just over a furlong long.

I have two pitches here, one being in tatts. The three-day May meeting is always very well attended and on Wednesday, Thursday and Friday people come to Chester for a good time. The traffic flow is abysmal and often gridlocked on race days as the course is close to the city's hotels, bars and restaurants but people bring plenty of wonga to spend at the champagne bars and eateries. There are queues for everything, including trying to get a bet on. A lot of folk have had a nice drink so the old saying that alcohol loosens the tongue also applies to the wallet but it is a hard racecourse to read, so results are surprising.

I have my own triple commandment for a good day's punting at Chester: ladies with short skirts and long legs are there in their thousands; fish and chips from the racecourse chippy are very nice; a low-drawn front runner, especially in the five-furlong races as horses don't come back very often if they get away.

It's the premier meeting in the North West and many Premier League footballers come with their clubs or just for a nice family day out. Liverpool and Everton and the two Manchester clubs frequently turn up. Sir Alex loved a punt here. (Hopefully he's well on the mend now). As an Arsenal man I'd have swapped him for Wenger but not in the Frenchman's early days. Let's give him some credit where it's due, *Sacre Bleu!*

The formidable owner Dr Marwan Koukash is always an interested spectator. He demands winners at Chester, employing very shrewd trainers like Richard Fahey, Ian Williams and Marco Botti. Those bleeding light grey colours have cost me a packet over the years but the good doctor looks like a man not to meddle with. I certainly wouldn't like to meet him in a dark alley after his horse had just lost a photo finish. So hearty congratulations on all your winners Sir, may you have many, many more. He might just read this book one day, best to stay on the side of the righteous.

A local trainer who always does well at Chester is the up and coming Tom Dascombe. I say up and coming because he hasn't been training as long as some of the mega names but he is probably already just behind the elite trainers. His horses can be devastating, always keep an eye on those that get backed.

Financed by the former Liverpool, Real Madrid and Manchester United football star Michael Owen at Manor House Stables, just north of Malpas, Dascombe is less than half an hour away from the Roodee so they love a winner there but also watch out for his runners at Haydock Park if ridden by the underrated jockey Richard Kingscote. They don't like leaving their money behind inside the bookies' satchels.

DONCASTER: Town Moor is home of the oldest classic race, The St. Leger, the longest in distance and last leg of the English Triple Crown races which is nearly impossible to achieve these days. Wonder horse *Nijinsky* was the last to do it in 1970 and it had been 35 years prior to that. To attain full fitness over a four-month period and over three different distances demands an equine superstar so I doubt whether we shall see ever another *Nijinsky* in our lifetime.

Another Yorkshire course not on my Christmas card List. I've had some diabolical days here punting, I always seem to do my bollocks. They say Yorkshire men are very mean with their money but they love taking my hard earned. A jinxed course for me. After a losing session I always head for Whitby's Fish and Chip Restaurant just off the course, down a side street near Leger Way. I'm determined to have one winning day at the Doncaster Races in the future and give all the staff a good tip, just to show my humble appreciation for their blinding fish and chips.

EPSOM: Wow! What more can I say? The Epsom Derby and the Grand National are the most famous races in the world. Of course, there's the feted Melbourne Cup, Kentucky Derby and Prix de L'Arc de Triomphe but nobody sets up a race better with our history, pageantry and panache like the traditional British.

When I was a kid, the Derby was always on a Wednesday but the great and the good in their wisdom decided to change to Saturday in 1995. I think the whole occasion lost a little bit of sparkle and mystique after that but they say money talks, bullshit walks. Maybe I'm a bit nostalgic for the fun-filled family days we had there but even now the event gets a nine out of ten.

I remember the 1995 race quite vividly, won by the classy unbeatable *Lammtarra* in those distinctive green and white silks. Everyone always associates the horse with my old sparring partner Frankie Dettori because of his subsequent wins in The King George VI and the Arc but up top on Derby Day was the "Choirboy," the late, great Walter Swinburn riding him to victory in record time.

The strange minutiae and technicalities of everything running up to the race was like a Dick Francis novel. The previous year, Lammtarra's young trainer Alex Scott was murdered by one of his stable staff after they'd had a vociferous argument about how the horses should be trained. Later Scott confronted the employee to give him his cards and the guy shot him in the chest at point-blank range with a shotgun. Something of over-reaction on any level and not an everyday occurrence in leafy Newmarket. That was one of backstory; another was that in the months leading up to the Derby, *Lammtarra* was a stricken and sickly horse.

He'd been transferred to the stable of *Godolphin* trainer Saeed Bin Suroor who did his level best to get him right but on the day of the Derby he hadn't run for nearly a year. He went off at 14/1 but if you knew the whole background story then you'd think it was a crazy price for the son of *Nijinsky*. He had won his only previous race at Newbury as a two-year-old in good fashion but the rest is history. As he was led into the winners' enclosure there were tears of joy but also tears of regret for the absence of missing trainer Alex Scott.

Lammtarra will go down in the horsey annals of history as one of the greats. Who will ever forget The King George V1 epic race with Pentire when the runner-up was going much the best only for *Lammtarra* to get back up to win by a neck. It was the same story in the Arc where he was overtaken in the final furlong but battled back to get his head in front again. This lion of a horse died about 4 years ago; what wouldn't I have given to own one half as good as that, equine par excellence. RIP old boy.

All the family used to go down to Epsom on the Sunday, there would be thousands of Londoners there mooching about for the annual, three-day entertainment extravaganza. The fun fair was a major attraction with its rides and stalls. I used to enjoy the boxing booths where any young man, pugnacious or bloody belligerent enough, could attempt to go three rounds with some tough old pro-boxer who knew every dirty trick in the book. Did I ever stick my hand up? Only when the sausage rolls were being dolled-out by my mother! It was a marvellous experience, even when plenty of rascals were trying to lighten your wallet.

The old card sharp trick, "find the lady", also known as "three-card Monte", was always a game to swerve. It looks easy. There are just three playing cards, face down; one red queen, two black jacks or aces and you need to identify the queen. The dealer might even let you win a couple of games at first to lull you in but as soon as the stakes are raised you can never locate the queen again, bamboozled by sleight of hand. Many have been taught an expensive lesson over the years but daft as it seems people are still falling for it.

The funfair used to be spread out over ten days long ago but was reduced in length as attendances fell away. I have great memories of fortune telling with crystal balls, pearly kings and queens, jugglers, stilt walkers, candyfloss, bumper cars and big wheels. I still hold a pitch opposite the grandstand and there's quite a large petition containing thousands of names trying desperately to get the big race to revert back to Wednesdays. I'm right behind that but then again, I am an old traditionalist. Knees up Mother Brown.

EXETER: When I first started making a book here it was known as Devon and Exeter. Just to confuse matters the locals call it Haldon due to its location on Haldon Hill. It's a beautiful course and area but it takes forever to get there down the never-ending M5. Just like my life, please God; it's a hell of a long journey. Its a shame that I don't take it anymore, the sheer logistics make it utterly pointless. I sold my pitch last year for peanuts, a real shame because I do miss the racing and the wonderful people but it's all down to tight economics of the modern bookmaker.

FAKENHAM: A really stunning course. I like coming here because it's worth the effort and I still hold one pitch. Turn left at King's Lynn and up past Sandringham House, then it's a few miles to the racecourse in sunny Norfolk. The staff here cares. It's all held together by Chief Exec. and Clerk of the Course, David Hunter, a lovely fella but not the one who ran the Crossroads Motel many years ago. A great National Hunt venue.

FFOS LAS: Fflipping easy to say but hard to spell and even harder to find when it was first opened in 2009. The Tote sent me to the first meeting here with my usual stalwarts Pam and son Nicky but call us thick, we couldn't find it. This was the first jumps track to be constructed in over 80 years, on the site of a disused open cast coal mine, making it Wales third horse racing arena. They encompassed new Flat racing as well as jumping.

I had done my research before going and it was 20 minutes from Carmarthen so how hard could it be? What did I know about the area? Sod all, allied to the fact that there was a distinct lack of sign posting. We toured South Wales for about an hour and a half. Everyone we asked hadn't a Scooby-Doo, many who clocked our English accents, just shrugged their shoulders. Nice. It was apparently slap bang in the middle of nowhere. It got that desperate, I ordered Pam and Nicky to look out for any man covered in coal dust, wearing a hard hat and carrying a Davy Lamp, that would be our get out of jail card but I think we actually found the course by accident.

In the car park there was more back slapping and high fives than at the Superbowl, it must have felt like this when Columbus discovered America. We proudly strode in to take our place in history. We set up minutes before the first race started, The Tote had arrived but it had been a really close call, one more wrong turn would have scuppered the day.

To be fair, there was a bloody large crowd there and we took good money. The canny Welsh were out in force and with the high hills in the background the course resembled an industrial Cheltenham. I've heard it's gone from strength to strength since that first day.

I've never been back personally but it was one for the bucket list. Apparently, there are now significantly more directional signs; being lost in a foreign land like deepest Wales where every field looks the same is not good for your blood pressure. I wouldn't mind having a holiday home there one day up on the north coast if I hit the racing jackpot again, so I congratulate the boys from the valleys for their great new horse racing venue. The last thing I would ever want is coming back home to Towyn and finding the Sons of Glendower have torched my thatched cottage, what would the neighbours think?

Plenty of money has been spent here, facilities are now top notch with talk of improving the capacity to double the present number. There are only good things to say about Ffos Las, this is an arena here to stay and on the up.

FONTWELL PARK: Love it, love it, love it. Situated between classy Chichester and Littlehampton, just North of the mighty Bognor Regis. What's not to like? Friendly people, cracking racetrack and a new grandstand. It's always very well attended, most Boxing Day meetings I come here in preference over some bigger tracks, in fact if I could lay bets here every day of the week I would. Her Majesty Queen Elizabeth the Second had her first winner here and John Francome also beat Stan Mellor's lifetime career winners at the course, so if it's good enough for the Queen of England as well as the King of Jumping, it's mighty fine and dandy for the cockney kid as well. Long may it prosper.

GOODWOOD: One of the country's best courses without a doubt and, like Fontwell, it's close to the moneyed and well-heeled populace of

Chichester. You definitely get some big wagers struck here, trouble is I've been on the receiving end of a lot of them. Can there be a better sight than the summer sun blazing down over the magnificent South Downs? It's not called Glorious Goodwood for nothing and in some people's opinion, the most beautiful racecourse in the world.

I would always stay at the Royal Norfolk Hotel in Bognor Regis for the multi-day meetings, all the tote girls used to stay there as well. We had some wonderful nights there until ex-wife Sue, a tote girl herself, put a strict non- negotiable stoppage on all that malarkey, another avenue of pleasure confined to the waste bin of history.

I can't speak for other bookies but I find it impossible to win here. There are lots of winning favourites while unlucky horses I had on my side in running have cost me dear. I still go all the time, hoping for the tide to turn but I have done my bollocks here more times than I can remember. Please God let me win one time.

GREAT YARMOUTH: Of all the places I go racing, this is the one racetrack I look back with super-stereo, rose-tinted glasses. I still enjoy coming here but most of the action has long gone like Woolworths' pick 'n' mix. I have had more ups and downs here than The Big Dipper on Blackpool Pleasure Beach. The three-day September meeting is still going strong but the golden, halcyon days are gone forever. Then, the holiday crowds were wading in with gay abandon; the mass hordes from the Midlands coming down the A14 have side stepped off to the sunny climes of Torremolinos, Zante and Bodrum.

The local businesses, owners of pubs, hotels and amusement arcades would get away for a few hours from their daily grind of counting money to hopefully share the wealth with us beleaguered bookmakers. I even had a flat cap with "alms for the poor" written on it for donations from the public after any bad day. This was the era of the great British holiday; every hotel, caravan site and boarding house was packed to the rafters so hoteliers and publicans would turn up with jacket pockets stuffed with every denomination of bank note. Even the girl from the ring doughnut stall near that big slide was carrying major wedge. All I needed were the favourites to have a bad day at the office which wasn't always the case but I know I'm up a tanner or two over these long, cruel decades.

The Britannia Pier would always book some great acts for the theatre. Jim Davidson and Roy Chubby Brown have performed there, in fact every year I've been going to Yarmouth Chubby seems to have been pulling big crowds in. I know he's not for everyone but my favourite clean joke of his (there's not many) is the poem Paul McCartney wrote when he was courting Heather Mills, "We lay upon the grassy bank, my hands were all a quiver, I slowly undid her suspender belt and her leg fell in the river." Not a number one but quite profound.

My writer Michael O'Rourke told me he actually saw Leslie Crowther on stage live at the very same theatre, I didn't realise he was that old. All I can say is "Come on Down!" Now that's a blast from the past. I hadn't realised that Mr Crowther had passed away so long ago; it was 1996, the very same year I was struggling for breath at Ascot. I don't believe in conspiracy theories but I'm going to ask Frankie Dettori his opinion on *The Price is Right*.

Anyway, enough of this gay banter, back to Numero Uno, me, Big Gary Wiltshire, *bon vivant* and all-round good egg. I loved the area and have always liked to get away for a few days in a caravan at Scratby Hall or California Cliffs which was nearby and although it was fuck-all like California, it was close and amenable for getting into Great Yarmouth and back.

It was around this period when I had my greatest day on the racetrack at Yarmouth. I went through it briefly on half a page in the previous book but I now realise that this was the eureka moment of my betting career. All my ducks were in a row, Jupiter aligned with Mars and for a few hours in the afternoon I was the luckiest bastard in Norfolk, apart from Alan Partridge of course.

They say someone's good luck is another person's bad luck, the Chinese call it Yin and Yang. Well that day, the unlucky person was the famous bookmaker Roy Christie. He was a good mate of mine and we used to be cheek to cheek, next to each other on the rails. Roy was travelling across from his hometown of Kettering in Northamptonshire with his son John who used to accompany him to all the courses, when their luxury motor broke down.

He never made it to the course, so with the ebb and flow of racecourse punters I picked up one or two off his regular patrons. Roy was a Premier League bookmaker, he had a string of shops that he later sold to Coral and he wouldn't bat an eyelid if someone wanted a five-figure wager. I was glad of the extra business but was taken aback when one of his heavier backers tried to get ten-grand on with me in the first race.

The guy was a famous local poultry farmer and was extremely wealthy, he was a man who got his kicks from backing horses. Now I know it wasn't the legendary Norfolk turkey breeder Bernard Matthews because I never heard him say "Bootiful" but I did catch "bollocks" under his breath after a couple of losing bets. I was in a quandary for all of three seconds; he wanted ten large on the 7/2 second favourite, my satchel contained the princely sum of two thousand five hundred pounds. If he won that would all be gone and I'd have to sell my house. What would you do?

A divine light was shining down on me that day. He lost the first three races and his bets never fluctuated; he was a ten-grand a race man, very nice if you can afford it but the bottom line was thirty thousand little beauties in credit for a quivering wreck of a man, a certain Gary Wiltshire. I was hoping he'd give up the ghost and bugger off back to his hens but the man was a maniac, he was certainly not for surrendering. This bout was going all the way, one of us would be in quagmire after the racing was over.

Races four and five came and went the same way, I was sitting on a mountain of money. Less than five minutes before the final race he hadn't been sighted. Maybe he'd realised the enormity of his actions and phoned the Samaritans? Fat chance of that, he came roaring out of the beer tent. I closed my eyes and prayed to God, just one more time Lord, don't desert a poor sinner now.

I had a hunch he would go for an outsider as he hadn't backed anything bigger than 6/1 up to then but the shorter priced horses hadn't performed for him all day, he'd had a well beaten second and a close up third.

Sure enough, he wanted 10K on a 16/1 shot. I did the maths in my head quicker than Stephen Hawking; after five losing races, he would be well over a hundred grand ahead if he could pull it off. A tough businessman like Fred Done or Barry Hearn would have definitely cut him down to a smaller stake.

I hesitated for about ten seconds, technically speaking I didn't need to accept any of the bet but 'morally' it was different. I had taken the man's money all afternoon and my undoubted reputation meant a lot to me, if word got out, things could get misconstrued. He wouldn't even be betting with me at the next meeting but that wasn't the point, the right thing to do was give him the chance to win his money back.

It was the craziest thing I've ever done in my life. My total assets, liquidated, couldn't pay him in full and he looked like the kind of guy who would chase you for the last penny. I was shaking like a leaf as the horses burst out of the stalls, if this outsider won my life was utterly ruined. It felt like the whole race was run in slow motion, I was undergoing an out-of-body experience. A horse and jockey in very similar colours took it up in the last furlong, 'Oh no, God, shit!'

I went a deathly shade of pale but I needn't have worried, the outsider was out the back with the washing as the weight of the world lifted off my shoulders. I did a little involuntary victory reel on my pitch. If the producers of *Strictly Come Dancing* had clocked my rendition, I would've been immediately installed as favourite for the next series.

All this happened because Roy Christie's top of the range motor decided to down tools. I knew Roy wouldn't begrudge me winning, he was as good as gold. He was one of the last gentleman bookmakers, liked by many and with few enemies.

Roy unfortunately contracted cancer approaching his eighties but he was still as sharp as needle. He asked his son John to contact Ladbrokes near the end of his life to enquire about the odds on him dying on his birthday, it gave him pleasure to think he could still take money off Ladbrokes even though he would be dead. John declined to do it but true to his premonition, Roy hung about until his eightieth birthday with his cake and candles before going to the big casino in the sky. Let's all hope God is a betting man.

6/4 he is.

Talking about dying on your birthday, the odds are 365/1 but the most famous coincidental one is very interesting. Samuel Langhorne Clemens, better known as Mark Twain the writer, was born shortly after Halley's comet was viewed in the heavens. He predicted during his life that, "I came in with Halley's comet, I expect to go out with it." What odds would he have got if there had been American bookmakers about in those days. Well the day after his loyal comet was spotted again 74 years later, he suddenly dropped down dead from a heart attack on April 21st 1910. Maybe he got too excited, we will never know. Halley's Comet is due back in 2061, the thing's like bloody clockwork but if I say I'll go out with it at the age of 105, it just might be pushing my luck a bit too far!

So I'd hit the jackpot. I must have been more flush that year because I wasn't in a caravan park, I was staying at the Cliff Hotel in Gorleston on Sea just down the coast from Yarmouth and ex-wife Sue along for the ride. The next day I ordered a taxi to get some dinner and beseeched the good cabbie to take us to a village where he would like to live; five hours later we arrived at Sandbanks, 250 miles away (no, just jesting, he popped us 12 miles up the coast to Winterton on Sea and that was bloody bootiful).

We both immediately fell in love with the place. After a cracking dinner we were mooching about the village before coming upon a lovely thatched residence, "Harbour Cottage." What a corker it was and what made it more homely and attractive was the "For Sale" sign reading £59,999. It was fate, it was kismet, it was destiny, we both knew we wanted it and I had the wonga. There was even the added bonus of a nicker back, it was full steam ahead.

I rang up the local estate agents, Aldreds of Great Yarmouth; 'Is it still up for sale?'

Yes.

'Do I want to view?'

No.

'Do you want to negotiate a price?'

No.

'When can you put a deposit down?'

I'll pay the whole amount on Tuesday.

Now that's how to do business.

I'd like to say we were there many years but Frankie's soon-to-be *Magnificent Seven* took care of that. Harbour Cottage went with all my other assets. I'd bought it for when I grew old as my retirement castle, when all the hustle and bustle of the betting ring became too much to bear. I still fondly remember sitting out in the back garden with a Cromer crab and a large G & T, golden days taken away all too soon. I've never told anybody this but after some meetings at Yarmouth, I occasionally drive up to the cottage, park up and relive old memories and always have a little sob to myself. I would love to buy that cottage again one day but it all looks financially impossible now. Maybe this new book will be a best seller, it's got my heart and soul in it, maybe I've got one last chance for glory, maybe

I can win the lottery, maybe I should count my blessings and say I packed more into one life than most but no one knows anything for certain and it's probably best that way.

HAMILTON PARK: This place takes me back to when I was courting Phyllis. The track is just south east of Glasgow and I snuck off quite a few times to try my luck punting here. The lovely long, wide straight means there are few hard luck stories. I still retain two pitches here though I don't venture this far north quite as often these days but it's always an enjoyable occasion with friendly, enthusiastic crowds, staff and management who are always first rate, a credit to all my pals over Hadrian's wall.

HAYDOCK PARK: I've no pitch here, it's simply too expensive for the returns you get but it is the scene of one of my best ever day's punting on my own horse *Vado Via*, well documented in Winning it Back. Stuck on the M6 with my good pal Gary Selby at the wheel, we looked no hopers of even getting to the course but "Fangio" got us there with minutes to spare having gone down narrow Lancastrian side streets like The Sweeney chasing a gang of bank robbers. I got a few lumpy bets on just before the off and the horse did us proud, staying on to win in her own inimitable way. A bucket of carrots was the least I could do afterwards, it was one of those days you look back on and cherish.

HEREFORD: The scene of another Gary Wiltshire success story when my magic mare *Vado Via* secured her well-earned retirement. We decided to breed from her and the very first foal was a colt who we decided to name after my admired number plate, M1 ODDS. He would go on to win his fair share of races. Originally trained on the Flat under the tutelage of the renowned and wonderful lady trainer Norma McCauley, he won four times but I fancied a shy at winning a hurdles race. As Norma was primarily a Flat trainer I had to swap yards, moving *Mi Odds* to the very shrewd dual-purpose trainer Ian Williams.

Now that man knew how to ready a horse to win when you absolutely needed one to strike. He still does, there's not many better and he's still the only trainer to have the distinction of having a winner at every track in Britain. *Mi Odds* schooled brilliantly and he was champing at the bit, so we entered him in a Seller at Hereford. In my eyes he was already past the post, nothing could stop him from bolting up in a low-grade race like this. Even the SAS regiment based there couldn't prevent a winning Wiltshire war dance.

His opening price was 5/1, I thought it would be rude not to get healthily stuck into that. The big man, light on his feet, sashayed left then right to the front of the queue, resembling Wayne Sleep's larger brother. The money was certainly down and the bookies were running scared. At the off, *Mi Odds* was 9/4 joint favourite; all we had to do now was the hard bit, win the bloody contest.

The race did not go to plan, early doors the horse was pulling a stagecoach, jockey, 'Double Diamond' Dave Dennis was doing all he could to keep the horse on a steady gallop. On Betfair he would've been at least 10/1 in running. When he clattered the third and second last hurdle, I had that sickly feeling in my stomach, surely too much had gone wrong in this race for him to prevail. But the horse was in the form of his life and *Mi Odds* brought home the bacon. Somehow, he stayed on to win by over a length, we'd only pulled off a right little tasty touch, very nice. There was just one more hurdle to negotiate, the obligatory post-race auction. There was no way I was ever going to lose him, I loved that horse. We'd wrapped moody bandages round his lower legs before the race; I have never yet seen a horse with the old dodgy bandage routine sold after winning a seller as it must put serious doubt into the mind of any potential buyer. Derren Brown could explain it all better than me.

The racecourse auctioneer John Williams (unfortunately not related to Ian) ordered the bandages to be removed so that was him off my Christmas card list. He bust a gut trying to sell my *Mi Odds*, the way he eulogised about the horse convinced me I had the next winner of The Triumph Hurdle at Cheltenham. He wouldn't let it go but there wasn't a murmur from the crowd and no bids either. I'd like to think the bandages were the main reason but the image of the very large owner in mafia-style long leather coat and sunglasses standing just behind the auctioneer and making the odd throat cutting gesture might have played a part.

Mi Odds never ran over hurdles again, my ticker couldn't take it. He returned to the flat and all in all he won 15 races; one hurdles, one turf and thirteen on the all-weather. He was my little Nijinsky, what I wouldn't have given for another few as good as him. That glorious day at Hereford is forever etched into my memory. He was never going to be sold, on the day I was prepared to go up to twenty thousand pounds to keep him. That relentless galloper was part of the family, happy, happy days.

HEXHAM: It's the only course in Northumberland that I know of. Taking a first and final run up there to punt was a last resort but I was determined to set foot on all the courses. The journey plays havoc on the car's petrol indicator, no matter how much jungle juice you put in, it's never enough. Still, it's better than cycling up there. I went in January and with the course actually 600 feet higher than Hexham itself the Arctic wind was whistling into places that were too sensitive to cope. It reminded me of a friendly Siberia without the Cossacks. It was too far, too cold and there were way too many sheep. It was definitely brass-monkey weather and even they would have needed a welder for a bit of sub-zero DIY. I'll be giving it a deserved swerve in the future.

HUNTINGDON: A pleasant enough jaunt up or down the A14 but that's as good as it gets. It's also home to the two big C's; Cinto, the finest Chinese restaurant in the universe and Oliver Cromwell the king killer. I'm sure if there is such a thing as reincarnation then I must have been a bleeding cavalier in a past life because I can't win here for love or money. That said, it's a fine course with friendly people and excellent facilities but after a day's racing all I ever have left is BFH; bus fare home. That was a phrase used by the late Jim Bowen who helped put darts on the map through the great hit programme Bullseye, 'You've got to love a bit of bully.' I for one would be poorer today if it wasn't for guys like Jim and Barry Hearn. Who would have thought 40 years ago that a pub game associated with drinking beer would now be shown on TV throughout the world and attended by thousands of mad, screaming fans. As Greavsie used to say, it's a funny old game.

KELSO: This will be a short one. Another course I've only graced once and it was actually the very last one on my list. But at least I could now be the pub bore, pontificating how I'd been to all Britain's racetracks. that was after I'd shown the regulars my collection of beer mats and pictures of different post boxes. It has been voted best small course in the North and I can definitely verify that fact. It is another bloody 70 miles after reaching Newcastle on Tyne but I'm doing Kelso a disservice as it's also been voted the friendliest track and I can vouch for that. They are still missing a trick though. If they want to see more of me, move the course from the Scottish Borders to the Midlands. I won't hold my breath for that move but one can only advise in life for one's own benefit.

KEMPTON PARK: One of the great, old tracks and a real staple in the past. It's only 15 miles south west of London's city-centre in affluent Sunbury on Thames, Surrey. This dual-purpose course has everything going for it. Kempton kept up with the times in 2006 when it became a floodlit, all-weather, day and night track that has actually become less popular in recent years. That is strange because it should do much better sitting in such a huge catchment area.

The attendances for the Flat seldom peak over 1,500 with one meeting last winter accommodating 350 hardy souls. I rarely come here although I still own two pitches. Of course, two or three of the jump meetings are rammed especially the famous King George V1 meeting on Boxing Day but I still go to Fontwell Park. What's the answer? I don't know is the simple response, it's a changing world. In 2017, the Jockey Club proposed to sell the land, move the races to nearby tracks then bulldoze the stands and build thousands of houses on the site. You could hear the outrage from Land's End to John o'Groats. The power of money will probably influence the final decision one day but everything is up in the air at the moment. Sadly I think the old lady has had her time, which is a crying shame because I've had some wonderful times here but memories don't pay the bills, and the changes of no-consequence pick up the reins to nowhere. She at least has a few years left before the final bugle but if you feel strongly enough, fight the good fight. Kempton Park has always been a British institution, we haven't got that many left.

LEICESTER: A good viewing track with many undulations in the long straight, running on to an uphill finish. I've always found Leicester folk friendly. The football team would turn up every now and again though they didn't do a lot of punting, in fact most of them stayed in the bar all day. I remember the Monday meeting after the Sunday League Cup Final in 1999. My Arsenal nemesis, the damned Spurs were playing Leicester City and ten-man Spurs won one-nil, scoring right on 90 minutes. I hurled my slipper at the TV but the cat made a stunning interception, if only the Leicester keeper had been that agile. Spurs had Justin Edinburgh sent off for an altercation with the angelic Robbie Savage, that man could start an argument in an empty room.

I was just pulling the hand brake up in the motor on the racecourse car park when a bright yellow Jaguar XJ-S pulled up in the adjacent bay and out of it slips this tall willowy peroxide blonde. I was right out of my car faster than Usain Bolt only to be utterly deflated when she turned around sporting a six-o-clock shadow. It was Robbie Savage. I was going to mention that he was a bit naughty the day before but I was speechless. Still, if anyone had clocked me talking to him my street cred would have gone right down. I know gentlemen prefer blondes but this was ridiculous.

For me, there are never enough people at the course to make it worthwhile but certain bookies have been going for years. I remember a three-horse race there when the two fancied horses were both 10/11 and the rag at 33/1. Coming to the last furlong the outsider was 3 lengths clear and the Martyn of Leicester board man was running just as quickly as the winner past all the bookies chanting 'Here we go, here we go, here we go.'

You wouldn't get that at Royal Ascot but they do like to have fun in the shires.

LINGFIELD PARK: Another track, like Kempton, which should be killing it but doesn't. It's not a course for me, no good at all for making a book. Firstly, you have to travel to the bottom of the M25 car park before crawling on to the busy M23 to go south. I hear it's about £21 quid to get in now and with a family in tow that's quite expensive. Once inside, facilities are not great; you queue for drinks, which are expensive, and the food is not cheap either. As you know, over the years I've designated myself as self-styled champion of the world fish and chip taster. Nobody has done more for great British grub than me but not only are the fish and chips expensive at Lingfield, they are rank as well. The potatoes might have been leftovers from the Irish Famine while the fish from the nuclear power plant in Fukishima. If anyone in the Lingfield catering department reads this, I'm joking of course but the fish and chips aren't good value for their substance. If you need someone for quality control, I'm your man, I'll come down for that but my laying days there are over.

LUDLOW: Delightful jumps course with a beautiful Victorian grandstand. It nestles in the scenic surroundings of majestic Shropshire, just off the A49, close to the Welsh border. I've been coming here for years and have 2 pitches on the rails and two pitches in tatts. It's difficult to win here, you mix the good with the bad and hopefully you can come out in front to ward off the bailiffs. Under the grandstand must be the oldest khazi in Western Europe, it's got to be over 400 years old. I needed to go on a body building course one year to muster-up strength to pull the cast iron chain. There was even a rumour that Arnold Schwarzenegger at his peak was training down there.

The main reason I keep coming back to Ludlow though is the food; it's the number one restaurant town in England. There are a bewildering number of great dining establishments here, many with Michelin Stars. What did you think I was coming for? The racing is just a sideshow. Don't forget, The Belly is never wrong.

MARKET RASEN: Another really beautiful course, just north east of Lincoln and in the middle of nowhere. It's well run, well managed and full of good memories for me. I have three pitches here and have done very well when the races have been on the Sabbath but a lovely place to take the family. Highly recommended.

MUSSELBURGH: I've never been a bookie here though I've been up here at least once because I had one of my horses run here. For all purposes it really is the Edinburgh course as it is situated just to the east of Auld Reekie. I actually flew up from England to Edinburgh Airport to watch the horse run but I can't remember the horses name, whether he was running on the flat or jumps, or how he performed. I guess he didn't win or I'd have clocked that but there were two things I was that day that I'm not anymore; flush with money and paralytic from duty-free spirits on the flight up. I must have been rampaging around like some mad laird from the glens because I recall nothing. We've all been there, how rude would it have been not to sample the single malt.

I've heard from other bookies and trainers that the facilities now are second to none. Millions have been spent and attendances are rising year on year, I can only congratulate the Scots on a job exceeding well done.

NEWBURY: A magnificent course, the pride of Berkshire, with views from the top of the superb grandstand that are incredible and panoramic. They run the Group 1, Lockinge Stakes here as well as many high-class National Hunt meetings.

They have great racing and attract huge crowds but I always seem to do my bollocks. It's an extremely well run venue but nothing seems to go right for me here. I've taken more than a few hammerings laying horses with the very long straight seeming to help horses with the best form reproducing it on the day. Not many upset results there apart from me having to be consoled with a large box of Kleenex and a larger Balti pie.

NEWCASTLE: I've never had a pitch here and any punting has left me with empty pockets. Getting a winner has always been next to impossible and I'm talking about picking winners before they laid down an all-weather, tapeta track in 2016. They have run the Northumberland Plate here at Gosforth Park since 1833, known locally here as the "Pitman's Derby." There aren't many colliers about these days but if the miners had come here with their redundancy money, hoping to reinvest their nest-egg, they'd be eating thin gruel. For me, Newcastle makes the National Lottery look like a shoe in.

I remember some of the turf sprint races when they would split into two groups; half would come up the stand rails, half up the far rails; two races in one, there was no rhyme or reason to it because there was no data or proof which side was best. Winners used to come from everywhere.

The first time I ever clocked Gosforth Park was as a young man in 1971. I was about 17 at the time when a group of mates and I went to see the British gangster classic *Get Carter*. That is one of the all-time great crime-thrillers.

I recall the scene on the racecourse when Michael Caine removed the sunglasses from Ian Hendry's face and suggested he still had eyes "like piss holes in the snow."

At that moment Caine, who had come up to Newcastle from London to find out who killed his brother, became an odds-on favourite to wreak havoc in the North East. There are not many southern trainers who have followed his example since but I've watched that scene many times, it crackles with tension and nervousness. I only found out years later that Caine and Hendry actually detested each other in real life. If you get the chance watch it, a great film.

Once the tapeta was laid down one would think results would become more predictable but in the years since it's actually got harder. All the bookies there must be millionaires but I don't bother any more, no one can predict the winners. If Jesus was a Geordie, he would be ringing God in Heaven saying, 'Excuse me Father, who do you fancy in the 7-15 handicap?'

'Stop bothering me bonny lad, I'm only the creator of the universe and master of all I survey but I gave Gosforth Park the cold shoulder years ago.'

So, God and Wiltshire have given up the Holy Ghost. My money up there always said two identical words and they always preceded blackbird. Bye, bye, leave well alone.

NEWMARKET: Known as Headquarters and renowned throughout the world as an equine centre of excellence. There are many premier trainers based here and everyone seems to know someone involved in the horse racing industry. I won't dwell on this one, most people know the score but I've always done well on the July Course, less so on the Rowley Mile. Both are great fun with pizzazz, colour and glamour alongside top, quality racing. I still get a buzz on the days of the 1000 and 2000 Guineas, waiting to see the next young superstar come flashing out of the stalls. One thing always mystifies me about Newmarket; you never clock any ardent mountaineers here, I think my old bet at Ladbrokes of Sherpa Tenzing riding Mill Reef up Six Mile Bottom has finally been voided. I'm absolutely gutted.

NEWTON ABBOT: Another trip like going on your holidays but I will always remember the track with fondness. Ace trainer Martin Pipe was deadly round here. His father David, was a regular bookmaker on the course, as was another good old boy Roger King. I eventually sold my pitch because of the travelling but what a good apprenticeship I had in the West Country.

Pipe was champion trainer 15 times and terrorised all of us bookies for over 30 years. His son David has taken over the reins and is a success story in his own right but there will never be another partnership like Pipe and Chester Barnes, his assistant. The former England number one table-tennis player was always distinctive with his mop of hair.

Pat Masterson, the Managing Director and his team always make you welcome. They won the Gold Standard award about 6 years ago, which was fully deserved, they do a great job. Pat is also a very knowledgeable football man who always gives me stick about The Gunners when we meet. I really miss Newton Abbot; the wonderful, amicable locals, the tight track with its short finish but most of all, that West Country atmosphere with no edginess at all.

NOTTINGHAM: My local course in recent years, Colwick Park also has a greyhound track in action four days or nights a week. Entry is not bad at seven quid a pop as well but the horseracing should be so much busier. The Nottingham urban area boasts 750,000, the M1 is close and the area is a sporting hotbed. Football, cricket, and water sports abound in the area so why huge crowds don't flock to the races is anyone's guess. I do go when possible. The standard of racing is good and all the leading trainers come here but this friendly track doesn't pack them in. I hope it doesn't become a white elephant in the future as the staff tries so hard. Come on Midlanders, have a day out here and support your local track.

PERTH: The most northerly racetrack in Britain but over the years it's a trip I've been prepared to take, especially for the three-day meeting in late April. The course is set in the grounds of Scone Palace but it's always miffed me that I haven't been invited to get my napper down in the palace bedrooms. What have William Wallace, Robert The Bruce and Mary Queen of Scots got that I haven't? Apart from breeding, money, power, influence, high standing and being Scottish of course!

I always used to look forward to my chats with "Fearless" Freddy Williams, the doyen of all Scottish Bookmakers who was a standing dish here. The man had balls of steel, known for taking on the multi-millionaire owners and gamblers at Cheltenham where he never batted an eyelid if someone requested a wager of £100,000 or bigger. John Magnier or J P McManus, they all came the same to Fearless. J P once took him for over a million in one day. What sort of idiot would leave himself wide open to losses like that? Ha! But joking apart, he was assaulted by armed robbers while returning to his hotel in Cheltenham one Festival. They got away with £70,000 but what made it worse was his daughter Julie witnessed it all. I was desolate in 2008 when a massive heart attack took him from the racetrack and us. His rock, Julie took over the business, a chip off the old block if ever there was one.

Lofty was the usual, designated driver when we went to Perth, it was a hell of a trek. Michael Palin would knock it back frequently but once there, it made all those long, tortuous hours hitting the asphalt worthwhile. Win, lose or draw, we made sure we had a bloody enjoyable time up there, food was never far from our modus operandi.

As a dyed-in-the-wool nostalgic, I always headed to Ginestrelli for a world-beating ice cream nugget that set me up a treat. After racing we would sample the local produce; Aberdeen Angus beef, venison and salmon, not all at the same time, mind. I couldn't get enough of the Scotch broth with crusty bread and butter, I'd developed a real taste for Scottish cuisine.

I was invited to go to Freddy Williams' bottling plant in Cumnock and Lofty came along for the ride when he discovered food and drink would be in the offing, he never missed the chance of a freebie. I met Freddy and we were given a grand tour of Caledonian Clear, which was a busy, state-of-the-art, modern day bottling factory. Afterwards Freddy enquired if we were hungry. Did Dolly Parton sleep on her back? Does a one-legged duck swim in a circle? We were bloody ravenous. He had laid on a bite to eat but when we walked into the office, we encountered the biggest pile of cakes I have ever seen. Freddie knew I had a sweet tooth but that sugar mountain would have kept the German army retreating from Moscow alive for a month.

Lofty's eyes lit up. There was Dundee Cake, shortbreads, Battenberg, Victoria Sponge, Madeira cake, Eccles Cakes and Swiss Rolls. We were representing England so we would have to make a good fist of it but half an hour later we were wasted. I couldn't eat another currant, I was starting to resemble Mr Creosote from Monty Python but I could have died when Lofty asked the manageress if he could have a doggie bag! I got him out sharpish. My heart goes out to Freddie Williams and to Scotland, here's to many more days amid the Perth heather and the skirl of the bagpipes.

PLUMPTON: Another belter of a track, I adore Plumpton. It isn't my luckiest course but even though winning days are a bonus, I love coming here to sunny Sussex, north of Brighton, on the beautiful South Downs.

Easily accessible by train from London, Plumpton is a great day out for all the family. I retain two pitches here where the chase course is particularly tough for a new jockey or horse. It appears quite flat but there are dips and peaks in certain places, which allied to the long, uphill finish, seems to catch many out.

Tony McCoy was the master here, he actually had his 3000th winner at

Plumpton. Such was his proficiency that if he had been riding a Blackpool donkey with 12 stones on his back, I would have had him no better than 6/4. Many a time I saw him put a horse to sleep here, keep things simple and come home ahead of all the others. I always kept him short whatever he was riding, I'd like to think that ploy saved me many thousands of pounds over the years.

PONTEFRACT: This Yorkshire track has a lot going for it. They always attract large crowds with its close vicinity to the M1 and M62 bringing punters in from all four cardinal points. I retain a pitch in Tattersalls but this is another white rose arena that hasn't put much into my meagre bank account since I started coming here.

The continuous, oval-shaped track is the biggest in the country at 2 miles and 1 furlong and there is always a huge attendance for their arduous race, The Pontefract Marathon Handicap which at 2 miles and 5 furlongs is only exceeded by the Queen Alexandra Stakes at Ascot. A horse needs to be a stayer here, especially with the uphill finish over the last two furlongs.

I remember one year it had been raining all week and the epic race was won by a horse from the yard of Aylesbury trainer, Ken Comerford (there's a name from the past) and ridden by the underrated Tom McLaughlin. I got up to win by a nose with the third half a furlong behind, it was that sort of crazy race in the mud. The Yorkshire folk do their own thing; they're a breed apart.

This area was home to a huge, mining contingent years ago so 'Ponty' had unique, special permission to proceed with the commencement of racing after three o'clock so the local miners could finish their shift and get on down and wager their hard-earned wonga. As the collieries shut and disappeared so did the late start. This unique course was also the scene of the first photo-finish camera in 1952, which stopped all the debate that had previously gone on. You don't ever rob a Yorkie in a tight finish, *'ee by gum.*

REDCAR: Yorkshire's seaside track, again it's just too far for me. I've been once in early summer to punt there on Zetland Gold Cup day and to be fair it was packed, it looked like half of Middlesbrough and Hartlepool were there. But I get a nosebleed coming up to North Yorkshire, or Cleveland as it was called when I last ventured up.

Apparently, a guy on the track told me, the straight mile track is the fairest in the country, being dead level from the starting stalls all the way down to the winning post. I'll have to take his word on that because I wasn't going to take a theodolite out on to the course and prove him wrong.

RIPON: Goodness, another track in the old Yorkshire North Riding, not such a long trek as Redcar but still a petrol guzzler from down south. I never worked the course but I've always enjoyed punting here. What a scenic, well-preserved, little track it is, very popular with the punters and especially on the day of The Great St Wilfred Stakes, a really valuable six-furlong handicap for three-year-olds and older.

David O' Meara has won it 3 times in the last 8 years, so always bear him in mind for the race. It's extremely difficult to win, in fact only one horse has ever won it twice, mainly because this is a real specialist's course; there are more undulations here than a Shar Pei's neck, or my belly when I was in my prime.

SALISBURY: A beautiful, charming old course that looks down on the city, cathedral and all. I've had a pitch here for many years but to be truthful, I've never pulled up many trees over that period. A lot of the big southern trainers come here with their starlets, two-year-old flying machines that have burnt my fingers too many times to comprehend. The racing is always top quality as the track is a fair one. I'm sure both Mill Reef and Brigadier Gerard raced at the track in their younger days and Stevie Cauthen definitely made his debut here, winning on Marquee Universal in his very first race. He was a great, charismatic jockey; America's answer to Frankie Dettori.

SANDOWN PARK: A majestic example of a racecourse. A lovely, dual-purpose track with five grade one National Hunt races and a group one race on the Flat, the legendary Eclipse Stakes. Londoners come in their thousands by car, coach or on the train from Waterloo to nearby Esher Railway Station.

Always a great crowd here. People love the place, including the late Queen Mother who declared it her favourite track. She wouldn't have to travel far would she and I doubt she would have gone second-class on the choo-choo. I retain two pitches here but as perverse as it seems, I'm not a great fan. I can take it or leave it, the main reason being there are too many bloody bookies trading here. Still, we are dropping like flies as the game gets a lot harder so hopefully, I can hang on for a few more years. There might only be the odd prime specimen of the bookmaker genus left at Sandown but otherwise I can only describe the place as blinding. Would I miss my trusty fellow layers? About as much as listening to Max Bygraves singing Tulips from Amsterdam.

SEDGEFIELD: The home of Tommo, his local, boyhood track and also the constituency of much-maligned former Prime Minister, Tony Blair; two legends in their own lunch time. But there is a far greater man standing there taking bets and in my opinion, the best bookmaker in the country in "Gentleman" Johnny Ridley who won *On-Course Betting Operator of The Year* in 2012. He's based in Shotton, a village between Newcastle and Middlesbrough from where he works the Northern tracks as well as some local betting shops. A credit to the art of bookmaking.

I've punted here a few times but County Durham is a mile or three too far north to make it worthwhile. In my time as a bookie, the course has suffered from under investment and has been close to shutting at least three times. Old racing stalwart Clement Freud once described the course as "all field and not much sedge," that quip nearly made him smile himself for the first time in twenty years.

It used to have the longest run-in after the last fence of over 500 yards, even further than the Grand National because the fence nearest the winning post was the water jump and under National Hunt rules that type of obstacle can never be the first or last fence. So, in 1994 the water jump was replaced by a plain fence which made it the final fence and much closer to the finish. It is now known as "The Johnny Ridley" fence due to his long sponsorship of it. Not only is the man a great bookie, he now has a part of the course named after him too. What great advertising, why can't I be half as clever and astute as that? Answers on a postcard please.

SOUTHWELL: People generally pronounce it Suthull but no one seems to concur in the town itself. Each time I go past the beautiful Southwell Minster I realise what talented people once worked these lands. That cathedral must be one of the finest examples of British architecture ever constructed but its location is really quite strange as the town seems too small to accommodate it.

A few miles up a country road sits the racecourse, a great big, galloping, all-weather track and a National Hunt turf course. Midweek fixtures here are not well attended, sometimes only a few hundred turn up. The stands have been erected to house thousands of punters but they never fill them. Is it a malaise of the county of Nottinghamshire or is everything now geared to betting shops and online betting? It saddens me to see the great facilities underused but you can't make people go racing.

The staff are very friendly here and the restaurant food is second to none. I was once the table adjacent to Ryder Cup star Lee Westwood, he was dressed all in black, like myself; us athletes know that this is the colour for men who need to hide a few pounds after a pre-season break, in my case replace pounds with stones. He was living in Florida at the time in an expensive mansion, it's amazing what one can earn hitting that little ball into a hole. Recently he split from his wife so she is entitled to half of his thirty million fortune. Cowabunga! That puts me in the shade. You girls do all right it seems; all my ex-wives live in their own homes while soppy bollocks is now renting but ladies, we can't live without you and you can't pee standing up.

The course can't support many bookmakers but the racing is fair. There are probably more shocks over the jumps but if someone is planning a coup on the all-weather, there isn't a lot to go wrong apart from a high draw in a 6-furlong race, you don't want to be racing wide on the bends here as you can forfeit many lengths. A quick word for the racehorse Tempering who won 22 races here on the all-weather in the 1990s. He won 23 in his career and got his head in front one day at Redcar on the turf, it really spoiled his clean sheet away from home. This chapter is called Horses for Courses and what a wonderful animal Tempering was for his connections. Every time he spotted Southwell from his horse box he seemed to improve beyond belief. RIP superstar.

STRATFORD: This was my local National Hunt track when I lived with ex-wife Sue in Hollywood, south Birmingham. It was about a twenty-minute drive to Shakespeare's birthplace and after my breakup I often quoted the bard on the way to the course, "I am one that loved not wisely, but too well" (Othello, act 5, scene 2). The story of my life I suppose though I never listened to Shakespeare's Sister on the radio.

The course itself has been improved over the years and a new grandstand was completed in the late nineties. I always enjoy the meetings here, I still have 3 pitches. The racing is of a good standard and riders need to be handy turning into the winning straight, it's less than 2 furlongs long with just one hurdle to be jumped. There is always a huge crowd for the last meeting of the season, which features the valuable and prestigious Horse and Hound Cup for the best hunter chasers. The country set and gentry always carry a good stash of readies to put on their favourite charges but the bookies do well because the race is so competitive. I'll leave the greatest writer who ever lived to sign us out, 'A horse! A horse! My kingdom for a horse!' Perfect.

TAUNTON: Another track that Martin Pipe made his turf. If you managed to hold him off at Newton Abbot one week, he would blitz you at Taunton the next. The man was a training genius for banging out winner after winner. The older, more experienced bookies knew that when the money was down, his horses seldom got beat, only a fool would take him head on. I kept his horses short and lengthened the opposition, there wasn't much more you could do. I eventually sold my pitch; Pipe was king down there and I wasn't about to become the skint court jester.

The racetrack itself was particularly sharp with hidden undulations and Mick Fitzgerald, the former ace jockey, once did a small montage of films featuring tricky tracks and highlighted Taunton. He named one fence in the straight "Tricky Trevor" because many had come to grief there. Whether it was a pig of a fence or Mick had enjoyed one Guinness too many on the day of shooting the documentary, I've no idea but I've now named my three-foot garden wall "Michael" in honour of the Irish legend.

THIRSK: How many racetracks are in North Yorkshire? Are they degenerate gamblers up there? They're supposed to not like parting with their money, "ear all, see all, say nowt, eat all, sup all, pay nowt," cheeky buggers. It's only 11 miles from Ripon up to Thirsk so the same people must go to both meetings and that A61 is always gridlocked with people in clogs and flat caps taking their pet whippets to the races.

I have done the holy pilgrimage one time; it's an unremarkable but fair little course. I have nothing bad to say but it feels like it's there solely for the northern trainers and jockeys to put on a show for the great Yorkshire public. In all my years I never heard anyone say, do you fancy a day out at Thirsk and if they did, any excuse not to would suffice for me.

Thirsk's one moment in the spotlight came in 1940 when the St Leger was transferred from Doncaster because of the war. There are still centenarians dining out on a Friday night at The Crown and Anchor, asking unsuspecting strangers or visitors to Thirsk if they were there on that glorious day, and when a travelling salesman from Wakefield looks nonplussed and replies, "no," they look down their nose and reply, 'Well, I was.'

That's why you will never see big Gary Wiltshire in Thirsk on a Friday night.

TOWCESTER: This was my local track when I lived in Milton Keynes and I absolutely adored it. I'm writing in the past tense because in August 2018 the business was put into administration. That included the horse racing and the later added greyhound racing which featured the Greyhound Derby.

This was a double blow for me as one of my all-time favourite racecourses closed. I had previously sold my rails pitch, so the financial aspect didn't come into it but I regarded these wonderful courses as old friends. We all grow up with them, they are a big part of our lives. With the greyhound franchise closing simultaneously it hit me more personally. Lord Hesketh had recently hired myself and Sharon to work for him inside the grandstand when the greyhound meetings were on, a very gracious offer of meaningful employment from "Lordy" that we both loved being involved with. What can you do, when one door opens another slams straight in your face but you dust yourself down, wonder how on earth Teresa May and Jeremy Corbyn got to the top of their respective parties, laugh your socks off and carry on regardless.

When Towcester Races was on a going day, with a big crowd and an electric atmosphere, there was nowhere better. It was a tough course as well, you had to be up with the pace coming to the tricky second last because the run to the finish had a severe incline. I always wanted a winner here with one my own horses but regrettably I never pulled it off. Tony McCoy got his 4,000th winner here, there can't be any more superlatives left to mention about this dynamic superstar jockey. We have all been privileged to witness the best ever jump jockey. As I write this second book in the winter of 2018, detailing the ups and downs of an on-course bookie, hopefully Towcester will rise like the mighty phoenix from the ashes of administration and be taken over by right-minded people who will once again bring back our equine and canine chums to run their race. Too many courses have sadly fallen by the wayside.

Here's the amazing list of horse racing tracks we have lost since the end of the Second World War. Some you will know, some will surprise you:

Newport 1948
Colwall Park 1949
Buckfastleigh 1960
Hurst Park 1962
Manchester 1963
Woore 1963
Lewes 1964
Lincoln 1964
Bogside 1965
Birmingham 1965
Rothbury 1965
Alexandra Park 1970
Wye 1974
Lanark 1977
Stockton 1981
Folkestone 2012.

Let's hope and pray that Towcester doesn't become the latest on that sad list. We need these social gatherings to survive and prosper.

UTTOXETER: The pride of Staffordshire and home to the Midlands Grand National which has been won by some class horses like Rag Trade and The Thinker. The course gets rammed in the spring, they coach in from Derby, Nottingham, Lichfield, Burton, Stafford and Stoke. Allied to the fact that the area is rural, with local farmers and horsey folk abundant, one might feel a layer of bets would regard this region as a land of milk and honey but nothing could be further from the truth.

There must be a million bookies operating here (a slight exaggeration maybe but I'm trying to paint a florid picture) then there are the part-time punters coming out on the local social club day trip to the races, we all know at least one. They kiss goodbye to the wife at the front door, she's made him his favourite cheese and onion sandwiches, passes him two tenners for his beer and bets and tells him not to come home pissed. Fat chance of that. My old man used to call them two-bob merchants. They still miss rationing after the Second World War and they always have an allotment to grow their own vegetables, most read the Daily Mirror and cheered when Piers Morgan was fucked off for faking photos of the army.

I'm obviously stereotyping certain people but when I was taking bets here the stake rarely climbed above a two-pound wager. At the end of the day all your notes had been paid out in winnings and we had a carrier bag full of shrapnel that nobody wanted to count and take to the bank the next morning. Such was the life of a modern-day, jet-setting, international bookie like myself. Why didn't I move to Vegas, become Engelbert's manager and just play the slots?

The racing at Uttoxeter is always competitive with fairly large fields. It's a galloping track and can quickly change into a quagmire after a heavy shower or two. It is great fun here but it doesn't keep the bailiff from the front door. The fences have been eased over the years with the second last once notorious for bringing horses down. The birch could have been used for corporal punishment it was that thick and solid, many times I heard people entreat 'Just get over the second last, please,' and that's including myself. I've seen horses ten lengths clear crumble at that fence. The PC brigade won the day with that obstacle, it's been consigned to history, and hopefully I won't be joining it any time soon.

WARWICK: In my opinion, this midland track is on the move. When Flat racing ceased in 2014 for the track to concentrate on National Hunt, it was an act of genius. The standard of racing on the level had been mediocre-to-fairly-good at best over the years but since focusing on jumping things have started to improve and the jigsaw pieces are falling into place.

The young management team here really make you feel welcome, they try so hard. I would never dream of selling either of my two pitches because everything is positive and on the rise, in fact, I can safely say without doubt that Warwick is one of my favourite tracks and if I didn't work it, I would definitely come here as a punter. A great, simmering success story that I hope will go on to bigger and better things, a thumbs up from the big man.

WETHERBY: We are back in Yorkshire again! Wetherby is mainly known for National Hunt racing but has done the opposite to Warwick in bringing Flat racing on board. In situ between Leeds and York, this track is trying to be all things to all men. They have spent millions here and the facilities have improved a great deal. Did Yorkshire need another Flat racing venue? That's only me asking by the way, time will tell. I know the cricket team need another Geoff Boycott, Brian Close and Fred Trueman but that's beside the point. In the past when I've stood here midweek, crowds were on the low side and there was a distinct lack of atmosphere. I haven't been for a while so I can't pass judgement on present attendances.

However, the Boxing Day meet and The Charlie Hall Steeplechase in October were very well attended and worth the drive up. I wish Wetherby the same as Warwick, every success in the future. Nobody in these uncertain economic times can knock people for investing in horse racing. *I'll see thee.*

WINCANTON: Not quite as far as Taunton, Newton Abbot or Exeter but too far for me these days. To tell you the truth, a quarter-mile walk to the shops to get some bread and a Racing Post is beyond the pale for this fading athlete these days. But it's the same old story, I let my pitches go because of the dire logistics of it all. Maybe, just maybe if I was 30 again (no madam not stone), I would again venture down to the West Country, after all, it's only Somerset and not a real ball- breaker in distance like the far-flung Newton Abbot. It's about time someone invented the transporter they have on Star Trek, it would save a fortune on petrol.

The standard of racing at Wincanton is definitely of a higher standard than the other West Country tracks and the superstar grey, Desert Orchid won here on six occasions. The track is fair with not many surprises, many of the bigger trainers come here with inexperienced youngsters to give them a safe workout before sending them on to bigger and trickier courses. local trainer Paul Nicholls pitches some of his promising hurdlers here. For the older horses, the chase fences aren't a gimme but they do go a fair old rattle from start to finish so the course favours galloping types though it's extremely hard to win here with a hold up horse. Wincanton has great facilities to go with top jumping races, it really is a course that I miss going to.

WINDSOR: Or as Her Majesty likes to tell me, Royal Windsor. I've been coming here as a bookie since the National Hunt stopped in 1998. Between April and October, if it's a Monday afternoon or night you can bet your bottom dollar that Windsor Races is on. They get good, strong fields, big crowds, plenty of betting, eating and drinking but for a bookie there is trepidation. One particular Monday might throw up a batch of unfancied ones while the following week six or seven favourites will knock your socks off. It's a very hard track to have an opinion about especially if the going changes in a day, all a layer can do is count the rosary beads, say ten Hail Mary's and hope the big man upstairs shows some clemency.

Monday 15th October in 2012 began like any other with the favourite going in at 13/8, ridden by Irish beanpole Richard Hughes (impossibly tall for a Flat jockey at 5ft 10 but too short to make the cut at the Boston Celtics). He followed it up in the second with the 5/2 fav when I glanced at my fellow bookies and pessimistically said, 'Here we go.'

They all knew my past track record with Frankie, one laughingly suggested I refrain from coming again on a Monday. Was I a jinx or a Jonah? We didn't have long to find out.

The run of short priced winners was broken in the third as Embankment won at 7/1 but Hughes was the jockey again. He had his hat-trick in double quick time, the alarm bells at that moment were all going off in the big bookies' bunkers. Why? Because there's always a few numpties in the betting shops who have a preferred jockey and back every horse he rides in doubles, trebles and accumulators. Hughes had eight rides but that was impossible wasn't it? Fuck me! Even I had forgotten about 1996 (not really but I like to raise the tension).

Once bitten twice shy they say so every horse Hughes was riding that day would now be *persona non grata* and that shrewd move paid off when the Irishman won the fourth on the 4/1 fav. I could hear the other bookies moaning and groaning. I had it short at 3/1 so never took a bent penny. Same in the fifth, Hughes on the 5/2 fav but was 7/4 on my board. He went in again and some of my learned associates were ready to pack up. Hughes had a nap hand, five out of five, he was on the verge of history.

In the sixth race he was on the favourite yet again, this time at 2/1. Would I be standing that? Not bloody likely! It was deja vu, I'd travelled this bumpy road before, lesson learnt a million times over. There was a stunned silence after the race as Hughes had only come third, the dozy pillock had cost me money. What was going on? How dare he ride a loser. I'm very fickle if someone has let me down.

I'm amazed by the guts and durability of some bookmakers though as plenty had laid it at 2/1 so they had their small victory. They were high-fiving and back slapping, 'The spell is broken,' said one muppet, but for me there were two races to come and Hughes was on two more favourites. In my eyes it wasn't anywhere near over and sure enough Hughes brought them both home at 7/4 and 15/8 respectively.

I had good results on the last two races, destiny can never be beaten. Some of the bookies at Windsor took a fearful caning, the big high street chains lost millions with the sevenfold accumulator paying over 10,000/1. One punting so-called "numpty" won 160 grand. I felt quite honoured to have been at the two venues when both jockeys had ridden seven winners but I'm still cheesed off I wasn't at Thirsk for the 1940 St Leger. Then again, I suppose two out of three isn't bad.

Frankie Dettori must still get asked about his seven winners, seven days a week, all round the world but the Richard Hughes magnificent seven doesn't have the same ring. Maybe it was because Windsor wasn't as glamorous as Ascot, maybe it was because Hughes rode a loser, and maybe it was because there wasn't a big, fat buffoon at Windsor willing to take all of Hughes' liabilities. Most probably it was because Frankie was the first to do it. They say no one remembers who is second but we shall never know the whole truth.

Frankie Dettori's face was festooned on posters, tea towels, Royal Doulton tankards, Beswick plates and Aynsley bowls. I never copped an eyeful of an eggcup for Richard Hughes but he got something worth much more than all that Stoke on Trent china piled up high because he got my respect. I've been trying for bloody years to make Frankie Dettori jealous. Seriously though, two great sportsmen working at what they love, totally different in so many ways but bonded by a hunger to be winners. Hughesy is now a top trainer and Frankie is still doing what he does best, riding big winners. We are all blessed to have witnessed most of that.

WOLVERHAMPTON: This forward-thinking track has not always had the support it deserves. When it first developed a floodlit track in 1993 (crikey! How can 26 years have flown by that quick?) it was miles ahead of the opposition giving Wolverhampton a monopoly on evening racing. Since then other courses have got involved, there is even a Floodlit Friday on the television now.

To be fair, Wolverhampton's fixture list hasn't gone down much from the 90 yearly meetings it used to get but in the early days it used to regularly run on most Saturday nights in the autumn and winter because no one else was capable of doing it. These meetings were generally full houses with the bars, food outlets and private boxes packed. You couldn't always get a seat in the massive, panoramic Zongalero's Restaurant. It gave you a fantastic view of the whole of the American-styled track.

Go now on a midweek afternoon and it's just like Southwell, one man and his dog syndrome. Sometimes only 200 people and half a dozen bookies are there. I partly understand Southwell because it's miles from anywhere but Dunstall Park is in the middle of a big city and not only that, the facilities are fantastic. I can't believe there is too much racing going on, people must be voting with their feet and betting in the comfort of their own home.

I had a pitch on the rails, but sold it along with the Southwell one to a certain Mr Michael O'Rourke. He's never forgiven me, but he's graciously scribbling a few lines for me here, so we are still good mates.

Don't worry about the West Midlands though, they are spending 26 million here, expanding the hotel, tarmacking the huge over-spill car park and in the process of opening a casino, which would be the first Racino in Britain. All is well here, as my Black Country mates Wayne and Barry would say, "bosting."

WORCESTER: It got an honourable mention earlier in chapter four regarding the flooding here, suffice to say I always took a pair of water wings with me when I came to Worcester. I still have three pitches and I've done well here in the past, it's a good galloping track for novices with an emphasis on stamina.

Someone told me here one day that when the grandstand was built in 1975 it was done so at the wrong angle. Those cowboy builders are always game for a laugh so apparently after the winning post when the horses go around the bend, they disappear from view. It could have been a lot worse, if all the horses disappeared just before the winning post, even David Copperfield couldn't have pulled off a stunt as good as that, though he did make the Statue of Liberty disappear. Put it back David, they want it returning, what's the point in keeping it.

Yes, I will keep rocking up here. The key problem is the River Severn; every time it rises a few feet, the racecourse and the cricket ground become nature reserves. Global warming is not going away they say but the Irish have come up with a solution to combat it, all new racecourses will now be built on the sides of hills, it's that simple, it's genius. They are even chartering boats to get the public on track, one can only stand back in goggles and snorkel to admire them.

YORK: It's only right we finish in Yorkshire as they seem to have more than half the country's venues within their boundary lines. York, without doubt, is the finest racecourse in the North. Many Yorkshire men will say it's the best in Britain but those shy and retiring types can be a trifle biased. But what a fabulous sporting arena.

They hung highwayman Dick Turpin here in 1739 prior to the racing; you can't beat a bit of death before the first race. It was a shame that Dick had to go in the morning, apparently, he was partial to a bet or two. The track has so much history. In 1851, 100,000 turned up on the Knavesmire to watch a match between The Flying Dutchman and Voltiguer, they were the good old days.

The standard of races is extremely high with the three-day meeting in August to die for. Every racing fan knows about The Juddmonte, The Nunthorpe, The Yorkshire Oaks and probably most famously, The Ebor Handicap. These races are witnessed by huge, teeming crowds, the atmosphere is electric and people come from all over Britain to taste a piece of the action.

Everyone loves York apart from a poor, old, portly geezer from The Smoke. As anyone who has read *Winning It Back* knows I had a day to forget the last afternoon I was working for The Tote at York. It was The John Smith's Cup meeting in mid-July, the crowd was a monster, every other punter looked like they had downed eight pints of the sponsors brew. It made Dunkirk, Marston Moor and the Poll Tax Riots look like a bible class tea party.

We were on the rails that day and it was my remit after the last race to count up and pack everything away. The problem was that a massive, drunken brawl kicked off yards away. Normally I'd take three steps back and watch the cabaret but I was holding folding to a Godly amount. I grabbed all the kit and made my retreat faster than Pacifists United. If you've been to York Races you know the traffic is horrendous, it took two hours to emerge from the car park. It was extremely late when I got home, I threw the moneybags in the safe and had an enormous gin and tonic, then hit the sack.

The next day, Sunday, was a day of rest. On the morrow we were standing at Windsor, I grabbed the bags and counted out the float with the small profit from York. It was only nine-grand short. Fuck my boots! I'd only left nine big ones in the hidden zipped up compartment at the pitch. Cut a long story short, I overtook Lewis Hamilton back up to Yorkshire. Arriving at the pitch, I closed my eyes as I opened Pandora's box, hoping for serendipity but looking back at me was The Queen on a solitary twenty-pound note, a thank you note for my carelessness. Some thieving bugger was going to have a good drink at my expense.

I cheered myself up at the superb White's Chippy near the racecourse with my lucky score. If there is a Mr White, I don't expect to pay next time I come up as two endorsements from me normally costs a king's ransom. Afterwards, I drove over The Pennines to Tote Headquarters in Wigan. The buck stopped with me, so I offered to pay the for the loss. I was Gary Wiltshire; my good name was far more important than the money. I was out of pocket but I'd done the right thing. I never returned to York. It was a hard day to erase from my memory but I think the downturn started in 2005 when someone with a warped sense of humour closed down the Terry's Chocolate Factory. You could nearly taste the sweet, chocolaty aroma that wafted over the Knavesmire when they were in full production. Were there ever better chocs than Terry's Old Gold Chocolate Box? They are now made abroad but somehow, they don't seem to taste the same. You all know what I mean, let's get Terry's back in Britain, preferably in my hometown. Yum yum.

So, those are some of my experiences on all of Britain's racetracks; some are good, some bad, some happy and some sad. They all have something to offer to the public, let's see if we can keep them all afloat. Some need our support a lot more than the others but as my wise, old pal John McCririck used to say, 'Come Racing!'

The halcyon days are not coming back, so we all have to cut our cloth accordingly, we have to diversify. I've always taken things like sunglasses to sell at the seaside tracks, we could do with Green Shield Stamps again too. The courses are putting on music events after racing and that might put a few bob in their pockets but I'm yet to be convinced betting and music people are a match. We need a proper survey done on what percentage bet and listen to music, it might even suppress the betting turnover, we just don't know. I tell you this though, if The Kaiser Chiefs, Paloma Faith and Franz Ferdinand were playing in my back garden, I'd draw the curtains before walking ten miles to watch The Wurzels. Simon Cowell, eat your heart out.

Boozing at racecourses is an increasing problem too. It's all well and good taking block bookings of young people on stag nights, weddings and birthdays but there has to be more security and less tolerance of aimless, violent behaviour. I told you how it cost me nine grand at York but someone will be seriously injured or killed on the racecourse soon. Don't let the few spoil things for the many.

All things said we have our heads just above water but we can come through covered in clover. That's the courses done and dusted then, let's now turn our attention next to my first love in betting; greyhound racing, a sport most people associate me with.

I bloody love the doggies.

* * * *

Chapter Six

GONE TO THE DOGS

Ballyregan Bob was a winning machine. He broke the world record in the 1980s by winning 32 consecutive races.

Man's best friend, ain't that the truth. When you're down in the doghouse, being blanked by the better half, your trusty hound is always happy to see you. I've always loved greyhounds, even before I got my first bookmakers licence in 1978. If I ever come back as an animal, I'd like to be reincarnated into a pedigree greyhound. They are rightly known as the 40mph couch potato; once they've whizzed about for 10 minutes, they have a lie down for the day. Lovely. If you knock one nought off their speed then that's a perfect description of me.

The ancient Egyptians revered greyhounds. These fine hounds were even being buried alongside their rich and royal masters and the only dog breed mentioned in the bible. What is not to like? You don't find labradoodles or cockapoos in there. Bugger me! What sort of dodgy breeds are they? You might as well go down the local dogs home and come back with a Heinz 57. A mate of mine has just started breeding bulldogs and shih tzus so for a few hundred quid you can have a pack of bullshits!

My first love in betting was at the greyhound tracks in marginal preference to playing at those marvellous point-to-point meetings. I was betting long and hard at a young age. I think it was in my blood: the sights, the sounds and the whole aura of the betting arena but I did worry that my gambling habit would send me down the plughole of unfulfilled ambition.

I then read an article in a Sunday colour supplement that said five out of every six Russian Roulette players thought that the pastime was perfectly safe. That was just my kind of percentage and that profound fact clarified everything, transporting me down the turbulent, lottery highway and moulding me into the man you see before you today; an absolute bloody nut-case.

Stony Stratford, the market town in North Bucks was where I made my first move towards a career of bookmaking. Standing at the Magistrates there, I thought I was a million-to-one against getting a licence. A man was supposed to have means to become a bookie in those days and I was living in a Milton Keynes council house with Scottish wife Phyllis at the time, with not a lot of money and even less prospects if things went askew that day and if I got the knock back.

As I sidled through the courtroom doors, my dad, who had always been my biggest supporter said, 'They won't give you a licence son, if they do, you'll be skint in two weeks.'

I gave him a slantindicular look, not knowing whether to laugh or cry. I stood in the dock like the condemned man in a kangaroo court but everything went swimmingly until the chief magistrate asked if there were any objections. Up jumped Sergeant Plod for the Old Bill, citing a wild night of drunkenness and disorder in Bridlington. I was looking round for someone else, not only had I never been to Bridlington, I hadn't a clue where it was.

My solicitor could see I was getting agitated and advised me to calm down and leave it to him as he addressed the court, 'My client had a good night in Bridlington when he was a youth, he is now a proper person who has relinquished the lure of the bottle. I believe any one of us could make a mistake at a young age and ask the bench to give this ambitious, forward-thinking young man a deserved chance.'

That speech was good enough for the Old Bailey and even my enemies would have given me a licence after that. Outside in the anteroom I told the brief I'd never been there but he assured me that was irrelevant, all would be well. We were out for twenty minutes when a friendly copper came over and I told him, off the record, that it couldn't have been me. He seemed to think that the police had brought the wrong papers so it was a good job I wasn't in the dock for The Brinks Matt Bullion Robbery. We reconvened, the three magistrates were smiling, 'Mr Wiltshire, we are more than pleased to grant you your bookmakers licence, good luck to you in the future.'

Yes! What a result. Through all the hoo-ha, I haven't mentioned my precarious financial situation. At that moment in time I was surely the most destitute bookmaker in the land but the session at court taught me one thing that I have always adhered to, don't go to bleeding Bridlington and get rat-arsed.

I started frequenting Nutts Lane flapping track in Hinckley. You had to be nuts to bet there, all sorts of shenanigans were occurring. I chummed up with a local guy named Joey Cope, he was the best judge of a dog at the track and over an educational few weeks he had marked my card to the extent I was confident of winning a few bob off these hardened local punters. Joey sadly died in November 2018. RIP old pal, you were my original pathfinder. Much respect.

Every Wednesday was flapping night, to me it was like Sutter's Mill and the Klondike rolled into one. There was gold to be found but not before borrowing the family allowance of eighty quid from Phyllis to fund the book. This was a regular procedure and not very professional but I did hear that when he first went into business, Richard Branson used a red, public phone box as his office. We all have to adapt to circumstance when we are fledgling operators.

On the next pitch to me was Northamptonshire bookie Lesley Wootton.

He was a doppelgänger for the late Bill Maynard who apparently based his character Greengrass in Heartbeat on Wootton after meeting him on the local dog tracks. I wonder if he ever found out that he was a greedy beggar who wanted to take all of the money all of the time.

In life you come across diamonds and bastards and Wootton was a strange combination of the two. As you can imagine, the meagre family allowance money didn't always stretch to the end of the meeting if a few favourites stormed in but Wootton would always lend me money to tide me through to the finish though not before he announced the fact to the whole stadium. He had a real stentorian voice; you could hear him in the next county. He was the Foghorn Leghorn of Hinckley. He wasn't discreet when he yelled, 'You cockneys got plenty of mouth but you ain't got no money.' I used to have to suffer in silence, looking sheepish but it got to the point where I would rather pack up and go home than be humiliated by him so I came up with a cunning ruse that sly Mr Foxy Fox of Foxtown would be proud of.

I'd become good mates with Gary Selby who you've probably seen in the past on At The Races giving advice on the American racing. A natural and knowledgeable maverick, Selby was clued up about anything to do with betting on dogs and horses so he teamed up with me as bookies clerk and very good he was too. We both agreed to take Wootton's pants down in the hope that would quieten him down. It probably wouldn't but his pants were still coming off.

It took a couple of months to set it all up. I'd been winning frequently at Hinckley so I hadn't needed a sub off Wootton for ages but I was gonna stick one right up him, only the once, just for my own juvenile satisfaction. I'd actually bought a decent greyhound, a black one called Exclusive Native for 400 hard earned sobs. He was trained by John Peterson and was a regular runner at the superior Oxford Stadium. We entered him three times at Hinckley under the name Black Trevor and three times he finished stone last. We were adept at stopping him when we needed to; a bowl of sausages before he ran usually did the trick. He really had stunk the place out which put us in prime position to enter him into a mediocre handicap race with hopefully a head start on anything else useful.

We found out that the handicapper had allocated us trap 2 and with a six-yard start over the scratch dog in trap six for the upcoming Wednesday night handicap. With no mishaps it would be like taking strawberries off a donkey.

Early evening Gary and I went to the Hinckley Island Hotel for some nosebag and coffee (Gary Lineker married Michelle there). We were meeting part-time barmaid Audrey who was the vital cog in our plan; if she could come up trumps, we would maximise all our potential. We had deftly schooled Audrey previously on what she had to do and this was a final recce before we went over the top. Wootton was a bit of a misogynist; a favourite saying of his was "all women are mug punters". so we would use that adage against him. Audrey had been given £155 in readies to place with Wootton as he would never, ever knock back a chunky bet off a female, he regarded it as easy money.

Audrey was knocking off at seven and the handicap race was the 4th on the card at 8-15. To be fair, we didn't know the woman that well, she could just fuck off with all the money and what could we do? And you know my luck with the ladies over the years.

Three minutes before the off, there was no sign of Audrey. All the dogs opened at 2/1 (generous we weren't) so it was time to push Black Trevor out to 5/1. I half knew Wootton would want most of the action on a dog that hadn't beaten one home in three races and sure enough he chalked up sixes. I was frantically thinking where the fuck is she when Audrey emerged from the crowd like a sainted Joan of Arc and got the whole 155 quid on with Wootton as easy as you like. He sneered at me with a look of disdain that said this is safely in my bag and that's where it's staying. I smiled back hoping I would have the last laugh. Before the off I managed to get £80 on at fives at the other end and Garry got £50 on at fives with Dave Smith of Loughborough. It had gone textbook so far as we stood back to watch the forthcoming jolly japes.

Black Trevor went past the one dog round the first bend and never sighted another, going on to win by 5 lengths. We'd only had it right off. Wootton was screaming at Audrey like a Gestapo Officer, "this wasn't your bet, whose was it, tell me who sent you?" I thought she was going to crack but she stood her ground, adamant no one else was involved. I was really proud of her. Wootton slung the winnings at her, he hadn't taken it well but that was the whole point. The profit, nice as it was, hadn't been our main objective though it would come in handy.

I had arranged with Audrey to meet at Barnacles Fish Restaurant car park at ten o'clock. The two Gary's turned up in a two-tone, light brown Mini, beige and rust. It had cost £300 less than Exclusive Native and the dog would have beaten it in any race. It looked to any bystander like we were trying to beat the Guinness world record for most people in a Mini but in reality there was only two of us in it. I was breaking the scales at 28 stone and the slimmer Selby was three stone lighter at 25. How those two sub frames never collapsed is a testament to the genius of Alec Issigonis and God-given good fortune.

It turned five past and ever the optimist I said to Gary, "it's only evens she comes" but seconds later headlights flashed us. Selby, wiping the beads of sweat off his fat forehead, came back with, 'Never in doubt for me,' as we both burst out laughing. We loved it when a plan came together. Forget about the A-Team, the G Men were in town and we'd bloody get on a plane as well, especially to Tenerife.

I handed Audrey a ton and she was over the moon. That was a lot of money in those days, it was like a lottery win for her but she had earned every penny. Before she left I whispered in her ear, 'Mum's the word,' and she understood exactly what I meant.

'Be lucky babe,' she nodded and disappeared into the night.

I loved being at Hinckley every Wednesday and Saturday. I would sometimes catch Wootton eyeing me up strangely, not in a sexual way but in a way that said I know you had something to do with that Black Trevor but I can't put my finger on how you did it. If he did know he never said a word to me, in fact it knocked a bit of spite out of him and we became a lot friendlier. I was winning more and more and he seemed to respect that and treat me for what I was, a damn good bookie.

It was an absolute pleasure working the Hinckley track on Wednesday and Saturday but it was still expensive bringing up a young family so on some nights I had to go back to the trusty family allowance, confident that nine times out of ten I could turn 80 quid into two or three hundred. To supplement this I would always head early next morning for the flower market, scouting for bargain priced flowers to sell on the mean streets. Nobody could say I wasn't a grafter but I was still fighting against my lifelong nemesis. I just couldn't stay out of the betting shops in the day. Rash, personal gambling was my vulnerability, my Achilles heel. I had to really buckle down and change my mindset.

The magistrates at Stony Stratford saved my life when they granted me my bookmakers' licence as I was in danger of becoming a lifelong, chronic, compulsive gambler until then. Afterwards, I saved 60% of my winnings for my float. It was obvious even to myself that taking bets off the public was far more sensible than spending afternoons sweating inside a high street bookie. It was an incredible wrench to do it as well. All my young life I had gambled away my money and win or lose, I'd really enjoyed the pastime but I now had a young family to support so I became a strict advocate to myself, cutting back the blind betting and saving the money for my career on the dog tracks.

I was coming to the end of my self-imposed apprenticeship at Hinckley and I certainly wasn't flipping flopping at the flapping but I needed to test myself at bigger, more professional NGRC tracks (National Greyhound

Racing Club). I was ambitious to make a name for myself and make a few more bob in the process and unbeknown to myself at that moment, both targets were not long in coming.

So it was time to say goodbye to Hinckley and without sounding like Billy Big Bollocks, I had outgrown the track and the weight of money that was being thrust at me on race nights. I left with a heavy heart but all those super memories are still with me. I learnt so much that would keep me in fine fettle for the future: the friendliness, the characters, the friendly banter and the basic *joie de vivre* of having my own betting business that was slowly and surely making great strides.

Talk about coincidences though, my son Charlie and his partner Beth have recently moved into their first house and the address is only 22 Nutts Lane, Hinckley. What are the odds on that happening? A young Wiltshire is on the prowl down there again. Sadly the stadium closed down in 2006 but my boy and grandson will carry on the family tradition of amity, there are no ghosts to be exorcised now. My lad has only christened his son with the name of Frankie. The bugger says I won't forget about him now, bloody right I won't.

My next track was Leicester. I was just getting my feet under the table and really enjoying myself on a NGRC track when it was suddenly shut down in 1984. It was bloody inconvenient that but the closure took me down to the dreaming spires of Oxford. Many brilliant students had graduated from here to become MP's, actors, poets and writers but the universities were not renowned for producing bookmakers. We all could basically read and count but a few of us thought a Royal Enfield was where the Queen kept her chickens. I always felt that women and maths were very complicated but at least maths had some logic.

The racing at Oxford was on Tuesdays and Saturdays so my schedule was practically the same. I was the new kid on the block here, the parvenu, the runt of the litter, 8th of eight in line but my clientele grew steadily. I was taking lumpier bets, loving every minute of it, I was born for this; the bigger the wager the better, I had ice blood coursing through my veins. Oh to be a young man again. I was invincible then, I was a Demigod, I was soaring with the eagles but most importantly I was making money on my own terms for Phyllis and the kids.

I recall one Tuesday in March that lingers long and lovingly in my memory. It was the finals of the Pall Mall stakes, a prestigious, category one race. It wasn't on TV or on SIS in the betting shops so the only way to watch it live was to come along to Sandy Lane for a night of top class dog racing over 450 metres that had just been transferred up from the now defunct stadium of Harringay. That evening thousands heeded the call, what an atmosphere. Little old me was still at the end of the queue, the number eight bookie.

My fellow layers and I discovered what the Russian Gunners at Balaclava felt like when 666 (unlucky number) armed men on horses charged at them. We suffered no casualties but by God we fended off some huge punts. My turnover at the end of the night was £69,000, taken on just eight races. A remarkable figure by anyone's standards and impossible in today's market at a provincial track but I would give my right arm to experience that again, I'm not joking.

My career was on the rise but an incident with one of the big three bookmakers almost halted it before sending me back to the Labour Exchange. All I was doing was bringing a bit of value back to the game but it seemed that a larger, greedier predator was not quite so philanthropic as your old pal Gal.

The catalyst for this misunderstanding was the new Friday afternoon dog racing at Oxford. BAGS was involved and all the races would be televised live into the high street betting shops but right away certain people were trying to manipulate the prices of dogs to suit their own interests.

A large bookies rep tried to shorten a dog I had chalked up at 4/1. He passed me a grand and I reduced it to threes then a minute later he gave me another grand and I left it at 3/1. He said, 'Shorten the dog up,' to which I replied, 'No, have some more on.'

He didn't and the price remained as it was. My reasoning was and the rep never knew this; I'd already taken a four thousand pound bet on another dog by a big, local punter and I was merely trying to get a balanced book. As luck would have it, both dogs got beaten; I won £6,000 and went home in better spirits than the rep and the heavy punter. Such was the world of greyhound racing.

As soon as I got home the phone was ringing, it was John Blake the General Manager from the track, 'Gary I've got to expel you from the Friday meetings but your position on the night meetings is unaffected.' I asked him why even though I already knew what the answer was but his reply of "no comment" only confirmed my suspicions. I thanked him for calling; I'd suddenly become a rebel with a cause.

The large, high street bookmaker had thrown its toys from the Silver Cross Perambulator and the lead rattle had fallen on yours truly. The fact I was still participating on the night meetings at Oxford had nothing to do with kindness from the chain. This was a time when the betting shops didn't open at night so they had no reason to shorten one. Mark my words though, if they had opened for evening racing I would have been signing on the next day, put on the dole with my career in ruins for not bringing a dog in one point. You could only call them ruthless bastards if that was their brazen stance.

The news went round the betting industry quicker than Typhoid Mary on a kiss-me-quick tour and I was invited by Channel 4 to appear on The Morning Line the following Saturday. If I played my cards right I could come out of this looking like a modern day, benevolent, Robin Hood even though I closely resembled his portly henchman, Friar Tuck.

Before I went on John Francome took me to one side and said, 'Be careful, Mac will try to trick you into spilling the beans on who the guilty bookmaker is.'

I thanked the champion jockey, he had always been one of my heroes. I didn't know John McCririck that well in those days, that was before we became friends but I knew he was a top media man who would stop at nothing to obtain a news scoop so I had my guard well up when he started his inquisition.

Big Mac started with a dolly, 'Are you a gambler?'

I went right on the attack and drove it to the boundary, 'John, you know all bookies are gamblers; some win, others lose like yourself.' Ouch! He didn't like that straight drive.

He went for the throat and tossed up the googly, 'Who was the bookmaker that was trying to push down the price of the dog?'

I hoisted that one up for six and the ball was never found, 'When I was a baby my mother would put a dummy in my mouth, not a tin whistle.'

In other words, I'm not a grass, never will be and as much as I loathed that bookmaker chain at that precise moment, there was never any chance of me revealing who they were. John didn't get his headline.

A short while later I was on the rails at Market Rasen for National Hunt racing and the same rep who had tried to shorten the dog at Oxford approached my pitch. I thought to myself he's got some nerve but I bore him no malice. He was a man like myself trying to earn a living. It hadn't been his decision to have me barred from the BAGS meeting. He pointed to a 16/1 outsider, 'A thousand on at 2/1 please Gary.' I realised that was my little thank you for keeping schtum. It was a great life lesson. Don't ever be a snitch; no good ever comes of it.

That whole affair lifted my profile with the public into the stratosphere.

Some people said I was a hero, I certainly wasn't that but I'd always been a working class punter myself and folk could identify with that. Once seen, never ever forgotten; a few pounds overweight, a winning Colgate smile and the odd gem of betting knowledge would endear me to many but not all and the odds of an expectant reappearance at the Oxford Friday afternoon BAGS meeting were still longer than those for the midget at the all-male, nudist dance party not getting poked in the eye.

I had twelve great years at Oxford but I reluctantly decided to give up my pitch there in the new millennium. Greyhound racing was suffering, crowds were down and most of my big paydays were now on the horse racing tracks. I was proud of what I had achieved in that fine academic city having moved up over the years from number eight to number one but the universe was in a constant state of flux. Betfair was just starting to flex its muscles and my piles were killing me. Something had to give but I just hoped it wasn't the inflatable rubber ring that had done sterling work since I first encountered Emma Roids.

I kept my hand in by standing at Milton Keynes Greyhound Stadium, which was closer to where I was living and where I tried a new approach by Betting without the Favourite. Selby was my trusty right hand man again and he came up with a fool proof scheme of wicked genius, Betting without the Winner whereby whoever backed the victor got their money back, you couldn't get fairer than that. In all seriousness we were extremely successful and over the years we both made some handsome money. Boxing day 2005 was a very sad day in my life, as Milton Keynes Greyhound Stadium shut down. My son Nicky had worked the pitch with me as well; it was our little family concern. It was so sad to see Groveway gone, I cried more than a tear; it was like losing a relative. When Oxford went in 2012, all my tracks had run their race: Hinckley, Leicester and Milton Keynes left holes in my heart, the dog game was going to Carey Street. I didn't give a hoot about the money; I just loved greyhound racing so much, I needed to stay involved. It was like a quest looking for a long lost friend, I would always be unhappy unless I worked a track.

In 2003 I had started working a book at the modern Kent greyhound track of Sittingbourne. It was situated in the industrial Swale area just off the Isle of Sheppey and had for many years been the main staging point on Watling Street for travellers going from London to Canterbury. With a fairly high populace and the busy M2 (just South of the old Roman Road) nearby, this greyhound track has every chance of being a runaway success. I was doing well here, most people knew my face from the Frankie Dettori Ascot Day, especially in the summer when the manic holiday makers swelled attendances but just like at Oxford, I found travelling and other horse racing commitments too much to overcome. I made my apologies and withdrew.

Roger Cearns approached me years later in 2009. The man is a one off; a superb promoter and entrepreneur who single-handedly saved the stadium when it was failing financially only months after it first opened in 1995. I've always admired Roger and was very interested to hear what he had to say. The bottom line was, after a lull, he needed another high profile bookie to assist getting attendances back up and to strengthen the betting ring.

The promoter had put his heart and soul into the venture and he asked me to return in his hour of need. I was a greyhound man through and through so I couldn't knock the geezer back even if I wanted to. Gary Wiltshire owed greyhound racing a great deal, it had saved my life and later on it gave me a comfortable standard of living. It was time to get stuck in and rescue the track; I couldn't bear to see another hit skid row. It would be really tough but if we all rowed the boat in the same, sunny direction we could make for the calmer waters before reaching a safe haven.

I came back and my great pal the governor, *Numero uno,* Curly Wilson was still there taking bets off all and sundry, it was like I'd never been away.

It was now known as Central Park Stadium and that name change obviously hadn't helped much but a change they say is always as good as a rest.

Lofty would drive me down there from Hollywood, Birmingham so it was a fair old jaunt. I was in my mid-fifties and getting jip from a weak bladder and diabetes so we always went early with our destination Leysdown on Sea, a delightful coastal village on the Isle of Sheppey. It had a high number of amusement arcades and even a nudist beach but we had always been trenchermen; we were there for the jellied eels and fish and chips. You couldn't beat going to work after a hearty nosh up; we always made a day and night of it.

I'd like to think the return of the profligate son had a vast bearing on the improvement of fortunes but truthfully it was down to the brilliant business acumen of Roger. Things were on the up when the track secured the rights to stage the finals of The Television Trophy in 2011. The competition had been an annual event since the 1950's and it came to Sittingbourne for the first time that year.

What made it a red-letter day for Sittingbourne was that a local trainer, John Mullins pulled off a remarkable win with *Knockies Hannah* at 7/4. The crowd went berserk, even the ones who hadn't backed the dog were cheering.

The distance was just shy of 900 metres and Trap 5 *Minnie's Penske* broke out like a cheetah with *Knockies Hannah* chasing from trap 1 round the first bend. The five dog led the one dog by about a length for most of the race over two laps, no other dog got a look in, then quite literally yards from the line *Knockies Hannah* started to pull the leader back inch by inch, before getting her head in front on the line. A photograph was called for but I knew she had got up and was paying out before the result was announced. I'd backed the stamina queen before racing so was as pleased as all the locals when she tore up the finishing straight, sparking amazing celebrations. That bitch had the heart of a lion and was a credit to her very good trainer John Mullins.

In 2012 the Greyhound Grand National (a great contest over 480 metres for some of the best young hurdlers in the country) moved over from Wimbledon. Central Park was on the up and up. The journey however was at last beginning to take its toll on my temperamental bladder. I was watering the flowers at least eight times both ways, forcing many close calls looking for somewhere to sprinkle. If anyone was into water sports I could fill a small swimming pool.

When the Kent Kings Speedway Team moved here in 2013, it was time for me to bale out. I'd done my little bit to avert the bailiffs from the door and the future was bright for Central Park and Roger Cearns. I know he appreciated my input and I enjoyed every minute at Sittingbourne. It just goes to show that anything in life is possible with a positive mentality. Roger is one of those charismatic men that talk and walk which is very hard to do today. My only regret is that I'm not a pound behind him.

So, from happy days at Sittingbourne in 2013 this was the period when my life started to come off the rails. We are chronicling that year to the present, which, even as bad as it was, still had laughs a plenty. But think of all I'd been through: my weight worries, the gastric sleeve, wife Sue leaving me and sleeping in the car, depression, a year in the greenhouse away from racing, banned by BAGS off the dog tracks and released by Sky Dogs through it.

If a novelist put that out no one would believe a word of it. At the lowest points it was about as much fun as watching a fire at the orphanage but I pulled through and will now press forward. Big Gary Wiltshire is a fighter and with all your help I will return better and stronger. Maybe this book will kick start my comeback to the TV; a lot of the current crop of young presenters are professional but they don't cut the mustard. We don't need bland; we want colourful characters with charisma. Take two great jockeys; Ryan Moore and Frankie Dettori, not a fag paper between them in riding ability but if they enter a room one lights it up and the other puts his head down. No problems, different strokes for different folks.

I would restore John McCririck to the screen tomorrow. He's knowledgeable and controversial but what's the point of having presenters who never voice an opinion. I hope I'm wrong but I think John at 78 might just have to put his 'Double Carpets' and 'Burlington Berties' to bed. Maybe a producer will take a chance on him, I hope so very much. I'm the wrong side of 60 too but I've still got a lot to say. You can't buy the experience I've clocked up over the years, like General MacArthur once said, 'I shall return.'

It's probably a bad quote that; I don't think he ever did.

Of course I had a few months in 2018 at Towcester Stadium thanks to Lord Hesketh and Chief Exec. Kevin Ackerman. They never forgot me, you find out who your real friends are in life when you hit the pavement. There were my wonderful years on the selected six greyhound tracks but the sad fact is five are now consigned to history: Hinckley, Leicester, Oxford, Milton Keynes and now Towcester have had the dreaded quote, "last one out, switch all the lights off."

Those tracks will not be coming back to re-join an ever changing, mad world. Maybe Towcester has a chance to rise again but my beloved dogs are slowly being phased out by so called progress and advancement. BAGS have tried to phase me out at the same time but surely most people associate me with greyhound racing and as a man who isn't going to knock a punter back if you want a pony on a 6/1 dog. At a time when tracks are struggling to survive, attendances are down and a malaise is gripping the industry, wouldn't you think someone high up in the running of our great sport would say, 'Let's bring the big man in from the cold, he's done his time, his heart is in the right place, he loves the greyhounds, how come we are not using him?'

Do you know what? I would harbour no grudges, bear no ill will and get on with anything they consigned me to. Will it happen? It might if the public get behind me.

Let's hope sanity eventually prevails.

* * * *

Chapter Seven

BETTING WITH KING BARRY

Trainer Bill O'Gorman had a record equalling 16 wins in a season with a horse. He did it twice with Provideo in 1984 and Timeless Times in 1990, a superb training feat.

The first time I made a book at Barry Hearn's Fish'O'Mania was 2005. I'd been asked to take over from the legendary Harry "The Dog" Findlay as the matchday bookie. For me, Harry was all that was and still is great about betting. He has punted on most sports including a huge 2 million pound wager on the mighty All Blacks at a past Rugby Union World Cup. That colossal investment went awry unfortunately but the joint-owner of the jumping legend Denman is still going strong today. Can I just send my condolences to him on his recent loss; we all lost an equine friend when *The Tank* left us last year in the summer of 2018. One hell of a racehorse and like his owner, built of sterner stuff than most.

Harry's great love and passion is the same as mine, we both hate to see our wonderful sport of greyhound racing being badly run. He pumped big money into Coventry Greyhound Stadium but didn't seem to get the backing he richly deserved and so that's another Midlands track gone to seed. No wonder we both have had to fight our inner demons in recent years. I can only salute Harry for his huge contribution to the world of gambling; it wouldn't be half the fun without him.

From Harry to Barry and what can you say about this man? He's a force of nature, a diamond dynamo from Dagenham. Born on a council estate, he has taken some fringe sports to the highest pinnacle; all they have needed is some Hearn investment, know-how, oomph and razzamatazz.

Barry's genius is finding sports that have potential then promoting them in his own unique way. In the seventies after becoming a qualified accountant he became the chairman of Lucania Snooker Clubs. He was requested one day to come to the Romford Lucania branch by the manager there. A skinny ginger-haired teenager was potting balls for fun and the rest is snooker history. Barry became the friend and manager of Steve Davis, one of the greatest cue men ever. Who could forget the 1981 World Snooker Final when Davis won his first championship beating Doug Mountjoy 18-12. I was watching at home when the winning ball was finally dispatched then this madman came charging across the arena and lifted Davis off the floor. I nearly choked on my buttered scone, it wasn't snooker etiquette but it was something I wanted to see again and again. The exuberance, the excitement and, of course, the manager's percentage.

That's why I love Barry. The man loves a deal, he will deal to his dying day; men like him are the catalyst for success. Let nobody forget there is no crime in making a profit when you give value for money. Is it a coincidence that Steve Davis was the first professional snooker player to become a millionaire? It was odds-on in my book with Barry in his corner.

In 1986 "Snooker Loopy" reached number 6 in the pop charts while Barry was promoting his snooker stars from the hub of his empire, Matchroom Sport in Brentwood, Essex. Gone were the dark old days of old men playing billiards in smoke filled rooms, watched by a handful of spectators. The Matchroom Mob, consisting of Tony Meo, Terry Griffiths, Willie Thorne, (the pride of Leicester loves a bet) Dennis Taylor and The Nugget accompanied the great Chas and Dave in a foot-tapping romp. RIP

Chas Hodges, a shock to us all last year. Jesus, we are losing some good men recently.

This was the brave new world of ace promoter Barry Hearn. He loved his boxing and was involved promoting Lennox Lewis, Nigel Benn and Chris Eubank to name a few. His son Eddie has taken over that part of the business now and is thriving with many world-class boxers. Barry actually introduced a TV knockout tournament called Prizefighter, which was televised all in one evening. Eight boxers would fight a drawn opponent over three rounds, each winner would progress to a semi-final and then to the final. It was another great, entertaining innovation.

Barry also promotes Pool, Table Tennis, Golf and Ten-Pin Bowling. Without his input some of these sports would never get a mention on the box but surely his finest hour must be the promotion of the pub game darts. Years ago the only darts you might see on television would be the latter stages of The News Of The World Championship which ran from 1947 to 1990. To be fair, the top darts players all wanted to win it (later names on the trophy included Eric Bristow, Mike Gregory and Bobby George) but darts was dying a death as a spectator sport.

I'm not saying Barry saved the game but once he got involved, he took it to a whole new level and smashed through the stratosphere. I regularly do the book on his darts nights and very enjoyable they are too. Barry has me as the sole bookmaker whenever it's possible at the venues and I'm always the only bookmaker at the fishing. He's another great man who goes down as one of my top angel's. Barry has had a lifetime interest as a keen fisherman so it was only natural that he came up with a unique angling contest. Fish'O'Mania has now become the nation's favourite fishing competition, a no-brainer really when you consider how many millions partake in the sport

Barry pitched his idea to Greg Dyke who at the time was the go-to man at London Weekend Television but the silly, old sausage knocked him back. I'd love a job as an executive at these big companies; if you keep getting loads of big decisions wrong they give you a golden handshake for millions, nice work if you can get it. Anyhow Sky Sports took it up and ran with it. The competition started in 1994 and is going from strength to strength but don't tell Greg.

So, I rocked up in 2005. I'd sold all my racecourse pitches to Tote Bookmakers at this juncture and was working for them as part of the deal. They looked after me very well indeed and it was little old Gal who turned up for his first Fish'O'Mania. On most finals day Bazza would turn up, not in a taxi but in a helicopter, it's the only way for a good day's fishing.

There have been a few different venues over the years and 2005 was at Hayfield Lakes, Doncaster. There were three previous winners in the field but there was a lot of money for local angler Marc Jones, a company director from Wakefield. He had a lumpy bet with me on himself at 8/1 and every canny Yorkshire man there wanted a piece of the action. I phoned head office. He had been 50/1 in the morning apparently and they had been knocked over with all the interest for him so I got the order to scrub him off the betting. The Tote stood to lose a small fortune if he prevailed but hopefully one of the previous winners could weigh in with more fish. He had already mentioned to me that he had played for Tottenham Hotspur for 5 years and that was like a red rag to a bull for a Gooner like myself so it was a double whammy.

Fair play to him though because from midday to 5pm he caught more weighty fish than all the others. Throughout the afternoon I'd been gleaning little bits of local tittle tattle and heard that Marc Jones had been coming down here for the last ten weeks to fish and put a game plan together, all perfectly legitimate and nothing wrong with giving yourself a slight edge. He only had one problem after the event, the winner had to take a running jump into the water to celebrate, not advisable if you can't swim but a time honoured tradition which is fine so long as you remember to take all your winning betting slips out of your pockets.

Afterwards he presented me with a pile of the mushy, unreadable betting slips but thankfully they were matched up within the week and he got paid out. He'd had a nice touch, The Tote had been given a lesson in match betting and everyone was a shade wiser. In all the years I've done the event I think I've only come out on top two or three times. These anglers are very shrewd; they know their stuff. They are also the salt of the earth, some of the finest people you would ever wish to meet. Although it hasn't been very profitable for me over the years, there is nowhere on that particular Saturday that I'd rather be than among the piscatorial punters. It has also raised my public profile no end with these enthusiastic sportsmen.

When the finals were at Cudmore Fisheries I always had to go past the Eddie Stobart compound at the traffic lights in Stoke-on-Trent (onto the Loggerheads road). It reminded me of years ago when the kids and grandkids were on a long run in the car with me, I'd tell them, "first one to spot a boys name on the front of an Eddie Stobart lorry wins a tenner." It kept them quite for hours on end.

A few years after my debut, one of the fishing finalists approached me an hour before the off to have a bet on himself. Nothing unusual in that you might say but when I reveal all, you have to come to your own conclusions. His name was Steve Cooke (the same as Lofty but smaller) and he wanted a 50 quid wager on himself. He wasn't among the front-runners in the betting but he had won the competition in 1999 so he knew his way round a tackle box. I accepted his money and shortened him a little in the market. Ten minutes before midday a guy from that year's major sponsor rings me asking if he could have a bet with me. Now they were a massive concern with untold billions, why would they want to lay off on me? When I'm in a corner my odds can only be compared with Dick Turpin's.

Apparently they had been inundated with money all day for a novelty bet, an ungenerous 20/1 for any angler in the final to catch no fish. They had taken so much cash that the bet was now evens; did I want to get involved? I told the guy, 'It's not my sort of bet fella but if it's of any consolation to you, I think I could catch one fish in five hours with a branch, a piece of string and a worm on a bent nail. These are career anglers, your money is safe.'

He seemed relieved after my reassurance, he was going to ring me back after five o'clock. I thought no more of it and carried on taking bets.

At five past five he rang again and he was overly keen. They had announced the first three, now they were giving out the losing fishermen's weights in descending order with eventually "and in last place Steve Cooke with no fish." There was a shocked silence. I relayed the bad news back to the sponsor's employee and I'm sure I heard a gunshot before he hung up.

The next day there was an official stewards enquiry and the Angling Association got involved but it went down a dead end street. Remember Steve Cooke had backed himself to the tune of 50 pounds and there was no case to answer. Sometimes these novelty and fun bets can go wrong. I recall in 2017 when Wayne Shaw, the Sutton United reserve goalkeeper came to the attention of the national press. He weighed in at 23 stone (bloody lightweight) when Sutton drew the mighty Arsenal at home in the FA Cup and he copped a load of publicity. He was actually a good keeper in his younger days and was in the same squad as Alan Shearer at Southampton.

Before the live television match, Shearer declared, 'I followed my dreams to the Premier League while Wayne followed the burger van.' It was quite a beautiful statement. Shaw was by far the biggest personality on the night, literally and Sun Bets got shed loads of publicity when they announced a novelty bet of 8/1 for Wayne Shaw to eat a pie on the sidelines during the match.

They had to pay out a five-figure sum when peckish Wayne produced a meat pie out of a paper bag in the eighty-third minute and started casually munching away. He claimed that he hadn't eaten all day and hadn't been involved with any of the betting but these things happen when companies advertise crazy bets; integrity can disappear. Wayne can have the last word in mitigation as he claimed, 'No, it wasn't a pie, it was a pasty.'

On that slim differential, a promising football career was destroyed; he was only 46 at the time. Wayne old son, you are a legend. We large sportsmen have to stick together; there is discrimination out there against us big lads.

I actually had a bit of luck at Fish'O'Mania last year in 2018 when a young, unfancied Brummie won the fifty thousand pound cheque. Pete Black from King's Norton became the youngest ever winner at 21 years of age. I had him in the book at 25/1 and he was a good result for me because he was up against a plethora of top experienced anglers. It was a marvellous achievement for the midlander. I think Sky Sports man Rob Palmer was on at those odds. He knows full well that most years I'm doing my bollocks. When he comes and interviews me throughout the day it's normally a tale of woe but in 2018 we both had smiles bigger than Zippy off Rainbow.

Boxing is a sport I've not had a lot of experience of but I was over the moon when Eddie Hearn asked me to do the odds at the Liverpool Echo Arena. If I recall, Tony Bellew the Evertonian was top of the bill but most of the undercard was priced up at 1/20, 1/25 and even 1/50 and these bouts duly went to the long odds-on favourites. I didn't see a lot of punting action and came home like One Round O'Riley but it was another string to my bow. Just call me Mr Versatility.

Now snooker is a game I love. I had the honour of being the bookmaker for Barry at the world famous Crucible, meeting up with John Parrott again and the wonderfully droll John Virgo, an absolute delight. Most punters have got their wagers on before coming but they can bet with me if they want to adjust their standpoint on procedures, not to large amounts of money on two runner matches but the buzz of just being there is reward enough.

I've done two out the last three years at the great *Ally Pally* (Alexandra

Palace) for The Masters Championship and Ronnie O'Sullivan comes alive at this event, so I keep an eye on him. It's a bit more boisterous than Sheffield but again not a fortune to be made. There are no mobiles or drinking allowed in the arena, still the crowd can get quite partisan. Jimmy White has been so popular here over the years but he only won it the once, way back in 1984.

In the past few years I've noticed the mind games going on between Barry and Ronnie. Whatever Barry does or says, Ronnie will have a little pop; nothing outrageous but enough to force Barry to make a defensive comment about what Ronnie has suggested. It's food and drink for the media and keeps snooker on the back pages. I can let Ronnie know that you can only push so far with Barry; he is a supreme operator. There will only be one winner there and it won't be the guy chalking his cue but all in all, a fascinating, psychological stand off to establish the alpha male.

One evening Barry invited Sharon and I up to the Holiday Inn Hotel, Stoke-on-Trent (just off the M6 junction 15) for a big charity auction night. He was man with the microphone and the local legend of darts Phil Taylor was ably assisting him. Now, I know The Potteries isn't the most salubrious of areas, but only Barry could have got away with his opening gambit, 'If I was in London, this item would make five thousand but here, let's start at five hundred.'

Do you know what? He actually got the five thousand; he should have been a root canal dentist. But I've always found the Stoke people to be some of the most friendly and generous folk about, just keep those tasty, cheese oat cakes coming.

Premier League Darts is now staple viewing on a Thursday night on Sky all around the country and I've been privileged to run the betting booth on many of these nights but one evening stands out like a sore thumb. It was at my local venue in Nottingham too, The Motorpoint Arena (formerly The Capital FM Arena), which also doubles up as an ice skating rink and is home to the ice hockey team Nottingham Panthers.

I'd been down at the Cheltenham Festival in 2014 and had come away about 800 quid up, which was nothing to be sniffed at, and if I could get a few choice, favourable results at the darts then everything would be looking hunky dory. I'd left Sharon in charge of the girls as I was going to be late so I left her with a few basic instructions. I got there just after the second match had finished so there were three games to go. Sharon informed me that they had taken good money and the biggest bet had only been twenty quid with most of the wagers as fivers and tenners. That was how I liked to roll, lots of small bets usually meant a nice profit after all the betting slips had been settled up.

Sitting down to peruse the not inconsiderable pile of slips, an ugly pattern emerged. In the first match Peter Wright had beaten Simon Whitlock at odds of 4/6 and in the second Adrian Lewis had taken out Garry Anderson at 4/5 (this was shortly after "Jackpot" had been double World Champion and was throwing much better darts than the previous few years). At least three quarters of the pile were wagers backing the five favourites in accumulators and the three favourites to come were Michael Van Gerwen, Barney and The Power. I thought fuck me! We're sunk. Three multiple world champions, how often do they underperform?

Now all you gamblers out there know the power of a big accumulator, it can knock you for dead, no matter how short the prices. I worked out that if the last three favourites won the odds were about 12/1 so every £10 bet was returning 130 quid back to the punter. I had a sickly feeling in my stomach and sloped off to the back of the hall to watch the carnage unfold, hoping against all hope for a miracle. Why couldn't I just be lucky instead of good-looking?

The players were just coming onto the stage. It was Michael Van Gerwen vs. Wes Newton from Fleetwood and the superstar Dutchman was rightfully a very heavy favourite but Wes on his night was more than capable of causing a shock upset. It had been a really long day so far and I was totally cream-crackered what with the long drive to Cheltenham and back plus the mental pressure of making a book there and keeping my wits about me. It sent me into sleep mode despite of all the thousands of chanting fanatics surrounding me.

Even asleep, I was dreaming comfort food, and in particular, Bispham Fish and Chips, the best tucker on the Fylde coastline. I love those suet puddings you get up there; I've had many a happy hour dipping chips into the mince and gravy; heaven, it doesn't get much better than that. Wes lived in Fleetwood but he was originally from Blackpool and I still like to get up to see the lights. I really enjoy it there, usually staying at the Viking Hotel on the South Promenade, an adult only establishment that incorporates the "Talk of the Coast" cabaret bar. I've had many good nights there. Lofty prefers going up the North Promenade to "Funny Girls", a burlesque cabaret bar on Dickson Road. I don't know about drag queens but you'd have to drag me up there to watch them.

I came back to the land of the living just as the MC was lauding Van Gerwen after his seven-one victory. Thanks very much Wes. Walking back to the booth I overheard Newton had averaged over 103 and that was the highest on the night bar Van Gerwen so what could you do? Wes had given it his best shot but the Dutchman was different gravy as per usual.

That just left me with two games to save my shirt: Raymond Van Barneveld v Robert Thornton and Phil Taylor v Dave Chisnall. I don't mind saying it but it was time to panic; if Barney and The Power won the outgoings were over eleven thousand big ones and I was holding on to a little under 6k at the time. I tried ringing Barry, no answer, so I got hold of his right-hand man, Matt Porter who was there on the premises. Matt is another good man who will move mountains for you.

He told me World Champion Super Middleweight boxer Carl Froch was there and if Barney won he would send him down. I told him we might need Mike Tyson and Hulk Hogan as emergency back up. He also added that if needed he would collect all the money from the bar takings and bring that down as well. So at least we had a plan. Fair enough, I'd worry about the money later and if the worst came to the worst, at least we had a bit of muscle and all the funds in place to placate the good folk of Nottingham.

I was helpless at that moment; fate would do what it always did. As an old Yorkshire cricket captain used to say about the upcoming day's play, "we shall see what we shall see" so with that wise mantra in my head I went and sat down in the back of the arena again. I wasn't a masochist or anything like that but if I was going to lose my shirt, at the very least I wanted to have my money's worth.

Barney, who had won the Premier League that season, raced into a 2-0 lead and I thought to myself, fuck it, just make a run for the doors now only for Thornton to come back with two legs to square it at 2-2. I was rooting for the wee Scotsman not just because of the money, some of my kids were half Scottish so this was a stand for national Celtic pride but that was a long way second to be fair. Vacillating one way then the other, at the end of the 9th leg Thornton was miraculously up by five legs to four so he only needed one more leg. Then the worst it could end up if he got it was a six all draw and that would smash all the fivefold accumulators to smithereens.

I had spoken too soon. How many times over the decades have we heard on the television that the Scottish team had snatched defeat from the jaws of victory? Too bloody many and here I was as a spectator seeing it happen again. Barney won legs ten and eleven to lead 6-5; the only decent advantage in the last leg was that Thornton was leading off with the darts so he needed to make them count. He started with a maximum, 180, the sweetest words I'd heard throughout the evening. I think Barney replied with a ton. Thornton only rattled three more in, 180 and he was miles clear. Barney put in a ton plus. Thornton's next three were a bag of nails but he had left 81 which could be got with two darts. Barney put in another ton plus but was back on 121.

It was all in "Braveheart's" hands and I think they were shaking even more than mine. The only way to go for a pro player was treble 19 then double 12. He looped the first dart right into the treble bed, it was the only time that evening that I thought I might just get out of jail here but he seemed to rush the next two, putting one just outside the double and the other one inside, leaving him double six. I couldn't take the cruel, awful pressure. I screamed out and it wasn't, 'Oh, jolly bad luck Bob.' In fact I think both his education and parentage were called into question. Barney could now go out on 121 and actually got the treble 19 with his first arrow, he then went for treble 16. This was getting too bleak to watch but thank God he put it just outside the wire. He followed it up with a single 16 leaving him with three darts at double 16. He knew, I knew and the big crowd knew and Robert Thornton definitely knew that the big Dutchman wouldn't miss again.

This was the first time in all of my life that I couldn't watch the action unfold, I had my eyes clamped shut. It had only been a few months since I'd come through the depression and this was pushing me right back towards fragility. That six thousand pound float was all the money I had in the world, the five grand that I was borrowing was a bigger hurdle to me at that stage than Dettori Day when I was over a million in debt. I was approaching 60 so it could be my last stand, they were going to try and bury me under an ice rink. We had three darts left, the man on the stage was also under immense pressure but he would still be taking home his match cheque that evening. Please keep them straight old son, I just couldn't watch.

I heard the initial obligatory *Oooh*; he'd obviously missed the first, then another, heart stopping *Oooh*. I didn't want to hate this man at that precise moment but he was putting me through the wringer then I thought, no, I'm the only one who has done this to myself and suddenly felt better. The huge cheer that followed had me jumping out of my seat; he had only nailed double six with his last dart.

The girls were over the moon; they knew by my demeanour that trouble had been near while Matt Porter came down beaming, "never a worry!" He hadn't been sitting in my shoes. Phil Taylor beat "Chissy" in the last 7-5, just like I thought he would. Can you imagine having to sit through all of that to the bitter end if Robert Thornton had not got his draw? It possibly would have broken me. After we counted up, we had won 360 pounds. One dart a millimetre the wrong side of the wire could have cost me over 11,000 pounds, a sobering thought. It had been a good job I'd been wearing my cycle clips though as my lucky underpants were a write off.

The next day I returned to Cheltenham for Gold Cup Day and won well again. A lot of things in life are about momentum and positivity; if you can get a good run going from a tight corner, you never know where it might take you. I know that near fatal close call gave me added confidence for the next few years; to keep on merrily striving, never to give up no matter what the day threw at you.

Now if people ask me who my sporting hero is I always tell them it is Robert Thornton, he really did save the day for me at Nottingham. He truly is the William Wallace of the oche. "The Thorn" (as Thornton is affectionately known by his fans), might just read this book one day. If you're reading this Robert, I owe you more than a wee dram my old pal and hopefully we will bump into each other at a darts event in the near future.

Ye'll tak' the high road and I'll tak' the low road,
And I'll be in Scotland afore ye,
But me and my true love will never meet again,
On the bonny, bonny banks of Loch Lomond.

After that last gasp get out on the night I adjusted my strategy slightly with any accumulators now watched like an osprey checking out a shoal of salmon though I still give 33/1 for a nine dart finish. I must still have a good heart over 22 years after Dettori Day. Why I put myself through it,

God only knows but I'm chugging on to 64, and I'm not changing anytime soon. I might even get a perverse pleasure by going through the mill. They say bookies and gunslingers die with their boots on but I'd like to go out like Basil Rathbone in a silk, smoking jacket, pyjamas and carpet slippers. Then again so would John McCririck.

I must put in another good word for Matt Porter, a mini angel under Barry's wing. He got his chance after excelling in Barry's Brentwood offices after previously working for the bookie A R Dennis. He's risen up the ranks at Matchroom and nothing is too much trouble for him. If I'm really busy at the darts, he will jump in and help with the bets. I've got a lot of time and respect for him.

If the darts venue is a good distance away, Barry will put you up in the same hotel as the players and it's always nice to rub shoulders with the new superstars. I owe him a lot. He is a man of the people, a trier and a grafter; you don't get rich watching Jeremy Kyle and Judge Judy every day. The next venue after that Nottingham near miss was at Leeds and it broke the attendance record with over 11,000 people at the First Direct Arena. Barry has a lot to be proud of. Former great players like Alun Evans, Leighton Rees, Cliff Lazarenko, John Lowe and Jocky Wilson all missed the boat; they were born 30 years too soon. Some of them have gone to the great oche in the sky but they would be utterly amazed at the renaissance of the humble game of darts. I bet Bristow's up there with them now, winding them up.

Once a year Sharon and I get invited to the PDC darts awards at the Dorchester Hotel and it's a great night celebrating all that has gone on in the previous year. We are only a small cog in the machine and are usually seated at the back but everyone is in evening dress and Barry never forgets you. He comes to our table and says, 'Look at you lot and your togs, you've got a few quid. I'm impressed.' I always enjoy going back to London but it's changed a lot since I was a kid. The salt beef sandwich shop is still there, so are a few bagel houses but all the greyhound tracks have gone. I'll never go back, I'm happy in Keyworth. Every day I drive past Gotham, near Nottingham where Gotham City was based on. I must get Sharon to wash and iron my Batman suit, mask and cape; there's still space on the racetracks for a betting superhero.

* * * *

Chapter Eight

RIGHT, SAID FRED

Each and every greyhound running these days can trace its lineage back to just one dog, King Cob, born in England in 1839.

Going back again to Dettori day in 1996 (hypothetically if one could go back ten minutes before the first race in a time machine, I doubt if many punters including myself would be laying the buggers), I noticed in the Sunday red top papers that a northern chain of bookmakers Done Brothers, had taken a bigger pasting than myself.

They lost over two million pounds that day, not a lot you might say for Betfred but this was in an era before the chain went nationwide. They were not the same powerhouse then having just under a hundred shops, mainly in the North and a far cry from the thousands they run today. As I was going through the kitchen drawers for a sharp knife, Fred Done gave out a statement, 'It was a great day for racing and I'm really pleased for all of our punters who have had their lives changed by this.'

I know mine was.

Now other larger betting companies would have come out with similar platitudes but PR men saying these things through gritted teeth is not quite the same as the head honcho pouring his heart out on a bad day for his firm.

Knowing Fred as I do now, every word he uttered would have been true and sincere.

When my two properties were sold quickly, I was actually homeless. It would be right back to humble beginnings and renting again, just like a vast number of people who have had this for long periods in their life while some folk have only ever known a rent book. That is not uncommon in this country, in fact it's getting harder and harder to get on the housing ladder. My guilty, little secret was I owned two Mercedes (one brand new) and I could so easily have changed my name on the logbook. But that wasn't my style so I decided they had to go too; how would it have looked if people saw me lolling about in a top of the range Mercedes whilst owing untold thousands? They were quickly sold and I acquired a very modest runabout. I should have followed Sir Bradley Wiggins example and purchased a racing bike which would have trimmed my waist and my wallet but if I'd done that, the old saying you never see a bookmaker on a bicycle would have gone right out the window. I don't think a yellow jersey would suit me either.

As you all know I sold all my racecourse pitches to The Tote, went to work for them and it was in that capacity that I first met Fred. It was at Haydock Races. Straight away Fred came over as a gracious and humble man, no airs or graces. I can pay him no finer compliment than to say he was one of the lads, money hadn't changed him one iota. We struck an immediate rapport and Fred very kindly asked me to speak on his Saturday morning Betfred Betting radio programme, broadcast live from Birchwood (just north east of Warrington, between the M6 and the M62). He has since moved to Media City Salford, a state of the art complex that also houses the BBC. Fred's first shop was less than a mile away from here so for all intents and purposes, the man has returned home like a conquering hero. I know I've a great face for radio but with these new wide screen TV's, the betting public can see what a fine figure of a man I now am, having lost a few pounds.

Mark Pearson, his brilliant head of media, always makes me feel welcome and I love talking about everything to do with the betting industry but I've a request for Mark, could you upgrade to an elevator please? There's loads of stairs and it's killing me going up and down; I was built for comfort not speed.

I've known Fred for over twenty years; he's my man. I've always looked up to him and Fred has become like a second father to me. I've always enjoyed his company and over the years have become very attached to the family. He was there for me in my moment of need and he knows that vice versa, I will always be there for him. Over the years I've rung him for a shoulder to cry on including one, disastrous Derby Day when I took a terrible pasting and I spoke to him over the phone. His shops had also taken a battering but he said, 'Get back out there tomorrow son, we'll get it all back.'

It was just the tonic I needed to keep my positivity up and sure enough, I won most of it back that Sunday.

I know Fred loves Manchester United, but can't stand the Glazers; he feels they are sucking the life out the club with the interest loans and dividend payments. He's been a season ticket holder for many years and has twice paid out early on Manchester United to win the Premier League in 1998 and 2012 only for them to be pipped at the post by Arsenal and then Manchester City. For me it was worth every penny because in terms of free advertising it was worth tens of millions. I know a lot of soccer people who only bet with Fred because he's a true football man.

Fred and his wife Mo knew how to throw a party and I've been to many of them but the one Fred put on for Mo's seventieth birthday was a bobby dazzler, no expense spared. The superb Russell Watson (the People's Tenor) was singing his mix of pop and opera while Heather Small and M People were performing many of their chart hits including *Search For The Hero*, *One Night In Heaven* and *Moving On Up*. It was great stuff, and with enough food and drink to sink the Queen Mary, I woke up with a sore head the next morning I can tell you but what a night.

Mo and Fred were teenage sweethearts. When Fred started as a back street bookie, Mo used to be the bookie's runner. She would always sign the betting dockets Mo 21. When Fred acquired his first shop after betting was licensed in the 1960s, he took the wagers and Mo kept the shop spick and span; they were always a team. Fred always said of their marriage that, 'Mo is a saint for having to put up with me,' but whatever Fred says tongue-in-cheek, you can take from me that they were one of the closest and best romance stories that I had ever come across. Then again my own track record wouldn't merit a Mills and Boon love story would it but it was so warming to see two people so devoted to each other.

But as nice as your life is, it doesn't exempt you from illness and like with so many happy families, the silent curse can come when no one is expecting and cause havoc. I'm not even going to give the disease credence by naming it but it affects most of us at some stage in our lives; we all have a friend or a family member who has crossed it's path. The pernicious C is no welcome visitor. They were talking about a cure for it when I was a young lad but very little seems to have changed in all that time; it's always maybe tomorrow.

I don't want to dwell on our mortality but Mo was diagnosed with it and Fred would have been devastated. Only people who had been together for that long would know the real pain and anguish along with the three daughters, son and grandchildren of course. We lost Mo in July 2018 following a brave and dignified battle against the unseen enemy. I was there for a beautiful service at St Mark's in Manchester and there wasn't a dry eye in the church. She was such a wonderful woman who I held very dear and was extremely close to. You feel so helpless in those awful circumstances but what could you do.

I decided unilaterally that I must act to try and soften some of the pain. No one could bring Mo back but maybe I could come up trumps with something helpful and unexpected. I rang up my old pal in Ireland, King of the Greyhounds, Dominic Magnone. He had 66 dogs so I said, 'Dom, pick me out the prettiest bitch with a good temperament, she must be able to run though.' He sent me back pictures of an unusual but beautiful bitch called *Lissatouk Snow* who was all white with some black markings. I knew straight away that this was the dog I was looking for.

I sent Dom the money for the dog and granted safe passage we were all set to rumble. Next step was an excursion up to Leyland in Lancashire. The day after *Lissatouk Snow* had been ferried across the Irish Sea I had renamed her *Mo Twentyone*, a change of name and hopefully a change of luck. She had been soundly beaten in four previous races in Limerick but Dom assured me the bitch would improve with experience and he was a man I trusted with my life.

Once in red rose country we headed for the kennels of ace trainer Pat Rosney and his partner Julie McCombe. The first thing they said to me was, 'Bloody hell Gary, we thought you were dead!' I had to tell them that rumours of my demise had been greatly exaggerated. We got Mo settled in. I had a DVD of Mo's last four races. But watching that they were both of the opinion that the bitch was a lovely dog but she wouldn't make the grade. I said let me worry about that, the dog is an improver.

The first trial at Belle Vue proved Pat and Julie wrong, *Mo Twentyone*, made the grading time so it was now time to inform Fred that Mo was back in Manchester. I'd put ownership of the dog into the "Mo's Family and Friends Syndicate" so I could take a step back, the job well done. It had all come together remarkably.

Lee Anne, Fred's daughter asked me, 'Why are you doing all this Gary? It's fantastic.'

I told her, 'Your Mum and Dad saved my life, without them I wouldn't be here today.'

I'd been holding myself together really well until then but a few moments after Lee Anne asked me that question the waterworks came on like a football pitch sprinkler. I retreated to the Gents to compose myself. It had been such a privilege to give something back and I really appreciated a positive response like that from a brilliant daughter. They had all been so strong as a family unit.

All winnings on *Mo Twentyone* would be going to the world famous Christie NHS Foundation Trust Hospital in Manchester. Mo had spent her last few weeks there and the care and love she got from the staff was staggering. I couldn't name all the nurses on duty but every last one of you are angels and in a cruel world, it gives you such a lift to see wonderful and dedicated human beings at work.

Mo Twentyone progressed throughout the summer and in her third race on September 9th 2018 she hit gold at Belle Vue. All the family were watching as she was put in the traps. Mo was more than quietly fancied at 9/4 and she came home in good style to win in a time of 28-56 seconds, looking a real nice prospect.

Fred actually went over to the kennels in Leyland with some family members and the grand kids to watch Mo in her home surroundings. He was there for more than an hour. I said afterwards, 'Why don't you take Mo home?' He was thrilled, it's the best thing I've ever suggested but no one knows more than me what it's like coming home to an empty house. Every night Fred gets home Mo comes to him, in theory Mo has never left and there is love in abundance. Fred has a new best pal and the dog lives a great life of luxury. It's a win-win situation and I bet *Mo Twentyone* appears on Betfred TV more than me and talks much more sense.

I class Fred Done and his family as close friends. His money is irrelevant to me, I can safely say that I have never asked Fred for a penny and nor would I; his friendship is more important to me than finance. He will say to me, 'Go and win a few quid son,' and that means so much to me, the humble son of a barrow boy who made a small fortune, lost a larger one and came out the other end intact.

Never the school prefect, I left with two unofficial A-Levels in Advanced Betting and Fish and Chip Shops of London. I saw more of the old bamboo than Dick Van Dyke when in those days the criteria was supposed to be "spare the rod and spoil the child." Well, Sir Rhodes Boyson, the headmaster at Highbury Grove School and later to be a right wing Tory MP, made sure I didn't get spared that much. The man was a maniac for corporal punishment.

The day I got reported as a 14 year old for absconding to the betting shop and getting an adult to put my bets on, I still remember like yesterday. Rhodes Boyson, his ridiculous, mutton chop whiskers bristling with indignity, gave me six of the best in front of the whole school. But I had the last laugh as there was a two-pound winning treble slip nestling in my pocket. Have that you big, bluff, bullying Lancastrian. I always thought for years that everyone was like that from the North West but he was just a one off. I don't know about the other kids but he scared the bloody bejaysus out of me.

Betfred is now the World's largest independent bookmaker but to listen to Fred, it's all in a day's work. The man is so modest, it's hard to fathom out how he is so grounded. He is as working class today as when he opened his first shop over 50 years ago. Fred describes his business as the Aldi of betting shops and that is where he has hit the nail directly on the head. Betfred gives value.

A lot of the major bookies today don't want to give anything away but on Betfred TV they have something called "Fred Pushes" where he picks out four or five favourites and pushes them out half a point from say evens to 6/4. He doesn't mind if they win, he doesn't care. He told me once, 'The people will punt with me for life.' He's right; you stick with the brand that gives you more or costs less. It will be a dark day if we ever lose Fred from an industry where his sponsorship is second to none.

I remember his finest hour was with Mo in the Cheltenham paddock, presenting The Gold Cup Trophy in 2015. He was willing to sponsor the most prestigious jumps race in Europe for years thereafter but someone on the committee thought racing was better served by having the cup associated with firstly a telecoms company with no obvious connection to racing then a cider company. That's all we needed, more advertising for alcohol. Why is racing selling it's soul to the wrong people? It upset Fred for a while and he said, 'If I can't have the best race what's the point?'

Come on Cheltenham; look after people in the racing industry. I'm sure Fred will get the race back but one thing's for sure, he won't lose any sleep over it. Fred Done; you are my friend, you are my mentor and you were there for me in my darkest hour. I love you and your family so much. May you enjoy many, many more years Sir; live long and prosper.

* * * *

Chapter Nine

WINNERS, VALUE, ODDS-ON AND LONGSHOTS

Arkle had the highest ever Timeform rating of 212. To put it into perspective; the brilliant Kauto Star was rated 191, truly amazing.

A few years after the gastric sleeve operation my surgeon told me I'd only had a 25% chance of coming through the operation without dying. He decided that as I was a betting man, he didn't want to worry me with the odds of coming through the procedure unscathed. Thank God he never informed me that I was 1/3 to die. Carpet odds on! I wouldn't have slept well the night before the operation knowing I was a heavy odds-on shot to meet my maker but it did prove to me that my theory on odds was correct. There are great 1/3 shots out there to be backed but sometimes a horse or individual is vulnerable, even at 1/5 or 1/6 or even 1/20.

Odds are only the opinion of people who see what they see and hear what they hear. A few years ago, it was solely down to a few experienced and knowledgeable bookmakers and judges of form but now Betfair rules the roost and most prices are determined daily by weight of money from the public with most of the major bookmakers offering prices just shy of the Betfair model.

In horse racing alone odds are affected by who the trainer is, who is riding the horse, the distance of the race, the draw, the going, the fitness of the horse and good or bad fortune in previous races. All these criteria can affect the price and, dare I say it, is the horse likely to run up to its merits or is it going for a canter round with no intention of running for a win or place? How many times have we seen horses doing all their best work after the winners are home and hosed?

When you have a handicap system for races, a few pounds off after a bad run or two never does a horse's future chances any harm but it's cold comfort if you were the poor sod who just backed it, vowing never to punt on the camel again only to see it hack up a month later against the same standard of horses it recently flopped against. I would recommend you take heed of the most famous line from the film All the President's Men, "follow the money." This isn't an exact science but betting stables put the money down when they expect their horse to win. On many occasions it will win but it can also come unstuck, indeed there might even be two or three stables in a race having a tilt; you have to read between the lines. I'd much rather see a shed load of money piling onto a horse I fancy than one drifting like a barge.

A horse that drifts doesn't often win but not always. Connections can have all their money on early or back their horse in bookie shops pre-meeting meaning that the horse is utterly friendless on course, which is exactly what they wanted to achieve; every point it goes out is pounds in their pocket. It's all part of the betting minefield and since horse racing began, it's why it has euphemistically and correctly been called "the glorious uncertainty."

These days I probably spend more hours in the betting shop than at the racecourse or dog track and I've made more money punting than taking bets for a living, especially in the last ten years. There are two important words that every punter should adhere to in VALUE and EDGE and if you have them on your side you will win again and again. But remember this; there is no guarantee in gambling. If you want a cast-iron guarantee, buy a washing machine from Currys. It just doesn't exist in the betting jungle which is full of wolves, hyenas and jackals and where if you show any sign of weakness, they will eat you for breakfast. It's strictly a poodle-free zone.

If you talk to professional punters, they are always looking for value in horses or dogs that are overpriced. The big bookmakers are nowhere near infallible, they do make mistakes and there are many anomalies out there but you have to put the spadework in with study, study and more study. Gary Player, the veteran South African golfer, once said, 'The harder I practice the luckier I get.' So get stuck into your formbook and scan your computer data on a daily basis and you really will surprise yourself on how lucky and competent you can get. Things can quickly fall into place.

Most pros work on a return of 52.5%. That's right, a mere 5% profit on all bets. It sounds easy but is much harder to do in reality. It's no good guessing, folk like Kevin Casey specialise on their thing (in his case foreign horse racing) but one can get involved in any sport be it snooker, golf or American Football. The world is your lobster as Arthur Daley would say; there are lashings of betting opportunities out there.

There's absolutely no edge at the casino or racetrack. In fact, if there is an eight-horse race with the jolly opening up at say 2/5 and the second and third favs priced up at 9/2 and 6/1 respectively and with all the rags at 20/1 bar; you'll be hard pressed to find many bookies on track going EW but it's an absolute gimme in the betting shop. It's a real bet to nothing backing the two semi-fancied ones EW with money back for second or third. It's surprising how many times the odds-on doesn't always run to form and it's invariably the next two in the betting who take the win. These instances are like buying money and you should look out for these opportunities in the high street bookmakers.

Bets I'd like to recommend amongst others include the Tote Placepot as this can pay huge dividends for small stakes and the beauty of the bet is you don't need a winner. All of you out there with seconditis, this is a bet tailor-made for you. It's not easy to win and you won't get it up every week but in my opinion the wait is worthwhile. If a few favourites have an off day then it regularly pays hundreds if not thousands, especially on a Saturday. The Quadpot is easier to achieve but if a few fancied ones have framed the dividend rarely gets into double figures. People who have gone down in their Placepots early doors can have another shy after the first two races have been run. Occasionally, after the odd day of upsets it can pay out a large dividend so don't let me put you off the bet but greedy old buggers like me gravitate towards the larger payback. You will harvest more returns consistently by backing in four races instead of six so the choice is entirely up to you.

The Lucky Fifteen is another cracker and full of value. It's basically a Yankee with an extra four single bets but it's a superior wager because if your first horse or dog goes down in a Yankee then you have already lost 7 bets out of the 11. In most bookies the Lucky Fifteen will pay out double or treble the odds on one winner so hypothetically, while one 5/1 winner on a Yankee returns zilch, the same horse in a Lucky Fifteen returns very nearly your money back. This can make a really important difference to your betting bank. How many other bets out there give you that sort of return for one winner out of four? It's one of my favourite high street wagers.

EW doubles are a bet made in heaven for the punter. Always look for races of around eight to ten runners with two or three strong contenders at the head of the market at prices of around 5/2, 7/2 and 5/1, then with nothing else really fancied, the next best in being around the 10/1 mark. Study the formbook; which of these will get the distance, go on the surface, etc. and all you are looking for is to get both your selections in the frame. Occasionally they will both win but getting two in the frame will give you a profit every day. Ten pounds EW on a 4/1 second and a 6/1 third in handicaps returns you £50, a nice profit of £30 and the second could have been beaten by 10 lengths. With this bet you win when you lose so long as both horses have finished in the frame. In the event of them both winning the profit would have been £340 for the win and £30 for the place giving you £370 with stake money back on top.

Always keep your discipline and don't back in every race. Carefully select races that give you an optimum chance of winning and never, ever chase losses; there is always tomorrow. If you think luck is going against you, come away. Devise a staking plan that suits your bets. DO NOT double your stakes every race on a losing run; that is the quickest way to the poor house or the mad house and lastly don't gamble with money designated for the mortgage or a rental payment, only bet accordingly with money that is disposable income. You can drink like a fish or smoke like a chimney if you like but what are your outcomes? Possibly a few more visits to your GP in later life but at least with spending your money gambling sensibly you will experience the greatest thrill of all; winning big now and then, going on holiday, buying a nice car, maybe paying off the mortgage. In this grey and stressful world, a nice winning Lucky Fifteen is the kind of good fortune that keeps us all ticking along. So, let's look at a few more sports that can give you all an edge for a profit.

I'm a lifelong dog man and it's hard to believe that 70 years ago attendances at the working-class tracks topped 35 million each year, only football was better attended. It has now dropped to present day levels of just under a sorry two million spectators per annum.

It looks like the only way to save the sport is to go for live, online streaming with the bookies. I'm sorry to say that, as a spectator sport, greyhound racing's glory days are sadly behind it. Why the demise? I just don't know but there has been a chronic underinvestment in the sport. Those huge London crowds at the tracks of my boyhood are a fleeting, distant memory. The sport will never die, there is too much money wagered on races but the on-course bookmaker is becoming a thing of the past as crowds evaporate and people preferring to bet online, in the comfort and warmth of their own home. I think the current number of around twenty stadiums is about right for the near future.

Let me mark your card on how I bet. You know I'm a forecast or reverse forecast man so I look for a dog that will lead and for that there is oodles of information out there in the racing papers and on the internet including a dog's fastest and slowest times, sectional times and even times to the first bend. If your dog can lead, he misses all the trouble on the first bend; the area of track where fortunes have been won and lost over the years. He might not always hold on but a fast trapper always has a chance. Perversely, I like to combine a speedball with a finisher; a dog that stays the distance as he will be doing all his best work in the second half of the race. He might get there, he might not but in theory I've got a leader and I've got a chaser and it's amazing how many reverse forecasts feature these types of dogs.

I rarely play heavy at Sheffield, Romford or Nottingham while Kinsley is a law unto itself; stick a pin in but I do like to punt at Crayford, Belle Vue, Hove and Monmore Green. You don't need to bet big if you are picking out forecasts, get one decent one in and it will pay for the night's entertainment. If you are playing to small stakes then back 1, 2 and 3 dogs in reverse forecasts and likewise 4, 5, and 6 dogs for twelve bets where you are guaranteed the winner; you then have two dogs against three for second place. It could also be the odd dogs 1, 3 and 5 plus even dogs 2, 4 and 6. You won't win a fortune but it will provide a fun night. So please everyone, support your local greyhound track where you can have a drink and a meal, bet with the track bookmakers or on The Tote and meet all your pals. It's still a great evening out.

Football is another good betting medium for a profit and I regularly play the bet, both teams to score. It does exactly what it says on the tin; if both sides get on the scoresheet in 90 minutes, you win. Avoid teams out of form like Huddersfield Town in their second season in the Premier League. They couldn't score in a house of ill repute. I know people who put on accumulators with eight to ten games involved and though the returns are great when they cop, they don't come in that often. My method is a little easier than predicting eight or ten full time results.

Another popular wager is under/over two and a half goals. If you don't consider a match will be open with plenty of goals, back under and you win if two goals or less are scored. On the other hand, if two attacking teams are playing, go for over which requires three goals or more to be scored. Top exponents of this are attack-minded clubs like Manchester City and Barcelona. There are hundreds of games played every week and your local bookmaker will price up any game for you.

Please don't forget the novelty and specials bets. If you know a good deal more about a local sporting event than the bookmakers who are pricing it up then fill your boots, it isn't a crime to be more knowledgeable. When aspiring goalkeeper Chris Kirkland was a young teenager his dad and a few good mates had a hundred quid on him to play for England at 100/1. It took over twelve years for it to happen but ex Liverpool and Wigan keeper Kirkland duly delivered, winning a lovely, ten thousand pounds for dad and co. He actually only played the once but that solitary cap was all that was needed to collect the dough.

If this sounds all too easy then let me put you on the back foot for a moment. In 2012 the African Nations Football Championship was being played while a young man sought to further educate himself. That day his student loan cleared into his bank account with the £4,400 that was supposed to feed, clothe and sustain him for all the tough months ahead. It certainly wasn't there to bet on the football. We've all been here though and with eleven minutes to go in a match, Angola were four-nil up against a wretched Mali team. In racing parlance, they were past the post. The lad wasn't shy at pushing his money out and the whole lot went on Angola at prohibited odds. It was the right bet at the wrong time. Mali pulled two goals back going into injury time but in the 92nd minute it was still 4-2, seemingly impossible for any team to get two more. But Mali did just that in the final two minutes, making the score 4-4. I know how he must have felt. He was extremely unlucky but until the referee blows that final whistle your money is never safe.

Who thought Leicester City could win The Premier League a few years ago at 5000/1? Not me for one. I actually heard a German punter won £45,000 at the last but one World Cup in Brazil, by backing his homeland in the semi-final against the hosts. He went for a correct score of 7-1 to the Germans. If he had put the bet on with me I'd have been questioning his sanity, so don't ever be scared of the longshot in a two-horse race; they do turn over the odds time and time again in sports like boxing, snooker and tennis.

A couple of pals of mine buy USA Today for the American Sport and they also trawl the net for information as some of the English bookies only pay lip service to all the great sport over the pond. Gary Selby me old mucker from the dogs knew his American horse racing as well as anyone I knew. There is money to be won on grid-iron football, baseball and basketball. A Canadian punter rightly chose all fifteen NFL results one weekend, staking 5 dollars and picking up $725,000; nice work if you can find it. In this shrinking world of ours it's worth a peek at what Uncle Sam has to offer.

Athletics isn't for everyone as, like cycling, it has a reputation for substance abuse but at the highest levels, the best athletes seldom get beat. Even at very short odds, it's better than letting all your money fester in the bank. Usain Bolt was a prime example, as was Mo Farah, who never lost a major race between 2011 and 2017. You could have made a living out of him and Frankel.

The toughest game of all though is boxing where in the old days the fighters took all the punches and the promoter took all the money. I'm happy to see my friend Eddie Hearn bringing back respectability to a sport that was once notorious for seeing old pros fleeced and discarded. I don't want to mention any name but hasn't that Don King got a wacky haircut? Enough said. It is still a great betting medium and a lot of the short-priced favourites win but one punch can change the aspect of a fight in seconds. In 1990, the Mike Tyson v Buster Douglas Heavyweight Title match in Tokyo was regarded as a near walkover for Tyson who was the undefeated and undisputed champion of the world. The Las Vegas bookies don't make many mistakes and had Douglas at 42/1 in a two-horse race but it all went tits up when Douglas knocked-out "Iron Mike" in one of the biggest sporting shocks in history. A reminder that we are all flesh and blood, no one is immortal.

Floyd Mayweather Junior is a huge punter who must be well on the way to billionaire status even after his stellar career has finished. 50 fights, 50 wins is not shabby at all and now he is taking on deluded cage fighters for millions but he still likes a wager as well. I think his biggest punt was in 2013 when he bet just shy of six million dollars on the hot favourites, Miami Heat basketball team to beat the Indiana Pacers in game seven of the NBA Championship Series and he won over 600 grand. It's a nice life if you can wager that much on a game of basketball but fair play to him, a legendary boxer who deserves every cent he made.

Do I hear the sound of leather on willow? These days cricket has become a popular way to make money and the shorter format of Twenty20 and one day matches have brought the game into the twenty first century with a bit more action and razzamatazz. There isn't much action in the county matches but there is money to be won on the international test matches. Most of the top countries are very hard to beat on their own turf as the ground staff will set the pitch up for major home advantage. Never wager a bet until you see who has won the toss; it's still a big advantage to be able to choose whether to bat or bowl.

Like in football, there are three outcomes and the shrewdies out there study the five-day weather forecast for the test. If the last two days feature heavy rainfall then the draw comes right into the equation so leave nothing to chance. The weather boffins are pretty accurate over a short period so just ignore Michael Fish if he says there's no chance of a large hurricane looming on the horizon.

One of the most famous punts on cricket was conducted in 1981 at Headingley, Yorkshire. England and Australia were playing the third test in The Ashes with Australia 1-0 up in the series and heavy odds-on to go two up. After both sides had finished batting in their first innings, Australia were 227 runs ahead and enforced the follow on.

At one stage England were 137 for 7 wickets. For all the realists out there that meant 3 wickets left, 90 runs behind with the combined might of the Australian team still to bat. Mission impossible had nothing on this as 500/1 England to win flashed up on a major bookmaker's advertising board; in my eyes, very mean odds. I'd have rather been at Rorke's Drift facing 4,000 charging Zulu warriors. The eyes of Aussie fast bowler Dennis Lillee lit up on seeing those odds so he got the team's coach driver "Geezer" to put 15 quid on for himself and wicket keeper Rodney Marsh who was also partial to a bet. The series has gone down in cricket folklore history as "Botham's Ashes" but England had a lot to thank Bob Willis and Graham Dilley for as well.

From that low point of 137 runs England managed to reach an unbelievable 356 with Botham scoring a ferocious 149 not out while Dilley batting at number nine scored 56 priceless runs and Chris Old at number ten added 29 more leaving the Aussies to score a paltry 130 to win. They would normally do that blindfolded but there was something in the air. Bob Willis, who was wicketless in the Aussie first innings, came steaming in like "The Mallard" but the Australian openers were playing within themselves and they scored the first fifty for the loss of only one wicket.

They must have put something a bit stronger in Bob's cup of Yorkshire tea during the break because he came back out like a man possessed. He was unplayable and Australia collapsed to 75 for 8. To be fair to Dennis Lillee who was batting at number ten, by scoring a gritty 17 he was trying his damnedest to win. So, it must have been foul rumour that as Willis ran in he was alleged to have said "come on you curly-haired, pommie bastard; just one more wicket." Bob duly delivered and clean bowled Bright to clean up the innings. England had won a remarkable match by 18 runs becoming only the second side in the history of test cricket to win after following on. Even though Botham got all the headlines, I think Robert Dylan Willis was the catalyst on the last day. His father was a big fan of Dylan but why would he name his son after the goofy hippy rabbit off the Magic Roundabout? Florence always used to do it for me so any younger readers here, just ask your parents.

England actually won the series 3-1 but there was a huge hoo-ha about Lillee and Marsh's bet that was alleged to have won them £7,500. Both denied the circumstances for years until Lillee published his biography in retirement where he admitted winning the money. I bet Rodney Marsh was over the moon about that, all he ever wanted was for the story to be buried away. If those betting patterns had happened in today's game there would be huge fines and banning orders, maybe even a life ban but back in the eighties the world of sport wasn't as money driven as today.

Has mega bucks helped some sports? The jury is out.

Darts is a game I make a living from. The scoring is volatile and a player's lead can disappear in just a few minutes but keep on the side of the good players. Van Gerwen is the man to beat now but Phil Taylor set the bench mark; he won absolutely everything and the Dutchman is trying to emulate him. Most of the top prizes are won by a few, select players. In the BDO events, stick with Glen Durrant; he's no spring chicken but is different gravy in that organization. The BDO weakness is that when a star emerges from within their ranks he is often head-hunted by the richer, glitzier PDC.

The player has to decide what suits him best; being a big fish in a smaller pond or taking on the great whites in the ocean. It's not unknown for players to suck it and see what's best for them.

"A good walk spoiled" was attributed to golf by our old pal Mark Twain but there's gold on those fairways if you know where to look. Golf tournaments are often won by players priced at 50/1, 100/1 even 200/1 and all of the big fields contain golfers who can play to a high standard but you have to find the players who are on form and can hold it together for four days. The big betting companies probably have only one or two price compilers for these tournaments so in every event players are overpriced, it's finding the right ones at the right times. There are numerous golf magazines out there giving form, tips and stats so it's definitely a sport to have a punt on with small wagers to win big money. There's one guy who bets on three-balls where bookmakers price up three golfers who are drawn to play together that day. He will choose certain threesomes and back the two outsiders so in effect he is laying the favourite but he has two chances to one. He looks for false favourites before making his move. I know he has won consistently season after season so sometimes you have to do an Edward de Bono and be a lateral thinker.

Gerry McIlroy always knew his son was going to be a great Golfer so when Rory was 15 Gerry wagered £200 that his boy would win the British Open within ten years. Nobody at the bookmakers would have heard of Rory, he wouldn't have even been on their radar so he got odds of 500/1. There would have been other admirers of Rory's talents at his local golf club but they didn't take advantage of what they saw. So if any of you see a young prodigy out there take a chance with a punt, the kid could be going all the way to the top. In 2014 at the Royal Liverpool Golf Club Rory McIlroy won The Open by 2 strokes. It was his third major and his timing was impeccable as it was the final year that Gerry's bet was valid. A nice touch indeed with £100,000 going to the proud dad whose son went on to be world number one.

Talking of Liverpool; I had an associate who was a Scouser living in Brownsville, New York for a few years. He was a boxing fan and hung around with like-minded Americans who told him about a local 14 year old who would be world champion one day. He clocked the name but never acted on it. Six years later that raw teenager was Heavyweight Champion of the World and Mike Tyson was his name. Even a £5 fun bet would surely have returned at least £5,000. Bummer.

Formula One is an extremely popular sport that takes place on every second Sunday between March and November. It's a betting medium to get your teeth into with about 21 races a season from all across the globe. The constructors' title has gone to Mercedes for the last 5 years and to Red Bull Renault in the 4 years previous to that while all the drivers winning for the last 11 years have either been German or British so that's a pretty good consistency if you are following past form.

Season 2019 has Lewis Hamilton and Sebastian Vettel installed as favourites again although Ferrari have moved up as second favourite behind Mercedes in the constructors' race. There are plenty of other nuanced bets you can wager on though including fastest practice lap, grid placings, podium finish, choice of tyres and how many finishers. Watch for weather changes too as some drivers excel in adverse conditions.

In 2001 one bookmaker offered odds on which Williams team driver would score the most points throughout the season in a head-to-head match, a proposition which I would liken to a serious novelty bet. Racer number one was the talented and proven Ralf Schumacher, not in Michael's class but a man who finished the previous season in 5th place. Racer number two was Juan Pablo Montoya who had come from the USA Indy Car Racing circuit; two totally different forms of motor racing, akin to each other as chalk and cheese. The bookmaker went 5/6 each the pair and was knocked over in the rush as people scrambled to get on with serious money for Schumacher. They quickly amended the odds to 4/7 for the experienced German and 6/4 for the inexperienced novice but still the money kept cascading in for Schumacher so they eventually had to bite the bullet and take the loss. A massive rick by the layers but mistakes can be found on most betting days, they are out there. Probably the only newbie in history of F1 who could have overturned those odds would have been Ayrton Senna but as he was God-like and a genius, he would have been the exception to the rule. If you think a sportsman is out of his depth, attack.

Richard Hopkins was a doting father who followed his talented son on the junior go-kart circuits. He hoped one day it would lead to great things but they kept coming up against this young kid from Stevenage who seemed to be on a divine mission to win every race he entered.

He had talked to the other kid's father and it was obvious the kid was heading for the top as all the big racing names were trying to sign him up. He nipped down to the bookies sharpish betting £100 to win £40,000 for him to win an F1 race before the age of 22 and £100 to win £50,000 to be world champion before the age of 25. Ultimately the kid did the business and Mr Hopkins had 90 grand in the bank thanks to the prodigy Lewis Hamilton. The old saying, *If you can't beat them, join them*, was never so apt.

Rugby League and Rugby Union are now huge, powerful sports on the television. Both codes have a marked advantage to the home team, similar to the football stats but the bonus is that there are very few draws making most games a two-horse race. A lot of matches run to form in rugby league but always get the team news before having a bet, it's a very tough, demanding and physical sport where a glut of injuries are not uncommon over a season. In union, the Six Nations is a good competition to bet on but study the home and away fixture list. The Rugby Union World Cup winners in past tournaments have mostly come from the nations of the Southern Hemisphere but the North is catching up. Ireland have a very useful squad at the moment and England and Wales are not that far behind and dare I leave out the unpredictable French. But the mighty All Blacks are still the side to beat; you can't beat a good old of Haka with a bit of tongue play.

Snooker is another of the sports where I bet and lay. There are no draws and its man against man so your opponent can't win if he's sitting in his seat all session. There are plenty of upsets and the youngsters are hungry for success while most are utterly nerveless and can all play. If there is a criticism it is where have all the characters gone? A lot of these young players are very robotic. While he is still playing and gracing the green baize, just thank God for the ambidextrous genius that is Ronnie O' Sullivan. He's deadly in the big tournaments like the World Championship, the UK Championship and The Masters but vulnerable in other events like the China Open. He has gone out of that in the first round four times out of the last seven so I don't even think he bothers going these days even though he has a billion fans over there.

So, before you put a penny of your hard earned on Ronnie in any snooker event check to see if he is happy and content or grumpy and morose. If it's the latter, be careful as Ronnie is a complex character who knows more about mind games than Sigmund Freud. He can go from hitting a ten-minute maximum in one tournament to losing heavily to a journeyman in the next. The man is an enigma. Barry Hearn me old mate, just keep him going old son; he's a diamond, maybe with a few minor imperfections but brilliant when he's shining. Long may he pot.

New balls please! It's not a sport I get involved with but tennis is highly popular on every continent and has a huge betting following. Again it is a head-to-head sport with certain players much better on certain surfaces. Most tournaments are played on concrete, clay or grass and a lot of players thrive on one surface though some great ones can play well on them all. If you are contemplating backing a player, have a look at his stats on the surface; it's the equivalent of soft or firm going for horses.

The women's game is hard to predict but Serena Williams is still kicking ass. Physically she is years past her best but she is a powerful woman, much the same as when Navratilova was too strong for most of her opponents. The men's game has been dominated for a decade by four musketeers, Roger Federer, Novak Djokovic, Rafael Nadal and Andy Murray. None are getting any younger and a new superstar will be coming through, maybe two or three so keep your eyes peeled. A lot of people make a living following the tennis and no doubt some matches are not always priced up correctly, especially in the early rounds. There are always plenty of good opportunities throughout the year for you to beat the book.

There are so many opportunities out there one doesn't have to even know anything about sport. Remember the novelties, politics, next Prime Minister, elections, Oscar winners, BAFTA winners, Royal baby names, Dancing On Ice, I'm a Celebrity (nice one 'Arry, King Of The Jungle, my mate, great man, Mr Redknapp, horse racing buff and one of our own), Eurovision Song Contest, The Greatest Dancer and The Voice to name a few. If you didn't know that you could win money watching your favourite show, well you can and it will add spice to your night's TV entertainment knowing your selection is closing in on the money for you both.

In football there is always a manager getting sacked from a club but you might have heard a whisper so have a punt; who has had a great sporting twelve months, get involved with BBC's Sports Personality of the Year, the lists are endless. I'm having a quid this book wins The William Hill Sports Book of the Year! Stranger things have happened, remember *Foinavon*? No? What do you mean? My bloody demographics are a lot younger than I imagined.

So you really can bet on practically anything. People have bet on what year the world will end, good luck picking up your winnings with that one; Aliens to be found, 1,000/1; Lord Lucan to turn up at Clackett Lane Services at 5,000/1 is a bit of a longshot. In 1995 a guy bet he would father a child in 2040 but he was 55 at the time! He must have had a Viagra upgrade. Somebody else has bet that Katie Price will be the next Prime Minister at 25,000/1. It's a shame she divorced him as Peter Andre would have made a fine Chancellor of the Exchequer. My personal favourite though was the wager made by a Glasgow Postman who must have come up with it posting letters in the Gorbals; it was his ticket to a new life of sun and sand. He got a million-to-one that Elvis Presley would fly a UFO into Loch Ness and hit the monster. Now there's a sight you don't see every day and who says the Scottish aren't optimistic?

Let's finish this gambling chapter with a guy who was a one off; a bit of a rogue, a bit of a rascal. He was meticulous in the planning of a coup; here was a man who had total commitment to emptying the bookies bulging satchels. Albert Davison (1938-2011) was a man of few words. I knew him on a nodding acquaintance with maybe the odd, gruff, 'all right.'

He was a man who didn't say too much and would seldom use a sentence where one word would do. Trusting nobody, the bookies never got to hear a whisper on any of his runners while the press and media were anathema to him. I kept his horses short, even ones with six duck eggs because on a going day they could leave that form miles behind and only one man in the betting universe knew when that bookie-bashing day was coming.

He was a horse racing trainer and professional gambler based in Caterham, Surrey. Even his staff members were kept in the dark as one observed, 'If he was about to land a decent gamble, not many would see the last gallop, he played his cards very close to his chest.'

These were the days before the compulsory overnight declarations of jockeys so Albert used to wait until the last possible moment before announcing his riders. His party piece was the each-way double which we heard about earlier from a certain rotund, good-looking talented bookie. He would run two horses in one day and if both placed, it was good profit, but if they both won then Bingo! You might even get a "goodnight" and a smile from him then.

Just before Christmas in 1987, at Folkestone, two of his horses Placed when *Prince Klenk* and *Matelot Royale* both finished second, the former at a price of 50/1 (equivalent to a 12/1 winner). That would pay for a bloody big turkey and plenty of roast spuds and sprouts that year.

Not a man to sit on his laurels, Albert had the same two horses out again on New Year's Day, 1988. He was obviously ready to rock and roll early doors that year. *Matelot Royale* had been entered into the 1-00 seller at Windsor where Albert had enlisted one of the few jockeys he really trusted in Dean Gallagher. The horse trotted up. *Prince Klenk* meanwhile was declared to run in the 3-30 at Leicester but Albert had bought a high speed motor with his previous winnings so he and Dean jumped in and sped to Leicestershire. It was a bank holiday so there was little traffic about and the deadly duo made it with plenty of time to spare. Gallagher mounted *Prince Klenk* and came home effortlessly by five lengths. I love it when a plan comes together. Albert actually talked to the press that day. He must have been taking his happy pills because the daft sod told them he was buying a helicopter to make journeys easier. I'd have loved to have seen him flying that in his ubiquitous flat cap.

But the race that really put the master plotter on the map and off the Christmas card list of many bookmakers actually happened a decade earlier and it was at Leicester again in the 1978 Christmas Opportunity Selling Handicap Hurdle. He loved that time of the year; he was like a selfish Santa filling his own boots. He was using two horses again but this time they were both running in the same race. He was planning an audacious sting on the unfancied horse; the five year old *Great Things* who was an animal with a history of leg problems and dire form. His last six races read 00/0-PP0 with his latest effort a week earlier when he was out with the washing in a Plumpton seller.

The two horses were declared for the race without jockeys of course. *Mini Gold*, a fair Plumpton specialist was at the foot of the weights while the no-hoper was *Great Things*. On the eve of the race Albert contacted the great Josh Gifford asking about the availability of two conditional jockeys. He puts forward Richard Rowe and Chris Kinane so Albert agrees to use them but doesn't say which jockey will be on what.

Richard Rowe, now a successful trainer in his own right, got to the track and went into the weighing room and suddenly Albert appears from nowhere asking him how many winners he had ridden. Rowe replies nine and then Albert asks about Kinane who had ridden four. Albert says, 'You ride *Great Things*, tell Kinane he's on Mini Gold,' and off he pops. Rowe looks in the Racing Post, sees *Mini Gold* is quietly fancied and *Great Things* needs a miracle. He swears under his breath; all the way up here to ride that plodder. Both jockeys go to the paddock but no horses and no Albert but then as the bell goes to mount up, the horses appear. As Rowe is nearly on the track, Davison comes through a crowd of people and grabs his leg, 'Don't bother coming back if you get beat.'

Just to make matters more complicated, a thick fog appears making things hazardous. Richard gets to the start and seeks out Kinane asking what his riding instructions were to which Kinane replies, 'To go as fast as I can, for as long as I can.'

So there we have it, one of the greatest coups ever attempted in British horse racing history with one jockey told to go like shit off a shovel and the other one gets a warning not to get beat. You could never say Albert didn't have his own style of doing things but it would never get in The Jockey Club statute book.

The fog soon worsened and with heavy going the conditions were terrible. The tapes went up and Kinane was off like a scalded cat; Rowe's horse was off the bridle after a couple of furlongs and he was rowing away. On the far side of the track visibility was appalling so Rowe hadn't a clue where he was in the race. Turning into the home straight he passed a few tailenders and his horse was starting to pick up. He passed a couple more and he was actually going better now than at any other time. Mini Gold led over the second last but he was out on his feet and he had taken other horses with him and much faster than they wanted to go. Coming to the last fence Rowe could see three horses in front of him but they were floundering. Great Things had them in his sights and Rowe got him up on the line though he wasn't sure he had won. Albert came over and said, 'Well done, I'll use you again.'

Coming from Albert that was like a 21 gun salute from the Queen; that was him being deliriously happy.

What everyone didn't know including the jockeys was that Albert had people backing the horse over in Ireland so on the course there wasn't a penny for him, he was totally friendless. Great Things returned at 33/1 and Albert was a rich man, winning about half a million in today's money. A few disgruntled bookies held the money back for a while but there was no case to answer so they coughed up. It was a brilliant training feat. Albert knew Great Things had one last race in him if conditions came right so for two years he patiently nursed the horse with bad pins for one last hurrah. The inclusion of Mini Gold was a stroke of genius. He was a decent animal who ensured a fast gallop leaving nothing to chance.

In his last two decades Albert fell out with the Jockey Club and had a bit of marital strife so the ex-wife made a few bob. He is survived by his lovely daughter, Zoe Davison who is now a very good trainer herself and nothing like Albert let me tell you. I hope I've done your dad proud Zoe, a legend and a real horse racing man.

* * * *

Chapter Ten

CHARACTERS OF THE RACE TRACK
(Angels and sinners)

The mechanical hare was patented by Owen Patrick Smith in 1912 and thus the sport of greyhound racing was formed.

As I come up to a pensionable age, I'm wondering is that all you really get from the government each week after paying in for 48 years? They really do spoil us. I can spot a good egg from a wrong un' within a few minutes of meeting them and I like to categorise them as Angels or Sinners. The angels will do you a good turn, even when it isn't in their best interests whereas the sinners will take the opposite standing; they will stab you in the back then twist the knife just when you need their help the most.

Some people never fail to disappoint but a good deed from somebody stays with you to your dying day. Thank God that for every single rotter out there slithering about in the long grass, there are ten loyal souls who will all go the extra mile for you. I'm going to name names, a thumbs up for a lot and a Caligula style thumbs down for a selected band of base, black-hearted individuals who put pain, angst and disquietude into my happy-go-lucky life. As most of you know from school, Newton's Third Law says that "for every action there is an equal and opposite reaction", so a bad turn should never go unpunished or as Big Gal likes to say, "he who laughs last, laughs longest." Through feast and famine, I've smiled, grinned, chuckled and guffawed, indeed the last picture of me scowling was coming out of a chip shop in 1979 after dropping a steak and kidney pie on the pavement.

That one still hurts.

ANGEL: First up is my great pal Tony Carroll, now a successful trainer plying his trade in The Vale of Evesham, Worcester. He's got a lovely set up, in beautiful surroundings and it's ideal for dual-purpose racing. Tony was my ex jockey when I had horses with the late David Wintle who we sadly lost in 2017. Tony rode a load of winners for me and he is flourishing as a trainer. If I need tickets or tips nothing is too much trouble. He is one of the game's nice guys.

ANGEL: Steve Cooke (Lofty) is my official driver and another of my close hombres who weighs in at about 24 stone. If Lofty, Gary Selby and I get together we can give the Roly Poly's a run for their money. He's a guy who has been with me through all the bad times. He actually did chauffeur work for other people including old pal Gary Newbon. I call him the chauffeur to the stars because for a period of time he was ferrying about Birmingham City and England legend Trevor Francis though he never got a tip off him, not even a pound coin. The first million-pound footballer must be saving up for a rainy day.

Roy Dotrice **OBE** was a different matter and the impressive, quality, classical British actor who recently passed away aged 94 used to put a twenty-pound note in Lofty's hand with a 'there you go dear boy.' Now that's the way to do it if you are reading this Trevor. And those were the days when a score bought you a lot more than four pints in the boozer as well. Roy's daughter Michele was probably better known than him because she played the ever suffering "Betty" in the long-running sitcom Some

Mother's Do 'ave 'em. I think Frank Spencer should make a comeback at BAGS, he might liven a few of them up.

Lofty has to be designated as an all-rounder because in the summer he used to drive an ice cream van for the Worcester firm Lannies. He had the prime pitch in The Malvern Hills and every Sunday morning he would have a queue half a mile long then every Sunday evening he would pay the office 80 to 85 quid. They would check the stock in his van and it always tallied. He frequently told them he'd had a bad day and when the manager asked him one Sunday evening why his takings for the last eight weeks had always been around eighty odd pounds, Lofty told them that he always served the same customers. They actually bought that and the answer was so good it bordered on genius.

After picking up the ice cream van at Lannies depot, Lofty would head straight for the cash and carry warehouse and buy 700 pounds worth of his own ice cream and then head for The Malvern Hills. The first 80 pounds of sales were for Lannies, then he'd sell his own gear. In my opinion it was one of the first great enterprise schemes in the Midlands. One glorious Sunday when the mercury popped 92 degrees, Lofty had to go back and forth to warehouse three times such was the demand for ice cream and lollies. They eventually smelled a rat and took him off that site which saw their takings rocket. Lofty was soon to become an ex-ice cream vendor, the cash and carry warehouse refrigerated section never recovered from the blow.

If you think Lofty was sailing close to the wind there, look away now. He used to place bets for bookie Lee Ibbotson on a Saturday and one Friday night Lofty was in a casino in Birmingham playing blackjack where he lost his £300 bank. He decided to play with some of Lee's two and a half grand that was calling to him from his car boot. You know what's coming next. He only lost every last shilling. All two thousand, eight hundred pounds had flown away and landed in the casino safe, all down to the turn of a card.

All he could do on the Saturday was stand Lee's bets and hope they all got beat, a long shot indeed as Lee was a very shrewd gambler. The writing was on the wall after the first wager, a £300 win and £150 place on a 33/1 shot. That would have been like a dagger through the heart when the outsider won. Lofty was another eleven thousand in the hole. That afternoon Lee Ibbotson got seven punts out of nine in, I bet Lofty felt suicidal. When stumps were drawn Lofty owed £21,500. He now had to phone Lee and give him the painful SP. That wouldn't be a call many of us would want to make. In fairness to Lee, there was no scream up and Lofty paid him back every penny in dribs and drabs and eventually all was right with the world again.

Lofty and Lee used to go on holiday together to Thailand. Lee had a dodgy back and used to visit a fantastic chiropractor there while Lofty would make a beeline for Walking Street in Pattaya where he would frequent the Sensations Street Bar for a few lagers and stiffeners. Then he would head to Beach Road, home of the iconic Hooters Sports Bar, for their wide-ranging menu of chicken wings before finishing the night off with some horizontal jogging. He would turn up at this local knocking shop which had a selection of 70 numbered table-tennis balls.

Now if you or I or any rational thinker hypothetically wanted to do this we would at least mull over the 70 runners and riders, checking over the current form. Lofty would just pick number 40 which was a girl called Sally. But sometimes she wasn't on parade so occasionally a ladyboy called Brian was number 40 and Lofty would wake up in the morning in bed with Brian. I'm expecting to see Brian and Lofty rock up at Funny Girls in Blackpool anytime in the near future. Sally must be broken hearted.

You've all probably sussed by now that Lofty lives in a universe almost all on his own. He won't use NatWest or Barclays, he has his very own Run Out of Readies bank; a guy called Darren Acton who used to own a cash and carry though not the ice cream one. When he is short, he pays him a regal visit and because there are no queues or interest, he prefers it to the high street banks. Trouble is these days the bank is rarely open. When Darren and his partner Scott Fraser see a Mercedes pulling up outside their house in Bewdley they know it's Cooky and quickly hide under the large kitchen table. They must have clocked his chronic flat-lining Experian credit score and decided discretion is the better part of valor.

In recent years Lofty was my regular driver down to the dog stadium at Sittingbourne. One morning we left really early and picked up my lad Danny on the way as I liked to take him racing whenever I could. Our plan was to catch a ferry, go to Adinkerke in Belgium and bring back about 600 quids worth of fags and tobacco before getting back in good time for the greyhound racing. All was going well as we parked up outside the supermarket but Danny being a tenderfoot abroad forgot what side of the road they drove on and got out the wrong side of the car. Forget about metric, a huge bloody juggernaut missed him and the car door by half an inch, it literally screamed past the poor lad. It was a bleeding close call and didn't do much for my nerves but Danny had the shakes. By the time we got back to customs he was convinced we would all be done for smuggling. He was in a right cold sweat, we actually had to get him some new strides on the journey back. I'm not sure he's a big fan of the European Union. Why can't they drive on the left like civilised folk?

Me and *Steve* had a lot of fun and adventures on the road to Sittingbourne dogs, we didn't class it as work. If we won, it was a bonus but food was always an integral part of the romp so we would leave Brum at 10.30am because Chummy's sea-food stall in Shepway shut down sharp at 2.30pm in the afternoon. There were fresh whelks, mussels and prawns but we usually had half a lobster each, washed down with two bowls of jellied eels. That was the best part of three score gone down our gullets but it was all about the food as well as talking a load of pony on the way down, not necessary about winning money.

On the way home win or lose, we would drop into Marino's chip shop for skate and chips while Lofty would always have a king-size chocolate bar for dessert; he had the physical constitution of a starving glutton. If we'd brought home as much money as we did extra calories over the years, we'd be world champions and multi-millionaires to boot but then again, we would have only spent our new wealth on grub.

One guy at Sittingbourne, Paul Vincent, was like a pro-punter and we couldn't beat him, no matter what. He was a well-known face about town and was always accompanied by his mate Kevin who ran a local boxing club. I don't think anyone ever gave them any grief as they both looked like they could handle themselves. It seemed like the only way you could beat them would be to clump Kevin over the bonce with an iron bar and probably then it was even-money the bar would break in two. I said to Lofty that we'd have to take them out for a slap-up meal to get them on side. We took them down to Herne Bay and by God they could put it away. It cost us a king's ransom but we became good pals after that and the other bookies were on the receiving end of their punts. Mission accomplished.

Curly Wilson would come over to us half way through the meeting and nine times out of ten, if he was winning, he'd ask us to join him in his local after the racing for a sing-song and a knees-up. We were right up for it one night as we'd won over two-grand and later on in the boozer were talking bollocks about buying a house close to the track to save on the travelling. I don't think we had another winning night there again for months but in our hour of glory we were going to become property magnates in Kent. A 10% deposit on a family newbuild down there would be forty-grand so we could but dream so we never became Kentish men.

Another night there in the pub we found out that the old boy in the corner had lost his beloved dog. So Lofty sidles over to the guitar player and puts a request in for Old Shep then the next minute there's forty inebriated, grown men singing really badly and out of tune, 'As the years fast did roll, Old Shep, he grew old, His eyes were fast growing dim, And one day the doctor looked at me and said, I can do no more for him, Jim.' The old lad in the corner was bawling his eyes out but I never found out if he enjoyed it or not.

Over the years I'd been in hospital a few times, mainly a few days or a week to sort out something relatively minor. Lofty would often visit, bringing with him a lobster; most people would come with their girlfriend or grapes but Lofty would turn up with a crustacean. I didn't mind, I was partial to one, the downside was the ward used to reek of sea-food afterwards. For example, I was having a six-day convalesce at the Spire private hospital in Solihull, the scene of my gastric sleeve operation. I'd been to see the head chef to set things up and so all I was eating was scampi. But instead of having the frozen stuff Lofty was bringing it in fresh every day.

Lofty came down one afternoon and realised there was an elite room-service so he was ordering club sandwiches and snacks like they were from the corner shop. The bill for food afterwards was three hundred quid but all I'd had was scampi and some soup, it was dearer than The London Hilton. He's like the visitor who brings you a bunch of grapes then proceeds to eat them all. It didn't matter a jot though, I was always glad to see him.

Another trip up to Scotland springs to mind with Lofty. We flew up as it was much better than all the relentless hours on the road and then we would hire a car from Glasgow to Perth. Once we were airborne over northern England, I asked Lofty where he had the money on his person; it's a sort of safety release valve question that always brings a pleasing reassurance when he shows you a big bulge in his raincoat (no Madam, that's not the front of his raincoat, it's an amply zipped pocket on the side. It's me he's flying with, not Brian). He tells me casually, it's in the luggage case so I said, 'Stop mucking about, where's the eleven-grand?' He really had left it all in the case and I felt as sick as a starving vegan who'd just won a year's supply of Cumberland sausages. It was odds-on the float was going to the baggage handlers' serendipity fund.

The rest of the journey seemed to take forever, like a long-haul flight to Dubai but after what seemed like a lifetime, we touched down and were the first to bolt down to the conveyor belt. I was utterly convinced it would all be gone, my faith in my fellow man wasn't nearly as strong as it had once been. We watched each and every bag and case come through like a surreal version of the conveyor belt in The Generation Game but we weren't arsed about any cuddly toy, we needed our readies.

It took an age for the bags to appear. It had already gone through my mind that a dodgy baggage handler had thrown our case and all the money into the boot of his car and knocked off early. That mad theory floundered into fantasy when our luggage came through right at the death. There were audible gasps of relief, every last note was present and correct. I'd falsely maligned those fine, diligent, upstanding men who dutifully look after all our property in transit but I made sure that I always carried the cash on trips after that. We were probably very, very fortunate to come away with a clean bill of health and our fighting fund for the races.

A lot of hobbyists like stamp collecting or trainspotting but Lofty doesn't go in for anything as banal as that; he likes visiting prisons, especially the car parks. Well someone's got to do it. He has now seen every prison car park in Britain, a proud achievement of his and one which I played a crucial, small part at the end. It was around Christmas time, there was promotional work to be done and I had to visit three Tote betting shops on the Isle of Wight.

Lofty got wind of it and he was like an excited schoolboy as the three prisons on the island were the last ones he needed to visit to have the full set in his locker. I think it was the best Christmas present he ever had as he took the wheel and we headed down to Pompey to catch the ferry. It just got better and better for Lofty as just in front of us was a big white meat van, rammed full of dour prisoners. Lofty was beside himself with joy, a stark contrast to the poor buggers in handcuffs who were going to spend all the festivities behind bars, far from home.

On the ferry we were having a coffee when a warden came in with a con who was wearing a bright, orange jump suit, Guantanamo Bay style. Lofty wondered where they were going, I said, 'Odds-on it's the gents, I doubt if he is going up the bar to buy him a pint and reminisce about old times.'

We arrived on the Isle and Lofty dropped me off at the first Tote bookies; he'd planned a route to take in the three prisons, Parkhurst, Albany and the now closed down Camp Hill. I was right in my element amongst the punters giving out presents to the loyal clientele of the Tote, scarves, wallets, ties and diaries; little things that made all the difference. There are more people who back online now than go in the betting shops, so we've got to give more back to the high street punters to get the shops buzzing again. It was a great day all round, Lofty had fulfilled a lifetime ambition and I had mingled with the wonderful racing public who really appreciated me having made the effort to be there. But I would have done it for nothing. Always a pleasure, never a chore was my motto and it was a warm feeling driving back home with fish and chips on the way.

Our crusades to Sittingbourne gave Lofty the chance to visit the prisons on the Isle of Sheppey. I didn't even know they existed but Standford Hill, Swaleside and Emley are clustered together so why didn't they just build one big one? That was another red-letter day for our intrepid Lofty but there was one dark episode when he was approached by two policemen outside the notorious Wormwood Scrubs. They demanded to know what he was doing loitering outside the prison for half an hour. I think they suspected him of being the ace getaway driver for a prison break but he responded with, 'Look at that car park officer, it's a beauty.'

Following that superb response, the cops immediately made him blow into the breathalyser but it came up negative, so they nearly detained him under the mental health act of 2007. You can't arrest a legend though and Lofty was allowed to go on his merry way with both officers eyeing him suspiciously as he sped off into the distance. Could you imagine Lofty turning up for Mastermind and being told by Magnus Magnusson, 'Steve Cooke you have two minutes on your specialist subject, prison car parks of Great Britain.' They broke the mould forever the day Steve "Lofty" Cooke was born. He reckons he's spent over a million quid in the bookies and at least as much getting lagered-up in his local The New Inn.

He's a man destined to go his own way in life, a trouper I'm proud to call my mate.

SINNERS: Tom Kelly and Jim Cremin. I've said my piece on them in the early chapters and I hate what they've done to me. I can take it bang on the chin any wallop that life throws at me but when it is outright lies then I can't let that go without recourse, I'm very emotional as I write this and do not want to go right overboard with anger and vitriol because life is too short to hate. I'm holding myself in as I regrettably regard them both as two pieces of filth for wanting to destroy me, my family and my lasting reputation with the British public.

Kelly, I thought was a friend until that greyhound bet. He had given me absolutely no inclination that he hated my guts before then but he was just biding his time with BAGS to blindside me and stab me through the ribs with his poisoned dagger. He had no qualms about trying to jettison my work and professional career into the sewer and for what? The Gambling Commission proved my wager was a winning bet, not a crooked one and the verdict was not guilty. Kelly was never going to apologise because he told me face-to-face how long he had been waiting to settle my score. I'm finished with him. If he has many mates, just watch your back lads.

Cremin was a friend for many years on and around the greyhound tracks. He was a capable journalist who knew the time of day. He actually rang me after the whole episode went around the betting industry rumour mill and I gave him the facts all *bona fide* but he preceded to write his own tissue of lies which were a crock of shit. He actually wrote that this incident could affect my job on Sky TV; that was the only true statement in his fabrication, especially when they unjustly sacked me.

When the Racing Post had to retract his whole report and apologise you'd have thought that he would have been the first person to ring and say sorry. I'd have begrudgingly accepted because to do that shows you are a man but the phone has never rung and even now when I see him, he looks away or turns to go elsewhere. Why would I want a friend like that? All the negativity from those falsehoods are not healthy so let's not waste any more ink on these sinners.

ANGEL: Stuart Clark the "Tater Man" is one of my very best friends and we speak on the phone at least two or three times a day. I first met Stuart when myself and Sharon were on holiday in Estepona, a lovely resort just down from Marbella at the very pricey Hotel Kempinski. I decided to treat Sharon to dinner one evening so we joined a small queue at the reception desk to book in. There was a right nimrod at the front of queue, whingeing to the young receptionist about the size of his bedroom quilt being too small to adequately cover the double bed. Whilst he was overstating his case, he constantly repeated that at 500 quid a night it just wasn't good enough. I could see by the female receptionist's face and demeanor that she couldn't give a rat's shit but his vocal tenacity eventually got him his bumper bed wear and the moaning Minnie triumphantly retreated to the restaurant much to the relief of everyone in the queue including my good self. It was akin to having constipation and swallowing a giant size bottle of fast acting Senokot.

We walked into the restaurant and the dozy *maître d'hôtel* only put us by the king of insomnia. For fuck sake, that was all we needed. He was with a very attractive, young, blonde lady and I thought he's punching well above his weight. Stuart was actually a horse racing man and he knew me off the television so I was warming to him by the passing minute. He asked me my general thoughts of the hotel; I told him it was a blinding gaffe but very expensive, you'd think that they would give you bigger quilts, my feet stick out the bottom. He was over the moon with that observation, 'There you see Ellie, I told you the bedding was substandard.'

I brought him down to Earth with, 'We were just behind you in the queue when you kicked-off, you daft sod. The cabaret isn't supposed to start until eight o'clock, leave it out.' He burst out laughing, he would do for me. In a quiet moment Sharon commented what a lovely father and daughter they were, I said, 'I'll give you odds of 2/1 they ain't no bleeding father and daughter, they're a couple.'

That would have been another banker bet I'd have won.

After the holiday we all kept in touch. Ellie turned out to be Russian but I don't think the vast travel logistics to St Petersburg helped their ongoing relationship afterwards. Ellie liked the finer things in life as long as Stuart was paying, she was higher maintenance than the Russian Royal Family and you know what happened to them. I'm sure Stuart stopped short of hiring a hit man and it just seemed to fizzle out like a lot of long-distance holiday romances. It was a good job really as Stuart's wife would have cut his balls off if she'd have found out.

Unlucky for lovely Ellie but lucky for the big lad. Like I said, we talk every day but not as much as Stuart does with Tony Carroll; he must bell him ten times a day, Vodafone would go skint without them pair. Stuart has been going racing since he was eight years old, he's the best paddock judge of horses and the fairer sex I've ever met. Top trainers at the point-to-point meetings will hang on his every word about their horse if he is asked to give an assessment and likewise Tony Carroll will bring out six to eight new, young horses in his yard to ask Stuart his opinion of them. He is rarely wrong with his evaluation.

I liken Stuart to a rural James Bond 007 as he leads a double life. He's had a helicopter, a private jet, property abroad, he goes skiing in France or Andorra and some of his lady friends have resembled Miss World, you'd never see him with a selling plater. Over the years he reckons he's spent well over a million on the high life, he spent 130,000 in one season alone. He says that his former life of living in the fast lane has come to an end and is a dead parrot. He is a reformed character apart from backing the gee-gees apparently but your Uncle Gal knows best, there's about as much chance of him turning his back on *la dolce vita* as nailing a blancmange to the ceiling.

His wife now has him where she wants him; on Saturdays he has to go to either the garden centre or shopping mall or even God forbid, muck out the stables. How long will the lad put up with that sort of malarkey? For about as long as I would contemplate bungee jumping off the Clifton Suspension Bridge.

The man has no money worries and only a few close friends as he's always suspicious of people's motives, especially strangers. I don't know how I got into his inner sanctum, maybe I'm keeping his potato business in profit with all my chip munching though I've never mentioned a Maris Piper or a King Edward to him yet. I think we just bonded through our love of racing; it's our overriding passion. If I go to the races there's no one I'd rather go with than Stuart Clark, especially if we are meeting up with the main man Tony Carroll. For two or three hours we can blissfully forget about the rest of the world and enjoy the racing and if we can kick a winner in then so much the better. I have many great memories with Stuart; my best mate, my confidante and a special human being.

ANGEL: Tim Brown is a good bookie pal and he's had a far worse time of it by a long chalk than any grief which has fallen my way. On the 22nd December 2016 he, his dad and a work associate were involved in a serious road accident when returning from a day's racing at Bangor On Dee to their home town of St Helens. Tragically, his dad Albert, a good friend as well, lost his life in the collision while Tim and Paul Sutcliffe were badly injured. It's been a long and hard road back. I know friends and family have rallied round for them and I speak to Tim frequently on the phone. He and his dad were brilliant bookies and I know Tim will come through this all the stronger. I'm thinking of you constantly mate, fight the good fight.

ANGEL: *James Hurn* is a welcome ray of sunshine in this dreary overcast world of ours. Once I was at Worcester races, doing my bollocks as per usual, when a guy walks over and says, 'Gary, I've got a car number plate for you.' Strewth! That was all I needed when I was groping around the bottom corners of my satchel looking for screwed up fivers: 'Leave it out mate.' I was a bit curt but it was the wrong time and place as I was well under pressure yet again.

A few weeks later he comes back with the aforementioned number plate and I was much more whimsical this time. I apologised for my lack of interest last scenario and enquired how much it was. James said and I'll never forget it, 'Who's talking about any money, it's a present for you.' I was knocked back by the kindness of a man I hardly knew and gratefully accepted his marvellous gift.

It read "P4Y GW" which with careful positioning of a black screw under the left-hand side of the four would appear as PAY GW. It was an absolutely blinding number plate for yours truly. This was a never-to-be forgotten moment for me and when I'm at Warwick races I always shake hands with James and chat to his wonderful family. It restores your faith knowing good people like these are all about.

ANGEL: *John Parrott,* my old sparring partner off the BBC was one of only a few to ring after my demise from Sky Greyhounds. He's a true friend, a true blue Evertonian and a former champion of the world at snooker.

He decided after a day at Ascot that he would accompany myself and Lofty to Central Park, Sittingbourne for a night of fun and frolics at the greyhound racing. As soon as he got in the car, he alluded that the aroma in the motor reminded him of his old chip shop in Formby. Well we did have a reputation, me and Lofty for enjoying a fine repast of fish and chips. In the back of the car were compartments for proper chip shop salt shakers and vinegar bottles, serviettes, knives and forks, sachets of red and brown sauces and wet wipes. John was amazed, he said we were professionals, Lofty said, 'We are better than that John, we are connoisseurs of the humble potato and the North Atlantic haddock and cod; dedicating our lives to ascertain the whereabouts of the perfect combination and our quest is ongoing.'

We partook in our daily pilgrimage to the chip shop that night, all three joined in unison; the cool, cockney kid, your man from the Midlands and a Merseyside legend and for ten minutes not a word was said as we beavered away. The silence was golden only for Lofty to break the spell with, 'I could murder a big bar of Cadbury's fruit and nut.'

Profound words indeed from the master muncher.

The former cue master is a proper pal, a very charismatic and knowledgeable presenter on a lot of sports and he has absolutely no edge to him at all. I hope one day in the near future we can team up at Auntie Beeb again and continue where we left off at Royal Ascot. My weight worries are strictly behind me because as you know, I'm only half the man I used to be. The partnership might be a good step forward for racing and whatever we were, bland and boring was never on the screen. I'll be seeing you soon, goodnight John boy.

SINNERS: George and Lee Irvine, father and son. I'd known George for over thirty years and classed him as a good mate. When the furore went up about my greyhound bets, George (who was managing director of SIS Betting) asked me to stand down for a while, get the all clear and come back shortly after. I know he was under considerable pressure from BAGS in the shape of Tom Kelly, which was understandable as SIS and BAGS had recently teamed up with Sky to transmit the outside dog race meetings.

Once I cleared my name and proved there was no case to answer, I eagerly expected George to get in touch but the contact never came. It was so hard to believe that I'd been given the old tin tack on the strength of lies, rumours and innuendo. I thought once I'd proven my innocence that things would return to normality but it looks like I've been the victim of a stitch up.

George's son Lee was my boss at Sky Dogs and seems to have conveniently lost my mobile phone number as well. Since my enforced holiday I've heard absolutely nothing from either father or son. I hope it wasn't a political decision to throw me on the scrapheap because I'm still out here trying my hardest and I've got so much more to give to greyhound racing. Could one of you two just pick the phone up please? If only to say how are you doing big man, it would be appreciated.

ANGEL: Michael Van Gerwen is a special sportsman and they only come around every twenty or thirty years. Phil Taylor had to pass the darting mantle over to him just as when cue man Steve Davis had to accept that Stephen Hendry was the new kid on the block. All the champions have a certain number of years in the sun, there is always someone younger and better coming through. Van Gerwen will have to take second stage sometime in the future but it could be a long time coming, such is his current dominance.

We all stay at the same hotels when Barry Hearn's Premier League Darts extravaganza is on tour. MVG often sees me and Sharon as he knows I'm the regular on-site bookmaker. He calls across in that unusual, mellifluous Dutch accent of his, "bookie family" then laughs out loud. I'm sure he thinks he's costing me a fortune but nothing could be further from the truth. I always keep him very short so when he wins, I win which is quite often. I still take bets for him for a nine-dart finish or the 170 checkout because to my knowledge he has never managed one or the other on my watch yet but the Flying Dutchman is that good, he could pull off both finishes on a going night. What fun that would be going home potless and shirtless.

He has an absolutely brilliant management team around him as well,

Jason and Will are super people who are very communicative and will always give you the time of day. So, Michael, far from being a darting sinner who causes me headaches, you are one of my angels. I'm always in your corner and if it's only for me mate, never get the yips, I'm relying on you son.

ANGEL: Barney O'Hare is the boss of the fabulous Bar One Racing from Navan, County Meath (just North West of Dublin) and a good pal. He invited me over a few years ago to promote my last book *Winning It Back* in his bookmaker shops and it was a real joy to witness and feel the warmth and hospitality of the Irish.

Lofty drove us over and we stayed at the main man's house. I had warned him there were two food fanatics heading his way but nothing was too much trouble. Barney is a proper person with a great family and his son Michael has actually been a racehorse trainer. While we were over Barney attempted a coup like his namesake Barney Curley and almost pulled it off as he got three in out the four. I won't forget my time there. Barney's a big asset to Irish racing and he regularly sponsors horse races, not to mention the mighty Crossmaglen football team. Another good guy.

ANGEL: Kevin Casey is one of the most extraordinary men in racing. A couple of these anecdotes might seem unbelievable but every word is gospel so strap yourself in, my old mate and bookmaker Kevin Casey is at the wheel and this is one helter-skelter ride you don't want to miss out on. Kevin has always been a ladies' man ever since I've known him; he likes women and they like him. It goes all the way back to the early point-to-point days when Bobby Warren used to shout over, 'Gal, Casey's found another one. Where's he finding them? He must be pulling them off the streets.' It certainly felt like that and at every meeting Kev would have a different woman on his arm. We were only jealous, most of them were drop dead gorgeous.

I lost contact with him for a while but about five years ago after I moved to Nottingham, we met up again when he was residing in Doncaster. He has two fine lads; 23-year-old Daniel who is a younger version of him and Brooklyn who is 12 and lives with his mother Andrea. So, I had found my old, true mate but I kept him away from Sharon; women were putty in his hands, remember.

Now that old adage, if you're lucky in love, you're unlucky in money is generally true but a lot of people including myself over the bloody years are unlucky with both. For most of his young life Casey was like a Ku Klux Klansman; he hadn't a racist bone in his body but he was a wizard under the sheets. There was a rumour that one night round at his pad the sex was that good, even the next door neighbours had a cigarette after. Not only that but he was one of the greatest judges of racehorses I've ever met, especially Arab horses and foreign racing. He is for the most part unbeatable in the bookies, they can't stand the sight of him. The fortunate sod not only used to get the girl but had enough readies to back it up with gifts of designer clothes and accessories before going night clubbing and ordering a huge Nebuchadnezzar of Moët & Chandon like it was budget dandelion and burdock. To be fair to Kev, he was a spender and South Yorkshire depended on him.

He is almost single-handedly the scourge of William Hill bookmakers. They have over 2,300 shops and Kevin Casey is barred from over a hundred. He has to wear elaborate disguises to get his bets on and he looked bloody ridiculous one afternoon walking in to a bookie in Batley dressed as a World War 11 Japanese Admiral.

His dad was a bookie and you could say he's gone from gamekeeper to poacher because he sold his betting shop in Town End, Doncaster in 2003 and handed in his bookmakers' licence in 2008. He's one of only a few shrewdies around who make money punting. There are plenty who claim to do so but reality paints a different picture, and he only backs in races where he has specialist knowledge.

One night at Fakenham there was a meeting featuring amateur jockeys riding Arab horses. Kevin who has always had a good eye for a promising jockey noticed one particular rider was head and shoulders above the others in style and horsemanship and this was confirmed when the aforementioned jockey got a horse up in a photo finish in a later race. He really had no right to get there but his talent pulled him through and so Kevin duly ringed his name in the runners and riders programme and thought to himself, I'd like to bump into that guy; there's possibly a nice little earner waiting. How right he was.

A week later at an Arab meeting at Wolverhampton while Kev was in the upstairs bar our jockey had a reversal of fortune. He totally misjudged his tactics and rode his mount a circuit too early but on slowing up after the winning post he noticed to his horror that all the other horses were still racing. He went after them and still finished second but the damage was done. Better jockeys than him over the years have gone for the finish too early, it's not quite as uncommon as you think.

The upshot was he was fined 150 pounds by the stewards which was not going overboard as a professional jockey would have been fined much more and possibly banned for a period of time. He moped into the bar later, his head down. Kev got into his eyeline and told him he was unfortunate and asked what he was drinking. He came straight back to the land of the living and extended his arm, 'Pleased to meet you, I'm Angel Jacobs.'

'I know who you are,' replied Kev, 'I'm Kevin Casey, me and you might just have some fun together.'

While they were chatting away, Angel revealed he was stony broke and couldn't pay the fine so Kev handed him 150 pounds, they were now bosom buddies. Throughout the rest of the evening they chatted about where Angel was racing in the next few months and was there anything Kevin could do for him.

Three weeks later Angel was riding at the Newmarket Town Plate meeting, one of the oldest fixtures in the world. He wasn't riding in The Plate itself, run over a distance of three miles and six furlongs but in a supporting sprint race of six furlongs. He was up on the heavy odds-on favourite which was owned by Sheikh Maktoum. I was actually there making a book and so was Kevin Casey who rarely attended this meeting, so I was surprised and pleased at the same time to see him there. It didn't look the strongest of races and the favourite seemed to have an outstanding chance on the form book. I was offering 1/2 on with some of the bookies going as short as 4/9 and I was considering joining them until I looked over at Casey's pitch where he was going a ludicrous 4/7 and he had a right queue getting stuck into that price. I was doing little business as there was no money about for any of the other runners, so I was quite content to twiddle my thumbs and watch events unfold.

A couple of the other bookies matched Casey's price of 4/7, I thought good luck with that then. Kevin had taken bundles at that juncture, so I was amazed to see him push the horse to 4/6 as another long queue quickly developed including bookies who had laid the horse at 1/2 and 4/7. They all thought Christmas had come early. A few minutes before the off he had the favourite at 4/5 and just on the off he took a couple of lumpy bets at evens, he was milking it for all it was worth. I pondered to wonder if the Maktoum horse had gone down to the start with three legs.

Casey was remarkably calm on his pitch, laughing and joking and counting all the money. I realised then the boy was at it, he had much too much horsey acumen to be giving charity to the public; that just wasn't his thing. The race had a tape start, with no starting stalls and as the commentator announced 'They're orf,' followed by, 'And one's been left at the start, he's at least ten lengths behind, it's the favourite.'

A huge, unanimous groan went up all around the racecourse, I'd not heard one quite like that since Cliff Richard began to sing *Congratulations* at Wimbledon after play had been rained off.

Angel Jacobs was doing all his best work late in the final furlong, a fast finishing fifth (try saying that after ten Stella's). He was beaten a good five lengths and there was no stewards' enquiry, no scream up and no room left in Casey's pockets, he was holding serious folding. I was a bit miffed I wasn't in on it, he could have told me as I was one of his best mates but then I realised for him to succeed he couldn't let the cat out the bag, loose lips sink ships. I consoled myself afterwards listening to the Leicestershire teddy boys Showaddywaddy singing Three Steps to Heaven on the racecourse and wished I'd have taken my brothel creepers for some fancy footwork on the dancefloor. Kevin had won well over five-grand on that race alone. He gave Jacobs a monkey and he was over the moon but there was still more to come. They would soon be returning back up to sunny Yorkshire where Kev would be invincible on home soil. All you Northern mums lock up your daughters now.

The equine circus was next in Beverley for the Bollinger Champagne Challenge Series for Amateur Riders. Our little maestro could go clear as the leading rider if he won on this day as he had ridden four winners previously, so he could go nap here. Casey was taking no chances with his golden goose, so he flew him up to Yorkshire where Angel was riding a horse called *Gymcrack Flyer* trained by Gordon Holmes. Casey knew from experience that the Holmes yard wasn't well known for having a stable punt and Holmes' normal bet was only around a score.

Angel later reported back to Casey that the governor had placed a bet of five hundred each-way on his steed. That would do just dandy for our Kevin so he quickly got to work, visiting a multitude of betting shops where he kept his bets fairly low so as not to set off any alarms. *Gymcrack Flyer* was available at around 11/2 and Kevin got more than enough on for satisfaction. The big coup was ready. On the day of the race, Casey gave Angel his instructions, 'You know, I repeat, you know, you must finish in the first three.'

Angel was blasé about the whole outcome, 'Kevin I shall win on the bridle, relax, man.'

The jockey was as good as his word as *Gymcrack Flyer* trotted up doing handstands and Casey had taken the betting shops for £28,000. No wonder people were beginning to call Angel Jacobs the "Cashpoint on Legs." All in all, it hadn't been a bad day at the racetrack.

Kevin gave his favourite jockey a bag of sand, a slap up meal at the Wok So Ever Chinese restaurant and a wardrobe of designer wear from a boutique in Bawtry. He even drove Angel back to Ely where the jockey lived with his wife Lisa and young son. Little did either man know on the trip back down to the flats of Cambridgeshire that they had reached the watershed of their association.

Going back to the Beverley winners' enclosure there was a doubting and suspicious Peter Murphy (husband of Sandy Brook, Secretary of the British Amateur Jockeys Association) who had hired a professional photographer and he was in amongst other media cameramen snapping away at a beaming Jacobs. The mug shots would be sent to interested parties in America.

The photographs fell onto the desk of Dick Milburn, Secretary of the Amateur Riders' Club of America and he validated that Angel Jacobs was actually Angel Monserrate, a banned American professional. The game was now up, the race was run, the murky pond was now crystal clear.

From that moment on things would never, ever be the same again, the good times would dissipate into memories and events would turn decidedly Pete Tong, especially for Angel who was about to experience a world of pain. Even Kevin Casey was utterly astonished when the bitter truth came out and shocked the whole British racing establishment. Porkies had been told on a grand scale to our equine masters and they certainly didn't like it up em.

Angel Jacobs had taken his wife's maiden name for in reality he was an American pro-rider who had been banned from racing for failing a drugs test. Even then he wouldn't take no for an answer as he adopted the name

Carlos Castro (a well-known marathon runner) and moved to the other side of The States where he carried on as an amateur jockey on the tracks of the Eastern Seaboard. He was eventually sussed out at Aqueduct Races in New York, arrested, handcuffed and taken out of the arena. After which he fled to England where he lied about who he was and wilfully forged his signature. It was only a matter of time before the cat was let out the bag as several investigative journalists had been on his case for a few weeks.

If Angel had been a run of the mill jockey, who knows how long he could have got away with the con but he was miles clear in the Bollinger Series and he rode like Steve Cauthen. He had even started to perform Frankie Dettori dismounts after he won a race for fuck's sake. No surprise a lot of racing people were eventually standing up and taking notice of his riding prowess, he wasn't actually your shy and retiring type was he. This was all months after the entrepreneurial Kevin Casey had spotted his vast potential; first is always first, second is nowhere.

The timing couldn't have been better for The Jockey Club as Angel had been booked to ride a horse for Her Majesty The Queen which was favourite to win the Moët & Chandon, Silver Magnum Cup over one and a half miles at Epsom. The race, also known as the Amateur Derby, is a top class and prestigious race. Could you imagine the hullabaloo that would have gone around the world in an instant if Angel had brought The Queen's horse home? A banned professional jockey who had a penchant for drugs riding a winner for The Queen. It was only hours from happening.

Once the story broke the press was camped 24/7 outside Angels' house in Ely so he phoned Kevin for advice. Casey told him to put Lisa and his boy into the motor and get up to Doncaster sharpish which is exactly what he did and they stayed for a fortnight at Kev's gaff. He fed and looked after Angel's family. The News of The World reported that Angel had gone back to America but he was lying low up North, waiting until his hearing with the Jockey Club. Meanwhile, the racing correspondent Claude Duval,

The Punters Pal in The Sun, ran a big story on Angel; he was on the lips of everyone in the racing industry.

The fateful day came at the Jockey Club in Portman Square where he was handed a ten-year ban. For a 29-year-old jockey that was a career breaker. He told the hearing that all he ever wanted to do since he was a poor young boy in Puerto Rico was to ride horses but he had gone about it the wrong way. He returned to Ely and found work in the catering trade but he eventually went back to America where his story took another downturn. One evening he was driving under the influence of drugs, had an accident and killed a passenger. At one stage he was on death row. Kev is trying to find out when his release date is, he is going to stand by him and help him out financially which I think is commendable. A promising life and career in tatters; it's amazing how many talented young men never attain their sporting dreams.

So sadly, one half of the deadly duo was in the slammer but that still left the Casanova of Castleford on the loose in this green and pleasant land. He had in his locker, as a bookie, one of the most outrageous ploys ever devised; one could only stand back and admire the sheer brilliance and audacity of it all.

On Arc de Triomphe day at Longchamp in Gay Paree, Great Britain wasn't just represented by runners, riders and trainers; they also had a bookie on number one pitch. What's that? Pull the other one, you can only bet on the tote in Paris. Well, my little vol au vents, that was before Kevin Casey and his team turned up and they stood opposite the winning post, right next to the French President's box. You couldn't make this up could you. Sometimes the queue was 50 metres long and the winnings at the end of the day regularly topped ten grand.

These events were reported for eternal posterity by Racing Post writer The Dikler who recalled, 'I spotted an English bookie and clerk taking more money than the Pari-Mutuel and they had longer queues than Tesco.'

Well "quelle surprise," it was only Monsieur Kevin and his crack band of lovable mountebanks. This went on for 25 years and in all that time they never got a single pull. There were a couple of handy hardmen on the payroll but they were never needed. The betting exchanges and online punting finally made the expedition unworkable but I think it was Britain's finest hour in France since Agincourt. Henry V would have been so proud.

Kevin now makes his living following the horses abroad and he says his days of chasing the women are over. His biggest regret was being young and foolish and losing the love of his life, his first wife Janet Casson (that's Kevin's real surname incidentally, Kevin Casey was his official bookmakers name).

Quite recently he split up with a nurse from Worksop, Susie Green whom he genuinely loved and it hurt him hard. He reckons he is now a happy singleton but don't you believe it. He's fifty-five, looks a decade younger, has a flash lifestyle, cologne, the clothes, the image and the next time we meet up he'll likely have some more eye candy on his arm. The man is mustard. His brother John Casson went over to California 25 years ago and became P.A. To Rod Stewart. In recent years he's performed the same duties for Paula Abdul and has become a multi-millionaire, living the American dream. A bloody talented family, it makes you sick.

Kevin Casey, you are a one off, a throwback to the good old days, one of the last great characters on the racetrack, a man for all seasons. We go back many years and we are still both out there. God bless old chum, meet up soon.

ANGEL: Guy Chadwell, is another good egg. Guy was in charge of Totepool in southern England and he worked at Betfred for over a decade before becoming Head of Betting at Ascot Racecourse. Three years back he contacted me with an offer. He needed one bookie to stand on the inside of the track (on the heath) for the Tuesday to Friday of Royal Ascot. It was mainly for the young mums and kids, it was a sort of ladies republic - with bets.

Over the last three seasons I've made some good friends. The ladies and yummy mummies bring me sandwiches, quiche and chicken wings, and it's great to see the kids having a whale of a time. I don't take a lot of betting money but I really enjoy going, it's something different and a lot less stressful than 1996 when Frankie went berserk. Guy has been a breath of fresh air since his appointment; he is very considerate to the on-course bookmakers' plight and nothing is a chore to him so long may he reign there. There's even been a sign installed on my part of the heath saying, 'This is a Kevin Casey free zone, keep out!'
Too bloody true.

ANGELS: Mark and Rosie Lowther are two really close friends of mine. I've known Mark since the Milton Keynes Greyhound Stadium days when he had dogs with Terry Dartnall. He is also keen on horse racing, mainly jumpers with Buckinghamshire trainer Phil Middleton who hasn't got many but the ones he has are quality. Mark and Phil often go to the races in a helicopter.

Mark and Rosie have a box at Ascot and I've been privileged to be invited. They are such fantastic, generous hosts; it will never be forgotten by me. I wish I'd have been up there in 1996. They both love their dogs and sponsor The Lowther Stakes and Eclipse Stakes races at Nottingham Greyhound Stadium which is a release from working at MSCM ltd, High Wycombe where they manufacture pumps and compressors. Work hard, play hard makes for happy families.

Recently myself and Sharon were invited to their box at Colwick Park; It's our local track and the Lowther's have been steadily pumping in prize money over the last few years, so they are very well thought of. The stadium is brilliantly run by Rachel and Nathan Corden who took over from their dad, Terry. They've worked so hard and the hospitality is second to none.

A good night was had by all and the highlight was a novelty race which Star Sports sponsored and made a book on. Remember me saying earlier that nothing good ever comes off these novelty bets, well lightning was about to strike again. Half a dozen guys were lined up for a one lap race and there was one fellow down on the track, Mark Pierrepoint (no relation to the hangman Albert, who wouldn't have hung around for this, sorry) who must have been 24 stone. He'd been backed in from 14/1 to 1/4 on. He had just the sort of physique and conditioning you need for sprinting, ten stones overweight and six big nights a week in The King's Head. He looked a natural runner.

They were off and the big man dashed away from the field. I didn't see that coming, not many did. He was shirtless and at the start he was lilywhite but half way round he was a rose wine pink and coming down the final straight he was redder than a sunburnt lobster. Surprise, surprise the rest of the runners were not gaining on him (most of them had backed him) but he took an age to fall over the winning line. He was nearly crawling at the end, he collapsed onto the floor like a winded, one-lunged baby elephant taking in huge gasps of air. Sharon was getting very excited next to me, she must have got aroused by all that wobbling flesh, flashing home to victory. I thought to myself it could be a good night when we get home but no such luck. She actually thought he was going to die after his exertions and she wanted to sell his relatives a headstone.

I'm all for the entrepreneurial spirit but I think her timing was slightly out. Five minutes after his heart stopped, I wouldn't have thought his mother would appreciate being asked, 'Do you prefer black marble or white Italian alabaster?'

Still it's the thought that counts. Sharon does bring her work home, she often tells me I would look lovely in mahogany and keeps showing me ads for burial plots in Undertaker Monthly. I keep telling her that's the last thing I need but she never listens.

So, thanks again my last two angels, the wonderful Mark and Rosie Lowther. We've had a lot more angels than sinners to sift through; one lot are surely going to Elysian Fields while a few lost souls are heading for the fire and brimstone of Hades. I'm sorry but you brought it on yourselves. When you mess with Big Gary you lose your very last chance of righteousness and redemption.

As Belinda Carlisle sung so sweetly, "Heaven is a Place on Earth," and it's always best not to argue with Cumbrians and redheads.

* * * *

Chapter Eleven

TO INFINITY AND BEYOND

Michael Dickinson sent out a record 12 winners on Boxing Day in 1982 as well as training the first five home in the Cheltenham Gold Cup

So that was the last half decade, all neatly chronicled for future generations of betting aficionados. It was a trifle unorthodox I must admit but I eventually came through it on my own terms, ready to reach the next level and hopefully on a steep, upward trajectory. I had some close scrapes: it was that bad a few Christmases back, that when I opened the first door on the Advent Calendar there was a bloody bailiff behind it. Talk about can't pay, we'll take it away. I had bugger all apart from Sharon and they wouldn't want to mess with her, believe me; within half an hour of meeting her they'd be giving her their dinner money.

I'm ready for my big betting comeback. If Dick Van Dyke can make a return starring in the new Mary Poppins film, there's hope for us all. I'm still a relatively young man compared to Tricky Dicky, he must be at least 126 years old. When I watched the original, I was wearing short trousers and eating ice cream from a tub, thinking to myself who's that geezer up there with the worst cockney accent in the history of film making.

The last part of my life has had some incredible highs and jaw-dropping lows. I don't think I will ever get over Sue walking out on me, it was like the ultimate betrayal of trust. I'm extremely happy living with Sharon and Jaimee but I still have horrible flashbacks to when the divorce proceedings started against me.

I parked up in Birmingham city centre and walked up to the divorce courts like a man in a trance. I'd been dreading this day. In my own, addled mind I wasn't accepting the situation and thinking maybe I could I get a last-minute reprieve like an innocent lifer on death row; maybe it was all a sick joke by Sue, she did have a strange sense of humour. Once inside, the enormity of the day hit me. In less than an hour I would be a single man again, the marriage legally annulled. I clocked Sue with her legal brief. He must have been the shortest solicitor in the Midlands as he came up to her elbow; he was obviously the best man for small cases. He looked me up and down as if I was a piece of rancid offal that he wouldn't feed his starving dog with. Here was a man who didn't like to waste time, he'd taken an immediate dislike to me.

We sat at opposite sides of a large table, the learned brief and myself on port side with Sue and Uriah Heep on starboard while the lawmen went at it hammer and tongs, running down each other's positions. After ten, facile minutes I'd had just about enough, I felt like flinging Sue's bloke through the sash window. It was only three floors up, he'd probably survive but murder through fenestration wouldn't have looked good on my CV. I wanted to scream, 'STOP! Come on love, let's just walk out.' But I let the day's procedures slowly amble back to normality. Sue wasn't asking for anything unfair or extravagant, it all went 50/50 and finished quite amicably.

Sue was gone in what was probably the worst day of my life. The whole episode could have destroyed me but I wouldn't let it; I had to stand strong even though little segments of it will stay with me forever. A last, clear caveat to finish this sad episode of my marital struggle was that while she was with me, Sue had her own small horse yard and gallop. She paid a guy called Martin 20k to upgrade the plot with some digging and building and they are now an item. Am I a man who is bothered? Not likely - six years has come and gone. Time is a big healer. One day I hope I can sit down with Sue and her partner and share a nice big magnum of Dom Pérignon rosé champagne. Sue and myself were together for over twenty years, and every time I look into my adorable grandson's eyes - little Frankie Wiltshire - I can see Sue in there.

What decent people do is look after their own like when an old pal of mine, Phil Briscoe the owner of Severn Sports and Leisure (a fishing related company) was going through a tough patch. He'd been divorced and he wasn't involved any more in a big fishing tournament that he had founded called the Maver Mega Match. He contacted me about a new £60,000 competition called The Golden Reel which would commence in 2017 at his home fishery of Larford Lakes, Stourport-on-Severn. I told him to count me in. He'd been very loyal to me, it works both ways in my opinion, so I wanted to reciprocate as much as possible.

Phil is a top man; a real diamond and his brainwave has really taken off in record time. Apart from having me there as the celebrity bookie, he has an 80-seater cafe and a new static caravan site for people who are serious about their fishing. The Angling Times and Colmic/Bag'em tackle are busy advertising and sponsoring the great new event so it looks like this one is heading north of the stratosphere.

The night before the big day, Phil puts up all the finalists and myself in a local five-star hotel where everyone enjoys a fantastic gala dinner as well as the important grand draw for pegs; the positions on the lake bank from where all the anglers must fish. It certainly isn't easy to predict if a high draw or low draw has any advantage but a few hours into the competition and the more skilled front runners will always emerge from out of the pack.

All the angling action commences at midday and they fish for five long hours. My step-son Liam comes down to give a hand and he's another who loves his nosebag so he brings a huge packed lunch in case I get the munchies in the closing stages of the afternoon. In 2018, the fifty-grand was won by the talented Andy Power from Wells, Somerset who I had on my side as he's a dedicated, young, prolific match-winning fisherman. Bring out the cider is what I say. So, cheers and big-ups to fab Phil, my old playmate. I will see you again at this year's final; I wouldn't miss it for all the tea in my Regency rosewood sarcophagus caddy.

As a probationary angel, I have to confess on a couple of occasions betting that I have erred on the side of the sinners; once as a young lad and once as a bookmaker trying to make my way in the world with not a lot of back up. My ten Hail Mary's were duly delivered with head bowed low and hopefully right after with a new clean sheet to go forth morally amongst the pure and righteous.

The first transgression was alluded to in *Winning It Back*. Mum and Dad had a caravan on Combe Haven Holiday Park which was literally only yards away from the where the Battle of Hastings kicked off in 1066. It wasn't widely reported back then but William the Conqueror had a serious dearth of good archers, so they were head-hunting right up to the day they sailed across the English Channel.

The Master at Arms took three late arrivals through their paces. The two bigger men were expert archers and were hitting their targets with great aplomb but the smaller guy was spraying arrows all over the Normandy coast. William met his skilled assessor later that day to enquire about the standard of the three new bowmen and the Master of Arms confirmed that the two large archers were top rank marksmen but he added that they would have to keep a close watch on the smaller one because that clumsy little bleeder will have someone's eye out.

Fascinating stuff, history but I was down in Sussex to win a few bob on the weekly camp Donkey Derby. We were staying there for weeks so I got to know the van driver Robin very well as he used to transport the donkeys in from Romney Marsh. I had previously noticed that two of the same eight donkeys they used every week were like *Shergar* and *Mill Reef* compared to the other six. Robin would mark my card each time because they all looked exactly the same and just to be on the safe side, I had this thick, industrial yellow crayon with which I would draw a cross on their rumps though you could only see it if you were really looking. There was a ten-shilling tote up for grabs and it was extremely rare for *Shergar* or *Mill Reef* to get beat. If a jockey was carrying a bit of overweight it could affect the result but I won race after race down there. Robin always made sure the two speedster donkeys never raced against each other as well. For this he was very handsomely rewarded each week with a large box of fruit and veg that Dad had brought down from the market. I used to go home after the holidays with my pockets stuffed with cash and Robin's family never contacted scurvy or missed their five a day healthy option. Happy, happy days in the sun.

Years later as a fully-fledged bookie but with a brood of ankle biters to feed, I lapsed again; I'm only flesh and blood at the end of the day. This was the only time on a racecourse that I chickened out and waved the white flag.

It was at Leicester Races as per normal and a quiet day saw me a few bob down after the first two or three races. I noticed a helicopter coming to the course from the east, over the old county of Rutland. I wondered, was it an owner, a trainer or jockey as a lot of very rich people travel to events by chopper. Why sit on the motorway half your life if you can afford to go up and over in a fraction of the time. That said, small planes and helicopters have a much larger accident percentage than major commercial airlines so if I had that much wonga, I might just stay down on terra firma.

The point is, small planes and choppers are not uncommon at the races, especially the big meetings but to fly in halfway through an afternoon's entertainment meant only one thing; the passenger in that helicopter wasn't coming to have a day out, he was there on serious business. As soon as he alighted from out and under the whirling rotor blades, I clocked who he was. It only the multi-millionaire, ace racing man, Michael Tabor; owner, shrewdie and large gambler. The man was not often a charitable friend to all us on course bookmakers, in fact Ladbrokes had just started to knock back his bets, such was his prowess. It didn't bode well for later.

I knew what he was there for as he had a runner in the last race which was a three-horse affair and I fancied the pants off the Neville Callaghan runner myself. It only confirmed my suspicions that his nag was going in. Tabor had excellent horses with Neville, the best probably being Danehill Dancer who won a few big races but is definitely better known for being a champion sire in Britain and Ireland. If that horse covered your mare, you absolutely knew that there was a very good chance of making a choice profit with one of his next generation.

As luck would have it, he decided to have a couple of lumpy, fun bets with me in the fourth and fifth races. A fun bet for Michael was anything just shy of five-grand and his selections both got beat. There would be a serious wager going on in the last race, for the time being he was just mucking about. I had decided the minute I saw him walking from the helicopter to the grandstand, that a certain bookie wouldn't be staying to partake in the sixth race, the money I had taken off him up to that moment I saw as irrelevant. I paid out the last of the punters who had bet on the winner in the fifth then I said to the clerk, 'Fuck this, grab all the gear we're off.'

Steve Ovett would have been proud of the way I glided from racecourse to car park in less than four minutes, mission accomplished.

Nostradamus had nothing on me as Tabor's horse turned the last race into a procession. He had got multiple bets on and I could even hear the bookies audible wails in the escaping motor when we were bloody miles away. Sometimes you just know this or that might turn sour; I'd had a grave, foreboding feeling about the last race. I'd never done a runner before that or since that day but my money and loyalty was to my family. Tabor wasn't a loser on the race so what did he care?

Well, I bumped into him at Sandown a few months later and he gave me both barrels; it was a right dressing down. I just had to take it, standing there like a contrite schoolboy. I was going to bring up the fact that when he owned the bookmaker chain, Arthur Prince I had been knocked back more than a few times trying to get 50 quid on a dog but decided to let it ride. Michael Tabor is a contemporary legend in the racing game. We still speak so there are no hard feelings. When he's not horse racing, he divides most his time between his homes in beautiful Barbados and Mediterranean Monte Carlo. He's grafted all the way to the top from humble beginnings in the East End, London and is another Great Brit who shows success is still out there for a trier.

Nobody said all aspects of life are easy. I remember back to South Ockendon when myself and Phyllis were attempting to climb the ladder of success and we'd only just got on the first rung with our first decent sized council house. We didn't know anybody in the area, it was just us with young kids against the rest of the world. I'm not saying the town was rough but the local Tesco was selling Father's Day cards in packs of five. After clocking that it didn't take the family long to move on and get on to the second rung.

Once I was making my mark as a bookie, or should I say after my joust with Frankie, my expanding girth and Californian smile would make me quite a well-known face with the racing public. Not as ubiquitous as big John McCririck but not unknown in households who had a penchant for horse and dog racing. I still think the day I lost in the two-horse photo-finish with Millie Clode to star in the prime-time game show, *The Colour of Money* in 2009 with old pal Chris Tarrant, stopped me getting my boat race into the living rooms of people who had no interest in betting or racing.

Would it have widened my public appeal? It's all conjecture but it couldn't have harmed my chances of appearing a lot more on the box but I knew I was in trouble when Chris said I was past the post. ITV had certainly spent decent money and pushed the boat out preparing for my role as "The Fat Banker." They'd had me measured up for five quality, pin-striped suits and dozens of Double Two shirts and they didn't come cheap either. It had even got me thinking, 'Jesus Gal, you've come up smelling like a giant size bottle of Clive Christian Cologne here.' But it was all dashed onto the rocks when Millie got the decision. It must have been close though, why would the TV company have gone to all that expense?

So, if you are living in the home counties, have any of you ever noticed a very large stockbroker or posh sumo wrestler walking up the high street, sporting a massive pin stripe outfit? I was over 35 stone at the time with a 68 inch waist and 78 inch chest so God knows who got the outsize clobber in the end but they never came my way.

Such is sartorial life.

Events could have been so different if I'd got the TV gig with Mr Tarrant but I can't say that my life has been unlucky. I've travelled the length and breadth of this wonderful country, meeting some of the greatest people who ever drew breath. If, at the start of my career, you'd have offered me half of what I've achieved then I'd have snapped your arm off. I was truly blessed the day I became a young market trader before graduating into a bookmaker. I've enjoyed every last minute of it, apart from when I was suffering from depression of course but people came to my aid and it was beaten back from whence it came.

I'm so content in my little Midlands village with its forty-odd houses and cottages. Sharon and Jaimee have been wonderful, sometimes I have to pinch myself to realise how lucky I am. Ex-wife Sue's family keep in touch and I get to see the grandkids while my own lot are thriving as I'm slowing down. They all have that quiet ambition inherited off the old man and I watch them like any proud Dad. You always want your sons and daughter to do well.

Occasionally we will have a big night out in Leicester at the outstanding Italian restaurant, San Carlo where super-chef Michele will make me an offer I can't refuse, namely Lobster Thermidor. Since my gastric sleeve operation, I can't eat meat, not even turkey at Christmas but as all of you know, I'm partial to seafood so even my old staple of haddock and chips is fine, only smaller portions these days.

Michele is a big punter but I don't give him tips, I just tell him to back his fellow countryman Frankie Dettori. If I'd done that instead of laying him, I could have bought the restaurant today, hook, line and sinker. We could have gone into business together and that would have been fishy heaven for me as the restaurant's official taster. Lofty could have even stood in when I was on holiday.

My old racing colours are still going strong, you might have seen them on Jeremy's Jet, owned by mate Stuart Clark and trained by Tony Carroll. They are the black silks with navy blue epaulettes and red cap that Mi Odds ran under with such distinction. I'd like to say that "The Jet" is a chip off the old block but he does his own thing. Stuart loves him to bits though so if he's happy, so am I.

So, what's left for me now? Certainly not retirement, there's a few good years in the tank yet. I still love laying at all the big festivals but I pick and choose the meetings I want to stand at. I love Warwick and Chelmsford; there's not many times I'm not there, even in the winter when they bring the betting inside. I appear twice a month on Betfred TV, giving my opinions on racing while Barry Hearn has me at his fishing, darts and snooker when possible. I'm so lucky to have powerful friends like that, they have stood by me while other TV people have let me fall to the wayside. I'd be lying if I said I didn't want to get back on Sky, I still have so much to offer.

If possible, I'd even like to get involved with the growing affliction that is problem gamblers; I'd love to give something back to the industry that has been so good to me. I'm sure with a bit of tutoring from an old gambler like me who has been there, done it and worn the Triple X T-Shirt, that I could stop a few young men or ladies travelling down the road to perdition.

I must inform at this late hour, an honourable mention for a few pals, firstly the indomitable Gary Newbon who was named in the 2019 New Year's Honours List as an MBE. It is a richly deserved honour for a man who has been to seven world cups and three Olympics. He moved from ITV Sports to Sky Sports with effortless ease, there is seemingly nothing he can't do. I don't think he will mind me telling you he is 73 years young but he has more go and energy than men half his age. The award is richly deserved. The only problem is the next time we meet he will expect me to curtsey but at the moment my knees are giving me grief so he might have to settle for a man hug.

A word also for Ed Nicholson, noted briefly at the start of the book. He's now the top man at Unibet and is the MC at both Bath and Chepstow Races. I think he's wasted not getting a slot on any TV racing channel, I'm absolutely amazed he hasn't got a job on the box. He's been in the game a long time and has the knowledge and acumen to go on to even better things if given the chance. As a horsey talent-spotter, he's one to watch. PS; If you go all the way to the top Ed, don't forget your old pal Gal, scraping a living in the shires.

Finally, I must give a mention for Hugh and his amazing staff down at The Hollow Bottom, near Cheltenham. It really is one of the best pubs you'll find in the Cotswolds and is the go-to place for racing fans after a day at Cheltenham races. As I mentioned earlier, they also host the best Festival Preview night of the entire year. It's hosted by Alex Steedman from Racing TV and he tries to keep the lid on me, Luke Tarr, Carl Llewellyn, Sam Twiston Davies and recently retired jockey Ryan Hatch. Being the night before the Cheltenham Festival it's a bit like Christmas Eve for punters and always pretty lively so if you fancy a decent night out, make sure you book tickets pronto.

Well the race is almost run but when I do hang up my satchel? It would be nice to settle somewhere on the coast and I fancy the Norfolk Seaboard, anywhere around Great Yarmouth. I have very fond memories of the area, it would suit me down to the ground. I haven't totally ruled out Los Jameos Playa on sunny Lanzarote but that would probably have to be a holiday destination. I absolutely love it there, we can all dream. I hope you have enjoyed my little story, there is just my heartfelt epilogue and jokes to come. This is the gift that keeps on giving.

As Tommy Cooper once said, 'Always leave them laughing.'
And he was the man to spread comic magic.

Thank you so much for going on my journey with me.

* * * *

Epilogue

Well, what a life.

Five years ago, I was practically homeless. It looked like Big Gal was a goner as well as a Gooner but somehow the Governor in the sky gave me one last chance of salvation. On top of that, what were the odds of me meeting up again with the lovely Sharon, who had ridden race horses for me thirty years earlier as my amateur jockey? Thankfully, after that long period apart, we are back together again as a partnership. It seems like destiny where those long, winding roads take you but it's so nice after a hard day's graft to come back to a place you can really call home.

These days, trips to the chemist to pick up our prescriptions are more commonplace than a night out painting the town red but we wouldn't swap a single thing. I can't tell you how fortunate I am to find happiness again after all that I've been through. I've been down to the dark depths and emerged back up into the blessed sunlight and that's the only way to live now.

The big house is gone, but the small, picturesque cottage we now rent is our little piece of heaven, it's where we can shut the front door and block out any problems. I love relaxing here without a care in the world until it's time to get my head down for therapeutic beauty sleep. My kids don't come around very often but you forget they are all adults now with their own lives to live. I would run through walls for each one of them and the welcome mat is always out, come rain, snow or shine. On the travelling side, my sister Jackie and her lovely husband Richard always go out of their way to make me feel at home whenever I drive down to Bournemouth to see them. Family is so important.

I absolutely needed to write this revealing book as people would not have believed how much my life has changed. I found it to be a cathartic experience, I'm so glad I got all this unwanted baggage off my chest. The television days are seemingly gone but I have the character, experience and knowledge to shine once again if someone gives me the chance. My name is my marker and keeps me going strong. People still stop me today and ask about that fateful day more than 22 years ago.

It changed so many people's lives so for that, thank you Frankie, *xxx*.

How strange with Cheltenham 2019 approaching that I've been invited to appear on five Cheltenham Festival previews, there's life in the old buffer yet. One of them features my all-time hero Martin Pipe OBE so what a buzz that will be and just for good measure I'm definitely standing as a bookmaker all that week. If the old health doesn't stand up then at least I'd have gone out with a bang at one of my favourite meetings, the incomparable Cheltenham Festival.

I'm still so lucky to find work on Betfred TV thanks to Fred and also at the snooker and dart nights with Barry Hearn. Thanks Fred and Bazza, where would I have been without those two fine gentlemen? Probably lagging at the back with the tailenders and also rans.

I've learnt in life, never be flashy or arrogant; that's not what I'm about and I certainly won't be going in that direction any time soon. Do I miss the money and the great, exotic holidays that I used to once love? Of course I do but what's wrong with Skeggy on a wet weekend? It's certainly bracing.

I always loved penny arcades with bingo and slots; we're British, we grew up with them.

Every time Yarmouth Races was on, I'd visit my old mate at Del Boys Cafe, Beach Road, Hemsby (near Great Yarmouth). That was odds-on in my book. We are all creatures of habit so if we have a good experience, we remember and return. I will never change and please God never let it happen. Money itself has never been the sole motivation for me. I've always said that the happiest times of my life were grafting hard early mornings on the markets, ducking and diving for a few hundred quid. When I was an on-course bookie, working most days of the week, year in year out and playing up thousands of pounds, it all came at an emotional cost.

It can ruin your family life and marriage chasing the filthy lucre all over the country. Sometimes you have to take a fall to realise what you once had and lost. Your own well-being is important; all the money in the world can't buy good health back if you're stricken with a serious illness. What's the good of being the richest bloke in the crematorium, you can't take it with you.

So, this is for all you great people out there, especially you lovers of a classic English tale of winning a small fortune, losing a much larger one and paying it all back while at the same time, marrying then losing wives one, two and three and thinking the grass was always greener round the corner before ending up with my beautiful partner, Sharon.

I've gone up more steep inclines and plunged down more sheer drops than the Blackpool Big Dipper on a bank holiday. I sincerely hope you thoroughly enjoyed the latest read because this was a book written from the soul for all you racing fans. My latest exploits have proved that Gary Wiltshire doesn't do things the easy or normal way but he will always try to do the right thing for friends and strangers alike. If you ever spot me working at the racecourse or having a social night at the dogs, come over for a laugh and a chinwag, I've got all time in the world for good, genuine racing people.

So, from the very bottom of my heart, I wish peace and providence to all of you.

Be lucky,
Gal
xxx.

The end

* * * * *

GARY'S LUCKY (FUNNY) 15

From Gary's bumper book of betting gags, here's fifteen rib ticklers.

1. A horse walks into a pub, the barman asks, 'Why the long face?'

The horse replies, 'All horses have long faces, it's a common adaptation found in numerous creatures evolved over many thousands of years for long distance running in an open plains environment.'

The barman says, 'Thanks for that, you've ruined my joke.'

2. A gang of young teenagers are playing Totopoly at a friend's house, his parents have gone out for the night, so he is making the most of his new found freedom. The drinks are flowing freely, but he has one too many and falls into a drunken stupor. Just before midnight he is woken by his returning parents, his pals have all gone home. He has terrible pain in his back passage, so his parents rush him to hospital, where he undergoes immediate medical procedure. Afterwards the doctor comes over to see the parents, who enquire about his health, he tells them, 'We have removed six Totopoly horses from his rectum, thankfully his condition is now stable.'

3. An American Greyhound with his lower leg wrapped in a bandage, hobbles into a saloon in Arizona. He sidles up to the bar and announces, 'I'm looking fer the man who shot my paw.'

4. A horse racing trainer visits the vet's and declares one of his horse's is constipated, the vet gives him a large pill and instructs him to put it in a long tube, stick it in the horse's backside and blow. The next day the trainer is back, looking sick and wanly. The vet enquires, 'What happened?'

The trainer replies, 'Unfortunately, the horse blew first.'

5. A man was at home reading his paper when his wife walks in and wallops him round the back of the head with a frying pan. He leaps to his feet demanding to know what's going on, his wife produces a slip of paper with the name Elsa Jean written on it, 'This was in your suit pocket.'

He explains himself, 'Darling, remember me and the lads going to the dog track last week, well Elsa Jean was a tip I was given, trap 6 if I remember rightly.' The wife had to apologise and bandaged his head for him, all was well. The very next day, the phone was ringing in the lobby, a minute later the wife comes in and clouts him even harder with the frying pan again.

'For God's sake what's wrong now?' the wife tells him, 'Your greyhound just rang.'

6. Frankie Dettori is in the parade ring, the trainer comes up, "Frankie we can't thank you enough, you are our last hope, 35 races the horse has had, stone last in all of them, if he downs tools today, the milkman can have him tomorrow." Frankie mounts up, after two furlongs they are twenty lengths last, he gives him an almighty backhander to the rump, no response, in fact he is going slower. He follows up with two hard slaps down the shoulder, nothing doing, the horse is nearly at walking pace, so in desperation he administers three sharp ones to the bollocks. The horse comes to a sudden stop, swivels his head round and says, 'Turn it in Frankie, I'm up at 4-30 tomorrow morning, delivering the milk.'

7. The trainer was giving last minute instructions to the jockey, when he surreptitiously slipped something into the horse's mouth, an eagle eyed steward came over and demanded to know what it was.

'Just a Mint Imperial sir, the old horse loves them.' The trainer then had one himself and offered another to the steward, 'Thank you, I don't mind if I do.'

The trainer then finished his instructions, 'Stay on the grandstand rail, you are an absolute certainty, the only thing that could possibly go past you down the home straight is me being chased by the steward.'

8. What's the difference between praying in church and praying at the dog track ?
Answer: At the dog track you really mean it.

9. *PUNTER:* Are you a gambling man ?
BUTCHER: I most certainly am !
PUNTER: Bet you a hundred pound that you can't jump up and touch the beef hanging from the ceiling on those hooks.
BUTCHER: I'm not betting on that, the steaks are too high !

10. A guy was walking by a casino and noticed out the corner of his eye, three men and a retired greyhound playing poker. His curiosity got the better of him and he went inside, he was amazed at the skill and dexterity of the dog. On a drinks break he confided in one of the players, 'Man, that's one smart greyhound.'

The poker player retorted, 'He ain't so cute, every time he gets a big hand he wags his tail.'

11. What do you call an Amish man with his hand in a horse's mouth?

Answer: A mechanic.

12. GAMBLER: I've had a terrible day, lost 12 out of 12 on the horses, then 8 out of 8 on the dogs and just to rub it in the 5 football teams I've backed have all got beat.

FRIEND: Well there's a Rugby League match on tonight, give you a chance to win some money back.

GAMBLER: Are you fucking mad, what do I know about Rugby League!

13. It was a quiet afternoon in a small independent Midland bookie's, an unfamiliar face ambles in and writes out a slip for the 3-30 two mile hurdle race at Uttoxeter, a two runner affair with the red hot favourite at odds of 1/10 on, he unexpectedly places a thousand pound wager on the outsider at 7/1. The ever friendly bookie tries to dissuade the man, telling him the outsider was a poor plater and had never won a race. He was adamant though that this was the horse he wanted to back, so the bookie shrugged his shoulders and took the bet. At the third hurdle, the odds on shot stumbled and put his jockey on the turf, the outsider who was ten lengths behind at the time, then went round in his own time to record his first ever win. As the bookie doled out the 8K, he confides in the punter, that he actually owns the winner and he never had a penny on himself as his horse is a right donkey. The winning punter makes his way to the door, but turns round just as he opens it and says, 'That really is an amazing coincidence, I own the favourite!'

14. A woman's reckoning on how men and greyhounds are the same creature.
1. Both take up too much room on the bed.
2. Neither tell you what's bothering them.
3. Both have a strange fascination with women's crotches.
4. Both have an irrational fear of the vacuum cleaner.
5. Both mark their territory.
6. Neither notices when you have had your hair cut.
7. Both are very suspicious of the postman.
8. Neither ever does the dishes.
9. Both fart frequently and shamelessly.
10. Neither understands what you see in cats.

15. A group of American tourists walk into an Irish pub in Dublin, A big Texan booms out a challenge, 'I hear you Irishmen regard yourselves as great drinkers. I'm willing to bet a thousand dollars that no man here can down twenty pints of Guinness in half an hour.' The bar fell silent apart from the scraping of a chair as a little local got up and left the pub. All the other Americans patted the Texan on the back, he'd put the Irish in their place, it was a moral victory for the good old USA.

Forty minutes later, little Paddy returned, 'Hey Yank, is the bet still on?'

The big Texan was right up for it, 'Sure is son, barman pull the pints and let's start the clock.'

Paddy downed pint after pint, he was struggling near the end, but finished the 20th pint with just five seconds to spare. Fair play to the big man, he paid up in good faith, but was curious to know where Paddy had gone when he had first issued the challenge. The Irishman replied, 'Well sir, to a humble man of means like my good self, a thousand dollars is an awful lot of money, so I went to the pub across the road to see if I could do it.'

* * * *

A man after my own heart, W C Fields, a guy who liked a drink, his grub and the odd expletive, was often found doing all three at the racetrack.

He once quoted that, 'Horse sense is the thing a horse has which stops them betting on people.'

I can only concur with the great man, but it would be a duller world without a cheeky wager. So a heart felt farewell to all my betting buddies, persistent punters and garrulous gamblers, let's hope lady luck and God given fortune, go with you in every step of your life,

From one of your own,

Big Gary Wiltshire.

* * * * *

The end

Also by Michael O'Rourke (and Faisal Madani)

Life in the Faz lane - The true story of Faisal Madani: Britain's most notorious fraudster...

A lively account of his life is crammed full of laughs, scams, revelations and not least of all, his 'bouncebackability'. Probably the most candid book ever written about football corruption and greed.

Also by Michael O'Rourke:

Black Eyes and Blue Blood - The Amazing Life and Times of Gangster Norman 'Scouse' Johnson.

Arguably the most unusual gangster story ever told... Black Eyes and Blue Blood combines violence and humour with an exotic twist of romance. It also offers a fascinating insight into the underworld on both sides of the Atlantic as Johnson mixed with some of the world's best-known gangsters, sportsmen and showbiz personalities....

Mainstream Publishing, 2008.

Printed in Great Britain
by Amazon